TEXAS

aredo

Gulf of Mexico

Rio Grande

Mier   Guardado Abajo

Chicharrones

ralvo   quin

Camargo

Rio Grande

Rio Sal

Reynosa

Point Isabel

Fort Brown

Brazos Island

Matamoros

los

ares

TAMAULIPAS

N

W   E

S

Victoria

The Mexican War Journal of Captain Franklin Smith

The Mexican War Journal

OF

Captain Franklin Smith

Edited by Joseph E. Chance

UNIVERSITY PRESS OF MISSISSIPPI
Jackson and London

Copyright © 1991 by the University Press of Mississippi
Designed by Sally Hamlin
Manufactured in the United States of America

94   93   92   91   4   3   2   1

The paper in this book meets the guidelines for permanence and durability of the Committee on Production Guidelines for Book Longevity of the Council on Library Resources.

Library of Congress Cataloging-in-Publication Data

Smith, Franklin, b. 1807.
    The Mexican war journal of Captain Franklin Smith / edited by Joseph E. Chance.
        p. cm.
    Includes bibliographical references and index.
    ISBN 0-87805-492-8 (alk. paper)
    1. Smith, Franklin, b. 1807—Diaries.   2. United States—History —War with Mexico, 1845–1848—Personal narratives.
    3. Quartermasters—United States—Diaries.   4. United States. Army-Officers—Diaries.   5. Ciudad Camargo Region (Tamaulipas, Mexico)—Social life and customs.   6. Rio Grande Valley—History. I. Chance, Joseph E., 1940-   . II. Title.
    E411.S643   1991
    973.6'28—dc20
    [B]   90-32026
                                                                         CIP

British Library Cataloging-in-Publication data available

Maps used as endpapers were drawn by Nancy Moyers, University of Texas, Pan American.

70180

To the memory of
Louis Steven deVries

Contents

Acknowledgments

Without the help and cooperation of many people this book would not have been possible. To these people I wish to express my deepest gratitude.

Photocopies of the original manuscript of the Franklin Smith journal were furnished by the Mississippi Department of Archives and History. I owe a particular debt of gratitude to Hank Holmes of that department for his help. Mary Lohrenz, Curator of Collections at the State Historical Museum in Jackson, Mississippi, was very helpful in locating information that appears in this book. Mary S. Dix and Lynda L. Crist, editors of the Papers of Jefferson Davis, located at Rice University, allowed me to borrow microfilm copies of the compiled service records of the First Mississippi Regiment and microfilm copies of the leading Mississippi newspapers from the years 1846–47.

The dedicated and able staff at the Pan American University Library were a constant source of aid to me. I would particularly like to thank Nicole McKelvy, Gerald Whittaker, Ken Brock, George Gause, Virginia Haynie, and Susan Hancock. Colleagues at Pan American University to whom I am indebted for sharing their expertise with me include Dr. Robert Lonard, Dr. Pauline James, Dr. James Maloney, Sister M. Geralda Schaefer, Robert Rodgers, and Norman Burandt.

I am grateful to the following persons who contributed materials and offered anecdotal data and suggestions that improved the quality of this book: Laurier McDonald of Edinburg, Texas; Gary Waggerman, Jon Harrison, and Gary Homerstad of McAllen, Texas; Alton Moore, Jr., of Pharr, Texas; Dr. Charles D. Spurlin of The Victoria College, Victoria, Texas; and Tom Fort of the Hidalgo

County Historical Museum. I owe special thanks to Al Ramirez and Jose Noe Gonzalez of Edinburg, Texas, who were able to identify the modern names of the villages in northern Mexico mentioned by Franklin Smith.

Introduction

Franklin Smith was born on September 25, 1807, in Baltimore, Maryland. He received an excellent education, at least partly from private schools in Washington, D. C., and studied to become an attorney. He married Ann Josepha Spence of Baltimore on March 5, 1839, and the newlyweds moved to Canton, Mississippi, where Smith became one of the first attorneys to practice in that city. He was elected district attorney in 1844 and in June 1846 received a commission as a captain of volunteers in the First Mississippi Regiment. This journal records his daily experiences as an assistant commissary of subsistence while he was stationed in Camargo, Mexico, from August 31, 1846, until February 6, 1847. Smith resigned his commission, effective April 14, 1847, returned to his wife and six children in Canton, and resumed his interrupted law practice. He died there on an unknown date and is buried in that city.

This brief account encompasses all that is now known about the life of Franklin Smith except what can be learned from the hefty 216-page manuscript that records his experiences as an army officer stationed in northern Mexico. Smith evidently attempted to publish this manuscript in 1855. In an introduction which has been omitted from the present book, he prophesied, "I am satisfied that the people of the North and South are about to have civil war on the subject of slavery unless the great mass of the people can be aroused in time to arrest the proceedings of the Demagogues who are hurrying them to the precipice."

Smith went on to say that the American public had made the glamorizing of war and heroic exploits part of its culture and thus could not understand or appreciate the true gruesome nature of such an undertaking.

But the dark side of the picture the miseries the disgraces the infamies of war—the lingering diseases the inglorious deaths, the profanation of the Sabbath the habitual drunkenness the blasphemy—the excess of youth, hope, health, and salvation here; thereafter the desolations of the hearth and heart in the Mexican war along the line of the Rio Grande have never been presented as fully to the contemplation of the American people until now. If such miseries belonged to men engaged *in a war of conquest*; it will be for the people of the United States to consider before they engage in civil war how much more humble and dreadful must be the scenes.

Smith's attempt to publish his Mexican War diary was unsuccessful, and the manuscript was tied with a ribbon and filed away in a trunk in a dusty attic to await discovery by a later generation. Such an event occurred in the early 1950s, when one of Franklin Smith's descendents cautiously allowed a typescript to be made and placed in the Mississippi Archives but stipulated that the family would have to approve publication of any portions. Researchers who have read the typescript, including John Porter Bloom and the editors of the papers of Jefferson Davis, have commented on the exceptional qualities of Smith's observations. Bloom, in his dissertation, quotes at least three of Smith's memorable observations and concludes by commenting that the entire manuscript is worthy of publication. Only recently has Franklin Smith's original journal been donated to the Mississippi Archives, and from this agency I obtained permission to reproduce the contents.

What I found in this manuscript was an amazing account of life along the Rio Grande during the turbulent years of 1846 and 1847 as recorded by a well-educated and literate man. To those of us who now live along the Rio Grande, Smith's descriptions of the river and its surrounding terrain sound strange. Accustomed to the Mississippi River, he wrote of "the current of the Rio Grande being more rapid than any current I ever saw." Such a statement is certainly inconsistent with present observations. Last summer, as I strolled along the banks of the Rio Grande at about the place Smith referred to, I threw a stick out into the river. It remained almost motionless in the still water. The dams on the Rio Grande from Elephant Butte to Anzaldua have transformed this river into a small, sluggish stream that offers no hint of its magnificent past. The native vegetation and the stands of *Sabal texana* palms Smith described growing along the river have been victims of modern agriculture; less than 5 percent of native brushlands remain in the lower Rio Grande Valley of Texas. This brushland provided a valuable habitat to the birds and animals found here, many of which exist in the United States only in this location. The local hunting season for the white-winged dove was cancelled for the first time this fall because of low population counts attributed directly to the scarcity of brush and trees for nesting sites. Smith's observations of the Rio Grande Valley in 1846 are valuable to us because they give us a sobering idea of what has happened to this virgin country during the last 139 years of our stewardship.

But reporting on ecology was not Franklin Smith's purpose in keeping this journal; he was providing an eyewitness account of the historical events taking place around him. Camargo became the gateway to northern Mexico for Zachary Taylor's army, and through its streets passed many of the leaders and future leaders of the United States. Smith carefully recorded his meetings with and impressions of the great, the near great, and the ordinary citizens of this country who had volunteered for military service in Mexico and have long since been forgotten. The anecdotes told about such men as Mirabeau B. Lamar, Sam Houston, Robert Patterson, Charles May, and Zachary Taylor present a private side to their nature that is often quite unlike their public image. Franklin Smith has left us with an amusing chronicle of the trials and tribulations of one of his favorite targets for ridicule: Maj. Gen. Robert Patterson. Smith wryly comments on Patterson's losing struggle to keep liquor from being smuggled into Camargo for consumption by thirsty volunteer soldiers and relates the conflict between Patterson and Col. Charles May, the bearded hero of Resaca de la Palma, regarding the clouds of dust created by horseback traffic through the streets of Camargo.

Smith arrived in Texas too late to participate in the battles of Palo Alto and Resaca de la Palma and was detailed to remain behind at Camargo when the American army marched from there to attack Monterrey. However, from Camargo, he was able to report on the heyday of steamboat transportation on the Rio Grande and furnish documentation on this neglected aspect of the Mexican War. His journal reports the almost daily arrival of shallow-draft side-wheelers at Camargo, about 130 miles from the mouth of the Rio Grande, to furnish supplies and transportation for American soldiers. Smith, as an assistant quartermaster, was one of those whose duty it was to organize the supply trains sent from Camargo to Monterrey and even further inland. These supply trains often consisted of more than 150 wagons and 1,000 pack mules and posed massive problems in logistics for the quartermaster of that day.

While busy with his many duties as a quartermaster, Smith still found time to observe Mexican customs and habits. He slipped away from camp one evening to attend a Mexican fandango. Another entry from his diary reports on Mexican funeral and burial practices. He was greatly impressed with the Mexican horseman's adroitness with a lasso and reported seeing Mexican rancheros on horseback roping livestock. This practice predated by many years the advent of the American cowboy with his roping skills.

Franklin Smith faithfully reported the gossip and rumors that circulated among the army camps in northern Mexico, giving us a view of the war more like the one seen by the ordinary soldier of that time. Much of the hearsay about army matters reported by Smith was often true. The rumors recorded by Smith were often the only documentation of the infamous guerilla war fought in northern Mexico in 1846–47 between the American army and the Mexican rancheros, since many of these brutal encounters would never surface in the official records. The picture presented by Smith of this covert struggle is ugly, and the stories of the many atrocities committed by soldiers on both sides contribute to the heritage of that war, the effects of which can still be felt today along the Rio Grande.

The journal of Franklin Smith in fact contains a wealth of interesting observations on the life and times of the Rio Grande Valley and northern Mexico in 1846–47. Those were exciting times, and Franklin Smith did a credible job of reporting them before he vanished into the mists of the past.

I transcribed this journal from a handwritten manuscript that was at times difficult to read. I have attempted to retain the spelling, wording, and intent of the author. Spelling of Latin and Spanish words has not been corrected, but all have been italicized. In some cases dashes have been replaced with periods in order to clarify the meaning. The ampersands in the manuscript were replaced with "and". Otherwise the text appears exactly as Franklin Smith wrote it. This manuscript was difficult for me to edit, because it contains so many observations on the men and events that are important to the history of south Texas and northern Mexico. Limitations on the book's size prevented me from commenting more on the people and events contained in this diary. Colorful characters such as Charles May, Antonio Canales, and Balie Peyton should not be forgotten in the rush of time. I have included a bibliography of selected diaries, histories, and newspaper articles on these subjects that will be useful to anyone wanting more information. Any errors in the text of the journal or in the endnotes are the responsibility solely of this editor.

Joseph E. Chance
Edinburg, Texas
October 8, 1985

The Mexican War Journal of Captain Franklin Smith

Chapter 1

August II–October I4, I846

A hard fight to no advantage
—*The Battle of Monterrey*

The United States declared war against Mexico on May 13, 1846, and shortly thereafter a quota of volunteer militia was requested from each state. Franklin Smith, like many of his fellow citizens, was eager to join the ranks of the volunteer militia on a mission to the Rio Grande, where, according to popular thought at the time, Gen. Zachary Taylor's forces were trapped. At the enlistment station in Vicksburg, Mississippi, many more men appeared than were needed to satisfy the state quota levied on Mississippi by Secretary of War William L. Marcy. Riots broke out among the rejected volunteers, and Gov. Albert Gallatin Brown anxiously appealed to Washington to expand the Mississippi levy to more than one regiment of volunteer infantry. This appeal was rejected in Washington, and after a lively competition among more than twenty-five volunteer companies of infantry, ten companies were selected and certified by Governor Brown as the First Regiment of Mississippi Volunteers. The ranks of the regiment from Mississippi were filled by young men from the upper social strata—the sons of the most influential and powerful men of the state. Elected colonel of the Mississippi regiment was Hon. Jefferson Davis, a graduate of the United States Military Academy at West Point. Davis had resigned his military commission in 1835 and was serving a term in the United States Congress as a representative from the state of Mississippi at the time of his election to the post of colonel. To balance military experience with audacity, the Mississippi regiment elected Andrew

Keith McClung to the post of lieutenant-colonel. Hot-tempered and high-strung, McClung was a noted duelist who came to be referred to by many in his home state as the "Black Rose of the South."

The ranks of volunteer regiments from other states, however, were often filled with unsavory elements from a rough-and-tumble frontier society. In the democratic tradition of the volunteer militia that dated from the time of the American Revolution, the soldiers from the ranks elected their own regimental officers. This practice was sorely abused by ambitious local politicians who bought and bartered for the votes that elevated them from the ranks to the officer corps. Many of these newly elected officers did not know the manual of arms and could not even drill their new recruits.

Franklin Smith, of Canton, Mississippi, was appointed at the recommendation of Colonel Davis to serve as Assistant Commissary of Subsistence for the Mississippi Regiment at the rank of captain. Smith's commission from Washington was delayed, and he joined the regiment later after it had moved from Mississippi to southern Texas.

Smith found the regiment stationed at the mouth of the Rio Grande on August 17, 1846, and noted a scene of chaos and confusion. The tents of thousands of men from hastily assembled volunteer regiments dotted the river banks from the mouth of the Rio Grande for more than twenty miles up the river to Matamoros. Three waves of volunteers had been hastily summoned from the United States at various times by Gen. Edmund P. Gaines, Gen. Zachary Taylor, and finally, by Secretary of War William Marcy. Most of these troops had been civilians only weeks before and knew precious little about army life and discipline. Soldiers ignorant about camp hygiene and what foods to consume in the torrid tropical zone soon fell victim to their environment, becoming ill and dying. Along the Rio Grande, the lowly amoeba felled many more Americans than ever succumbed to the Mexican musket.

Volunteer officers, often referred to derisively as "mustangs" by their counterparts in the regular army, could not be relied upon to enforce order in the ranks of their regiments. These politically sensitive officers knew that every soldier who survived the war would be a potential voter, and they tempered discipline accordingly. The standards of discipline for volunteers varied greatly from regiment to regiment. Some volunteer regiments which were never to see any military action made their shameful war record entirely by attacking the helpless civilian populations of southern Texas and northern Mexico. These men's crimes against civilians that went unpunished included murder, rape, and theft. To this day, American visitors to northern Mexico reap a harvest of ill will for the illegal acts of their American volunteer forefathers, committed more than 140 years ago.

The American army had performed marvelously on May 7-8, 1846, at the battles of Palo Alto and Resaca de la Palma and had driven Mexican forces south of the Rio Grande. After a pause, the Americans crossed the Rio Bravo del Norte without opposition and occupied Matamoros.

But by early August 1846, that was about as far as the American army had penetrated into northern Mexico. President James K. Polk was fuming in Washington at the supposed reluctance of American forces to take the offensive and prodded General Taylor to take prompt action. Polk had ordered Taylor to capture northern Mexico and establish an overland route of attack into central Mexico. The key to both of these objectives was the capture of the Mexican city of Monterrey, capital of the state of Nuevo Leon. Monterrey, a city of about 10,000, was built astride the principal pass through the Sierra Madre Mountains along an ancient trade route that connected northern Mexico with the interior of the country. Scouts had informed Taylor early in June 1846 that the direct overland trails from Matamoros to Monterrey were without an adequate water supply. Taylor, therefore, decided to move the troops to Monterrey in a more circuitous route, along the Rio Grande Valley to Camargo and from there to Monterrey along the valley of the Rio San Juan. As there were no overland routes paralleling the Rio Grande, the decision was made to use American technology to develop a water route. Troops and supplies were to be shipped by high-pressure shallow-draft side-wheel steamboats up the Rio Grande about 125 miles to Camargo. There was only one problem: the United States government did not own any such craft.

In the summer of 1846, the American army lay idle along the banks of the Rio Grande while agents of the Quartermaster Corps scurried up and down the Mississippi, the Ohio, the Cumberland, and even the Chattahoochee rivers to contract for steamboats. The United States government hurriedly bought and leased steamboats and negotiated freight contracts with independent steamboat operators. The government was able to purchase some new and well-designed shallow-draft steamboats such as the Colonel Cross and the Corvette but also found itself the owner of a few worm-eaten veterans such as the Mercer and the Enterprise. Steamboats began to course the mighty Rio Grande by late July 1846, as Taylor initiated the first leg of offensive operations—the transportation of troops and supplies to Camargo.

The regular army stationed in and around Matamoros was to form the nucleus for the offensive against Monterrey. Because of its small size, this expeditionary force had to be supplemented by volunteer regiments. However, many problems were associated with the use of volunteer militia. The United States Constitution stated that volunteer militia were to be used in the defense of the country but was silent about the use of volunteers in an offensive force. Could volunteers be legally used in an army to invade a foreign country? The many volunteer regiments waiting along the river had been inducted into federal service for various periods of time such as three months, six months, one year, two years, and the entire period of the war. A regiment whose enlistment period was due to expire in a few months would be of no use in a protracted campaign. The troops and officers of many of the volunteer regiments were undisciplined and poorly trained. Such troops would create more problems for an invading army than their use would merit. But some of the volunteers would have to be used, so Taylor set about to select carefully the volunteer regiments that he would transport to Camargo. He disbanded and sent home the three-month volunteers and ordered the remaining volunteer regiments left behind in camps along the river to guard the supply lines and depots along the river route.

One can only imagine the amazement that must have been felt by the citizens of Camargo, accustomed to the quiet pastoral and ranching life of northern Mexico, at seeing high-pressure steamboats and hearing those shrill whistles for the first time. They must have experienced even greater surprise when they discovered that the passengers aboard the steamboats were also of the shrill, high-pressure variety. In a matter of a few short days the sleepy city of Camargo became a center of bustling activity. Supplies and rations brought from the steamboats were stacked in the principal square, and this stack quickly assumed mountainous proportions. Troops were seen being drilled in the city, and the loud voices of Yanquis were heard giving commands during the day and drunken shouts during the night. Passing through the streets of this small border village during the next two years would be the men destined to lead the United States, both politically and militarily, for at least the next thirty years. No city in the United States, except Washington, D. C., could boast of playing host to as many future presidents, senators, ambassadors, and generals, as well as scoundrels, as the tiny Mexican village of Camargo.

Camargo was placed under the control of Gen. Robert Patterson, a volunteer who had made a fortune in private life as a manufacturer in

Pennsylvania. Patterson was given explicit orders to maintain strict control of the city and to prevent the volunteers and camp followers from turning Camargo into an open city, which was what had happened in Matamoros. Shortly after that town's occupation, American camp followers, gamblers, and shady ladies had rushed there to ply their trades. The quiet city of Matamoros quickly became a den of delights for the flesh. Previously quiet nights became punctuated with raucous laughter and the sound of small arms fire. In the mornings, the bodies of Americans lying face down in the streets bore mute testimony to the tragic actions that resulted from love spurned, a misdeal of the cards, or a fatal lack of communication skills. The bodies of Mexicans found on the streets were generally the result of confrontations with a lowly class of American volunteer soldier that preyed upon the citizens of Matamoros with virtual legal immunity. General Patterson was determined that this sorry spectacle would not be repeated in Camargo.

The regular army troops in Camargo staged a dress parade on August 18, 1846, and an impressive line of troops that extended more than three-quarters of a mile passed in review. This review was probably the largest that had been staged in the history of the United States Army up to that date. The next day at sunrise, the advance column of General Taylor's army crossed the Rio San Juan on a makeshift system of planks laid between the steamboats moored in the river to advance overland against Monterrey.

The city of Monterrey was captured on September 25, 1846, and, as reported by Franklin Smith, Lieutenant Eaton passed through Camargo on September 27, 1846, on his way to Washington to deliver the news of the surrender. The dispatches were delivered to President Polk by October 11, 1846, at the end of a very rapid sixteen-day travel time from the Mexican battlefield. Polk was unhappy about the terms of the city's capitulation and felt that General Taylor had exceeded his authority and shown bad judgement in granting a conditional surrender and armistice to the Mexican forces trapped in Monterrey. The American soldiers in northern Mexico agreed with President Polk's assessment, but the American press lionized Taylor's third military victory against Mexican arms. The American people had begun to sense that Zachary "Rough and Ready" Taylor might be the right man next to occupy the White House.

Tuesday 11th   It being reduced to a certainty that the steamship McKim Page Master would sail this day in which we were to embark for Brazos[1] I sallied out and made a few purchases among which were an India rubber cape and leggings—called on Col. Hunt who gave me orders to proceed to the mouth of the Rio Grande and report in person to Col. Davis[2] for temporary employment and to report by letter to Col. Henry Whiting[3] asst. Qtr. M. General as my superior for permanent orders Col. Hunt informed me that my name was on the list of those to be carried over at public charge by the McKim and to go aboard when I liked—went aboard about sunset myself and Capt. McCausland and the boat pushed off about 10 o'clock P.M. Very boisterous passage every body sick—boat rolled terribly on Thursday the 13th storm was so high that all the horses and mules aboard to the number of 9 or 10 were thrown overboard—It was a dreadful sight the mules and horses got loose and ran into the cabin at the same time—chairs tables and trunks were dashed to pieces—the mules and horses moaning and falling about the blood spouting the well rushing out of the cabin and the sick crawling and retreating to their berths. This was a dreadful sight—The steam and the season made the cabin so hot that it was impossible for me to sleep in it. I ate nothing from Wednesday morning until Sunday during the whole passage I staid on deck day and night fair and foul weather.

Sunday August 16th   reached Brazos Island landed on the sand about 12 o'clock. I never experienced such heat from the sun in my life—never saw so many flies—shewed my letter of instructions to Mr. Hill asst. Qtr. Mtr. and he gave an order to the Capt. of the steamer "Rough and Ready" to take us on board and to our respective stations. There were four of us Capt. Gordon Ky Capt. Graham Id Capt. McCausland Oh and my self

Monday August 17th   left Brazos in the "Rough and Ready" and finding the Mississippi Regiment at the Mouth of the Rio Grande stopped there. Found a great deal of sickness among our men—an hour or two after I arrived walking with Dr. Halsey[4] he asked me if I knew what that firing meant (there were guns firing just out of the camp) upon my answering in the negative he informed me they were burying a man. What is his name said T. W. Ellis[5] of the Yazoo volunteers. I used to know the man a bright eyed fine looking fellow who lived a short time ago at Camden Madison County.

Tuesday 18.   Ordered by Col. Davis to go to Brazos for the rifles[6] that were there and to inquire for the balance went in the "exchange"

steamer boat brought over, Wednesday Aug 19th, 15 boxes of rifles 2 of swords lease grant in the steamer Cinn. [Cincinnati]. The others not arrived at Brazos—expected hourly in the Revenue Cutter Le gare [Legare]

Thursday 20th   The Col.'s heart being altogether set [ink smudge on MS] on military glory ordered me back to inquire if the rest of the arms had arrived to have them transported to his camp immediately. I had to ride through the hot sun at 12. and when I got to Brazos I did not know whether I was living or dead. Indeed I expected every moment to fall from the horse with the sun pain. Informed that the Legare had arrived and that the remaining 37 boxes of arms were all on board the Cincinnati and would come round next morning at 9 o'clock—my trip was altogether unnecessary returned same evening—

Friday 21   closed on the accounts with Capt. AGH [Hill] of the temporary Qtr. Mrs. acting—

Saturday 22nd   Deviled to death trying to get the old muskets boxed up in time to go to Point Isabel[7]. After trudging about in the sand and heat 3 or 4 hours the boat nevertheless got off. left some of the arms Lt. Col. McClung[8] returned to my tent. Sick dreadful headache aching and pain in all my limbs owing to Col Davis at night and the hot sun laid on my blanket went to sleep as well as the flies would let me—they sting dreadfully—had a perspiration in the night.

Sunday 23rd   —better—walked out of the camp and found some men digging a grave—upon inquiring I found that the man was Nive Davis[9] that had died yesterday. This man was a private in the Marshall guards Capt. Taylor's company. I am told he was one of the stoutest and most thorough going men in it. The evening that I arrived at this place Dr. Halsey requested me to walk with him. When we reached the hospital tent I stood at the door while the doctor walked in. While the doctor was examining the other patients and prescribing a man lieing [sic] at the door of the tent near me was talking incoherently. Doubled up in the sand "Take care of your head you are a dead man oh! to shoot a man so, but die die die!" When Dr. Halsey came out I remarked he is delirious. "Yes he will die in two days" Not quite prophetic as to days but entirely so as to the death—buried Sunday at 8 o'clock in ground two feet deep

at the Mouth of the Rio Grande alas nor wife nor children more
will he behold nor friend nor sacred home

Monday August 24.   Col. Davis and part of the troops left in the
steamer Virginian for Camargo[10] everything hurry scurry—Lt. Col.
McClung returned from Point Isabel about night—

Tuesday August 25.   All confusion carrying down tents etc. guns
gun boxes pots and kettles to the landing got aboard the steam boat
"Col. Cross"[11] all the troops sick and all numbering about 400
men—officers and privates inclusive this evening—got up steam the
next morning and left for Camargo.

Wednesday August 26.   Started at sunrise in the "Col. Cross" This
was one of the boats purchased by Capt. Sanders[12] at Pittsburgh.
Purchased to run the Rio Grande at a low stage of water. The water
being now up even with banks of the river the boat large broad and
flat bottomed and drawing only a foot and half of water. The
current of the Rio Grande being more rapid that any current I ever
saw[13]—it is with great difficulty that she could stem the current. In
spite of all efforts she was constantly running ashore driven on by
the current. Tuesday night a man[14] died on board of the boat one of
the Marshall guards—There was a calling for the Dr. a hurrying to
and fro of rough men to the aft of the boat where the sick were—it
was said at 10 a man was dying the well went to sleep in the morning
it was announced that the man was dead. His comrades went out
early in the morning to procure a coffin and dig his grave. The rude
coffin was ready the grave nearly dug but steam was up the living
and the dead were taken along together. When we got four or five
miles up the river Lt. Col. McClung commanded the boat stopped—a
shallow grave was dug on the right bank of the Rio Grande. The
dead man wrapped in a blanket was buried unknelled uncoffined.
The grave was not ready when the dead man was brought ashore.
He was laid down some ten yards from the grave. Men had grown
familiar with death. I dont think it is too much to say that of all the
crowd there standing none looked on the operation with any other
feelings than a matter of business. While the dead man was laying
there I noticed but one man who looked at him as if thinking on
death. He was a sick man and as he fixed his eyes on the corpse of
his comrade the words "He steadfastly gazed on the face of the dead
and bitterly thought of the morrow" occurred to me. The banks of
the Rio Grande up to Matamoras are low for the most part but

there are many splendid localities for plantations—The land is rich as that of the Nile covered with the Georgia cane and chapperal [*sic*] and adapted to sugar rice corn cotton. In many places there was corn ripe and near to the ripe corn a second crop growing green as grass of various heights from 6 inches to 10 feet. The trees are scattering and low not higher than the ordinary blackjack. They are the musquite [*sic*] tree and other varieties of names of which I could not learn. For some twenty or thirty miles along the east bank in the neighborhood of Resaca De La Palma was to be seen a species of palm tree[15] very beautiful. Burrita[16] is a miserable little village of some dozen huts but lies high and fortified by an embankment. The land from Matomoras to Camargo all along both sides lies high is well adapted to cultivation and when the Anglo Saxons get to work on it will lay the region of the lower Mississippi in the shade. Let the government do as it may the Americans will in a few years occupy both banks of this River along the whole levee. The darkness flies before the sun; Laziness cowardice and ignorance must give way before industry courage and intelligence.

Thursday 27th   continued our voyage in the evening an officer high in command in the army called my attention to the fact that there were a greater many boxes of wine and other merchandise put out on the front lower deck near the bow of the boat not marked from the U. S. nor any officer. That doubtless they belonged to the Captain of the boat in violation of express regulations as published and put up in the cabin:—That from these articles being put out convenient to be landed it was doubtless the intention of the Captain to land them at Matamoras; that his great complaint about the boat not running better was that the boat was too deeply laden that it was an outrage that he should cheat the government out of freights and by helping to overload the boat retard the passage; that he thought it was my duty as asst quarter master to have the facts investigated by lodging a complaint at the Qr. Mrs. office when we arrived at Matamoras. I took a witness Capt. Holland[17] and went down on the lower deck and found some four or five piles of wine boxes containing 12 to 15 boxes in each pile. And there was also other boxes. I consulted with one of our officers what I should do he said he thought I had nothing to do with the matter. I reflected on the matter the boat reached Matamoras about 8 o'clock A.M. on Friday.

Friday August 28th I made up my mind to the line of my duty. I went to the Quarter Master's office in Matamoras which I found after some trouble. I inquired for Col. Whiting he had gone to Camargo. I stated that I was ordered by Col. Hunt at Orleans to report to Col. Whiting. I stated my name and office and asked for Capt. Montgomery[18] the Q. M. at that point. I was politely addressed by Capt. Montgomery as the man. I stated to him that I was green in my office and hardly knew the distinguishing line between duty and officiousness: that an officer high in command had called my attention the evening before to boxes of wine and merchandise which it was supposed belonged to Capt. Birmingham Capt. of the boat: that the boxes were still on board and doubtless would soon be landed: that I felt it my duty to mention the subject for such action as his better judgt would dictate. That very likely Capt. Birmingham could give a satisfactory explanation and that I hoped he could. Capt. Montgomery's reply was promptly made "sir you have done your duty you would have done wrong not to report such a case. I will have the facts investigated immediately." He turned to a young man and directed him immediately to go down on board the "Col. Cross" and see how the matter stood. I knocked about the city of Matamoras a while saw drinking and gaming everywhere and when I got down to the boat I found the boxes and goods above spoken of on the shore under guard. The result was that a great many more goods were found in the hold besides those which I had seen all the property of the Captain or private goods. The boat was detained in arranging this business until late in the evening. Capt. Birmingham was discharged the property seized for the freight and a new Captain, Capt. Pratt employed. Matamoras is a good large city of about 12,000 inhabitants. The houses in the suburbs made of up right or sun burnt bricks covered with cane. However in the town brick all doubled doored and windows barred as all the houses in Mexico are. Flat roofs no chimneys. The Mexicans are very cleanly man and woman have on course [coarse] clean cotton clothes and bathe in the river or lakes at least once a day. This account will suit I believe everywhere. We left Friday evening and right about 10 o'clock the "Col. Cross" was driven into a corn field by force of a current and shivered one of her wheels. Unfortunately for the imprisoned cooped up disagreeably situated passengers the water was too high up over the ground to admit of going ashore without getting wet up to the knees. Many of our youngsters did not mind the water and next morning scattered over the surrounding country.

Saturday August 29   The carpenter and blacksmith assisted by mechanicks found among the volunteer laboured hard at making a new wheel. In the evening a steamboat came along and took us higher up the river to a dry high landing near a large Rancho[19]— beautiful place elegant land beautiful lake near the house.

Sunday August 30   at 10 o'clock the wheel was done steam up and the boat about to start when the steamer "Rough and Ready" coming down haled to know if some box was on board being answered in the affirmative she ran along side but came upon us too fiercely struck our rudder and broke off the upper part [of] it. Here was another source of vexation and delay. The carpenter had to work to mend the rudder—got ready again at 4 o'clock and began ascending the river. That night about 10 o'clock the current struck the boat in sheering off from a point and drove it against a tree which grew out from the edge of the bank and leaned over the river crash crash crash went a part of the pilot House guards and some of the staterooms. All confusion and alarm. got clear of the tree finally and went a few miles and laid by for the night with the determination of the captain and all others high in authority not to run in the night any more.

Monday August 31   still moving upriver every body dissatisfied unhappy the boat fetid and stinking and many very many sick. I was suffering dreadfully with the universal complaint diarrhea so hot such a dreadful stench from the necessaries, biscuit half cooked no place to poke one's head in where a moment's comfort could be found night or day. The sick strewed about, some delirious and crying out for their friends. I became so weak that I could scarcely walk. Ah, how bitter were my reflections when I thought of the death that I felt certain would soon overtake me and thought of my wife and children and that in spite of their hearts entreaties I had voluntarily left home to suffer such a fate. Nothing particular further occurred except that one man[20] fell over board and after shrieking for help a few minutes was just sinking as the mate with a few of the hands in the yard caught him by the hair—another fell over next day and swam down the stream like a duck holding his hat in his right hand all the way and was nigh the bank when the boat overtook him. Another wandered too far one day when we stopped to wood and came running to the shore his name was Kinkaid[21]—The Col. commanding ordered the boat forward. Kinkaid that night got aboard another boat and when we arrived we found him at Camargo. Our passengers on board the "Col. Cross" the *distingue* were Major Genl. Patterson[22] Major Abraham Van Buren[23] Paymaster Major Burns[24] Do. Capt. Reynolds[25] asst. Qr. Mr. Lieut. Henshaw[26] Col. McClung and Major Bradford[27] of the Mississippi Regt. We passed the town of Rhinoso[28] [Reynosa] without stopping the place is very high and well fortified and a few brave men might have defended it against all comers but the poor devils delivered up [the] town without striking a blow we arrived at Camargo Friday evening the 4th Sept 1846 when we reached the right bank of the San Juan [river]. When we were to land and encamp I found on ordering the forage ashore that 10 sacks of oats were missing. I had received at the Mouth of the Rio Grande of the asst. Qr. Mr. Capt Ogden[29] stationed there fifty sacks of oats. We took six horses on board at the mouth and got Col. McClung's horse (which had run away or been stolen) at Matamoras three days after we left the mouth which made seven in all. As a sack of oats was wanting (they contained 2 bushels each) I marked it down and had it taken from the hatches. In this way 16 sacks were used, leaving 34 due me. Major Genl. Patterson had six or 7 horses and mules aboard and Major Van Buren had 2 or 3. It was said among the hands and servants that Genl. Patterson's servants used one sack of our oats. Genl. Patterson had gone into the Town [Camargo] when the defciet [*sic*] was discovered by me. Capt. Pratt requested me to go across the river in the Cross and see Genl. Patterson that doubtless I could get the matter settled as soon as I saw Genl. Patterson—it was then late in the evening I waited on the Col. Cross sometime but Genl. Patterson did not return. I waited until near dark I went over the river in a ferry found out Capt. Holland I learned from him that the sacks landed 24 were brought within the lines and were under a guard. I then inquired for my baggage no one knew anything of it but soon Capt. Taylor told me and Capt. McManus[30] that they found my trunk bag of stationary and lantern lying by themselves on the shore. No one had thought of them. It was only an accident that they had not been whipped off. I found my baggage at my friend's Capt. McManus' tent. And hunting out the forage found a sentinel in charge and directed him not to let anyone have any oats without my orders. I then had my baggage taken down to Capt. Holland's tent with whom I had made an arrangement to mess. I should have mentioned that while waiting on board the steam boat on the Camargo side for Genl. Patterson Capt. Reynolds one of the new asst. Qr. Mrs. from Tennessee being about to leave the boat to report himself to Col. Whiting asst. Qr. Mr. I thought it a good idea for me to do the same thing so I went with him. Col. Whiting remarked that I looked sick. I told him that I had been sick with diarrhea but that I got clear of it and was then initially well except debility. He asked me if I felt well enough to take the field. I told him certainly and that I knew riding would entirely restore me. This was near night he told me very well you will go forward and told me to call in the morning and get written instructions. When I called in the morning what was my surprise to receive written instructions to remain at Camargo with Capt. Crossman[31]. The secret was this Capt. Crossman heard from the Capt. of the steam boat that night that there were on board 2 Qr. Mrs. one named Reynolds a delicate weakly man one named Smith a hale stalward man from the mountains of East Tennessee. What does he do but post off to Col. Whiting and lay claim to Smith that he wanted back a man and now Reynolds wished to remain at Camargo as his Tennessee friends were stationed here under Genl. Pillow[32] and I wished to go on by all means with the Miss Regt. The next day Genl. Taylor Col. Whiting and the regulars took up the line of march for Seralvo[33] [Cerralvo]. In the hurry of departure an effort was made by Genl. Patterson and Capt. Crossman to get the order changed—but he would not trouble anymore about it—except to direct Capt. Reynolds to remain with Genl. Pillow. This is the history of my being ordered to stop at Camargo as I understand it.

Saturday Sept 5th   early in the morning left the Missi Camp and went over in the ferry boat to see after the oats. All was landed and I could not see my remaining sacks. I found Genl. Patterson in his dressing gown told him I had no doubt from what his own men and the crew of the boat said that his men had used some of my oats. hinted we ought at least to share the loss. He said it was altogether uncertain that he had bought a vast quantity of forage etc. etc. Servants could not be relied on etc. etc. Finding from his views on the matter that nothing could be done I returned to the camp—as I landed on the opposite side I found a Mexican with milk and hot wheat cakes. I who had been living on pork and crackers for two weeks—bought a tin cup of the milk and a loaf—It was 8 or 9 o'clock—never was any repast so grateful. Some of my acquaintances coming by prevented me from shame from buying more. Entering the camp I arranged the requisitions after a great deal of trouble to cover which had been issued and such further forage as was required and turned over to the forage master the sacks which remained. It was my intention to advise Col. Davis of my new orders but he had gone out of the camp and did not return until about 2 o'clock. When I showed him the order of Col. Whiting he seemed somewhat mortified and said if I had shewn it to him before he would have got it changed but Col. Whiting and Genl. Taylor had then left. I told him I did not know myself that I was to leave until I got the instructions nor had any idea of it and that I had mentioned the matter at the earliest moment I could. There the matter dropped. I went to Col. Crossman's office with my baggage. About night he inquired if I had any place to board at. I told him I had not. He suggested that I had better go down for the evening on board one of the public steamers that they would charge me ½ dollar a meal that he boarded in a spanish family, that they had taken him with reluctance and he did not know whether I could get in. I told him I would go aboard the boat as he suggested and in the mean time would be much obliged to him if he would try to get me board in the family he boarded in. This he promised to do: I went aboard the "Whiteville" (commanded by) Capt. Dunn. Supper was over—he had some ordered. A very good one. A very polite man Capt. Dunn son of the old Sergeant at arms to the Ho Reps. Major Carnes was aboard to whom I had been introduced—advised with him he said he would resign—I told him I believed I would—In course of conversation with Major Van Buren I mentioned my great disappointment dissatisfaction and disgust at my new position and that I had concluded to resign but the great misfortune was that I had got so far into the business that I could not resign in an enemy's country without mortification and subjecting myself to the jeers of enemies and the doubtful sympathy of friends. "No captain" said he "no captain dont think a moment of resignation—. The first great duty of a soldier is to obey the word of command—obey orders— whatever disposition they make of you submit to it without a murmur it is the only way—you can not resign here in the heart of the enemy's country. Every officer is apt to think his duties arduous and position difficult. We all have our trial I assure you". I was greatly disturbed in mind Major Van Buren soon left with his specie to follow and overtake Genl. Taylor Major Carnes remained but engaged in conversation with others. There I sat on the guards of the steam boat solitary and alone. I was greatly relieved to be joined by an acquaintance Dr. Patton[34] of Raymond Hines County Missi. He had volunteered a private in the Raymond Fencibles and got the appointment of surgeon in the army through the instrumentality of some surgeon belonging to the regular army who had noticed his treatment of the sick while traveling together in a steam boat from the Mouth. He was on his way to the post to which he had been ordered to wit Matamoras: where there was an immense number of sick and a scarcity of Physicians. He was much concerned like myself at being detached from our regiment but he had much greater reasons to be pleased than I—more pay and a comfortably agreeable place. We talked of the past and present and at a late hour retired. I tried to sleep but could not. After a long time I sunk into a troubled slumber from which I was awakened by the drum and fife playing "Hail Columbia" some fresh troops were coming up. Thus aroused I in vain endeavoured to sleep any more. My situation my wife and children—my mind was on a rack. With a body tottering from the loss [of] health and sleep and mind disturbed with harassing reflections I repaired after Breakfast to the office of Capt. Crossman.

Sunday Sept 6th This was one of the busiest days /God forgive me and my country/ of my life. Genl. Taylor had left the day before : the troops were to be sent on and anybody to be received and detached—a thousand demands on the quarter master department every hour. Riding post to the landing and back issuing orders and seeing them executed took up the day. I dined today at my new boarding House (Capt. Crossman got me admitted) Don Gaspar's. I found my boarding house a very delightful place—Don Gaspar was a native of old Spain born in Seville—He emigrated when young to Mexico and settled at Camargo a merchant where he married a Mexican lady—one of the aristocracy a very good looking short fat woman educated and accomplished as highly as the country would admit of. She has one sister and two nieces living with her. They seem to be very well behaved and modest young women. Every day when we went into Breakfast and Dinner It was *buenos Dios Capitano, Buenos Dios Senior*. Every night it was *Buenos Noches Capitano buenos noches senior*. When I first went there while there was hope that the Mexicans would make a stand at Monterey they seemed to be in a good spirit Capt. Crossman would say good humouredly *Viva Republica Americana. Si viva grande Republica Americana*. They would archly reply *Viva Republica Mexicana si Republica Mexicana La grande nation*. Capt. Crossman Ampudia[35] *no valiente much Mearo* and would shake himself as if trembling with fear. They would blush and laugh at the Captain's affectation of fear and Paredes[36] *el Presidente valiente il vent a Montere*. Then when they heard that Santa Anna[37] was at the head of affairs they were evidently delighted—and seemed to regard the whole matter as settled. With all Santa Anna's faults and misfortunes he is still in their hearts their great man. Had he won the battle of San Jacinto or rather had he not lost it so disastrously he would have been their idol—and the god of their idolatry. They [were] used to meeting us in the eating [of] Breakfast Dinner and supper—retire when we commenced eating and return to our companies after meals if they found we had not left. Frequently we sat after supper on the back pavement—we in chairs and they on a sofa in front of us and then we would try to talk to them using such few spanish words as we knew but calling in the aid of an American a brother boarder a Mr. Gilpin would offer to interpret—said Gilpin under standing both languages well. Twice they sent out and brought in good guitar players from among their neighbours who played for us delightfully. Thus passing my time and sleeping soundly every night in a nice bunk in a tent which I pitched by the side of Capt. Crossman's in an orange grove, my spirits returned, my health was perfectly restored.

Hope elevates and joy brightens my crest.
I once more thought of my dear home and all there so dear to me as if I live once more to see them. What poor devils we are.

Poor pensioners on the bounties of an hour. Goat's milk good coffee soup sweet bread mutton chop pure water and the smile of a woman can work wonders on a sick man who has been living in the sand and physicked on government crackers and fried pork. At least this was my experience. And whoever does not believe in it must be a city clerk or the keeper of an oyster cellar. For five or six days before I left Don Gaspar's there was an evident change in the deportment of the *senioras [señoras]*—They were seldom found in the room to greet us as we came nor did they come out after supper nor was there any thing in our deportment to invite a return to the old customs. The Americans were every where exulting and proud— Capt. Crossman's good humoured references to Ampudia's running from Monterey were no longer received with a laugh but with an air of melancholy and look of incredulity. The reason was that during that period reports and letters had reached the Americans assuring them that the Mexicans had fallen back from Monterey and Genl. Taylor in the act of taking possession. But the Mexicans in Camargo on the contrary had reports and assurances that Genl. Taylor was not about to take Monterey was likely never to do so and that so far from the Mexicans falling back on Saltillo they were strongly fortified at Monterey with an overwhelming force and that there was about to be brought a desperate battle another sort of an affair to Palo Alto or Resaca De La Palma.

From Monday Sept. 7th to Thursday Sept. 24th   my life was pretty much the same staying with Capt. Crossman in his office by day eating with him at Don Gaspar's and going to sleep when he did in my tent whose door was a few steps from his. There was but little diference between our habits except as to rising in the morning. The good Captain without awaking me would go quietly from his tent at sunrise or before walking off softly in his buckskin shoes while I would nap an hour or so longer. I found that taking more exercise and being more exposed to the sun than I had been accustomed to that if I did not sleep in the morning I was certain to get sleepy in the middle of the day or after dinner. When our meals were ready a Mexican boy would come over to the office and say "Capitan soupper ready" The men in the office taught him at least how to call the different meals. This boy whose name was Gerotaya about 12 years old was very smart considering he was Mexican and so impressed was he with the superiority of the whites that if any one said to him interrogatively Mexicano he would indignantly reply *non No Mexicano! Americano*. Five or six days after General Taylor left news was brought to General Marshall[38] in command of the volunteer troops stationed on the opposite side of the river that there were ten thousand Mexicans about thirty miles off. Everything

was hurry and excitement. Genl. Patterson had six pounders mounted in the plaza ditches[39] dug across the streets which could be shut
up without inconvenience and first ropes and then chains stretched
across the principal thoroughfares—The regular officers laughed
very much at the ditches and the ropes. They said that the ditches
which were on the side next [to] the Town were on the wrong side
of the embankment. That they would be no hindrance to the enemy
but devilish good places for them to fight from. As to the ropes
they could be easily cut in two by the first horseman that came to
them. Genl. Patterson also issued an order directing all persons not
Mexicans or connected with the army or in government employ to
leave the Town by the 17th[40]. The Mexicans in the Town became
greatly alarmed. They were much frightened at the preparations for
battle and the reports. Men women and children could be seen
hurrying into the country. The town was nearly depopulated. During the period above mentioned there were a great many discharges
of the soldiers on account of sickness. It was my business to give
them passports to the Mouth of the Rio Grande which it afforded
me the greatest pleasure to do having witnessed their sufferings.
When Mississippians or Marylanders would come to me sometimes
tottering with disease at other times carrying a whole graveyard of
melancholy in their looks my soul would yearn towards as did
Joseph towards his brethren when they came to buy corn but like
Joseph I had to act on the motto business before pleasure and
instead of embracing them as I felt inclined to do, I would with
apparent nonchalence examine their surgeon's and commanding
officer's certificate and write the permission to go on any public
boat to the Mouth of the Rio Grande There were some very
cunning names to write. One that struck me as utterly profane
"Christ Shene" of the Ohio Volunteers—The idea of a man calling
himself "Christ" in a Christian land is utterly shocking. He seemed
to be of some of the German tribes—I suppose his parents were
Hessians or Bohemians—He was a poor miserable scarecrow wretch
doomed perhaps to answer for the sins of his parents in giving him
such a name. I mentioned this strange name to some of the clerks
one of them said the name should not surprise as there [were] no
more common names among the Mexicans than Jesus and Christ—
that office we were then doing business in belonged to a woman
named Mary Ann Jesus. After that I thought of the maxim of

Horace *"Nil Admiran"*. There was a great time when expresses were being started for Headquarters. They were carried by hired Mexicans who were employed at $45 a month and everything found them. They were furnished with the fleetest horses—equipment of the best materials and the best arms. They carried the despatches in a pair of saddle bags which were secured against the weather by skins and the flaps sealed. These they were to deliver into Col. Whiting's or Genl. Taylor's own hands and none others. When the express arrived it was equally or greater an occasion, in would come the Mexican generally in the evening with a look of triumph and satisfaction his saddle bags in one hand his whip in the other the chains of his spurs gingling [*sic*] as if forty prisoners were marching in irons. During the above period Texans on the way to Matamoras were attacked by the Mexican Rancheros—one Texan was killed—The survivors when they got to Matamoras returned with a party of fifty men and in revenge laid waste some three or four ranches. A party of five or six Texans who had been left behind at Mier[41] were attacked while on their way from Mier to Monterey and killed their brains knocked out and their bodies mutilated. Having partially recovered their health they were on their way to join their regiments—when I first came into the office a half a dozen orders would be issued per day for coffins. At last all the lumber gave out and Capt. Crossman told the applicants that they would have to give their friends a soldiers burial—i. e. bury them in their blankets without coffins—the thing was soon understood and the applications ceased entirely. Hundreds of America's noble and generous sons sleep in this soil without having received the rites or the decencies of Scripture—But more blithely will they come forth at the sound of the resurrection horn than Kings from beneath the ponderous marble which sycophantic favourites have reared upon them. A few days before I removed to the opposite side of the river Col. Taylor[42] the head of the Commissary department arrived with specie en route for Monterey and Col. Riley[43] a fine noble soldier and his splendid regiment the 2d infantry. I like Col. Riley mightily he is a noble man besides he is a native of Baltimore. Some days after the report had reached Camargo that there were ten thousand Mexicans in the neighborhood Capt. Crossman finding no one else would do it and being anxious as to the fate of one of his expresses who was two or three days behind his time sent out a spy to ascertain the truth as to the whereabouts the numbers and the intentions of the Mexicans. He hired at a small price a Mexican in whom he could rely who under the pretense of selling pelonceau (candied sugar tied up in rolls about the size of Bologna sausages) was to go to their camp and while selling his pelonceau gather what information he could. He set out Saturday 12th and spent Sunday 13th in the Mexican camp and returned the next day. The news he brought was that instead of 10,000 Mexicans there were only 300 that these were rancheros and citizens of Mier Rhinosa Matamaras and Camargo. That they were some 20 miles from Camargo that they were under the command of Canales that their object was to cut off communications between Camargo and Monterey and plunder the wagons pack mules destroy small parties and above all seize the despatches intended for Genl. Taylor. Capt. Crossman told Col. Taylor of these things but there had been so many everlasting false reports that the Col. did not seem to give the account much importance. He started on the 19th with some Dragoons who had been sick and a few surgeons and others going on to join the army. Having learned on the other side of the river something further of the hostile designs of Canales he requested Capt. Crossman to ask a company to be sent from the 2d Infantry. Capt. Crossman unwell that evening from a fall which he had received during the day from his horse got me to see Genl. Patterson on the subject. Genl. Patterson at once issued the order for the company to set forward by times in the morning (it was night when I called on him) which he sent to Col. Riley by his orderly. He at the same [time] directed me to inform Capt. Crossman to furnish one or two wagons as Col. Riley might require. The company commanded by Capt. Anderson[44] left next morning about an hour by sun. In the evening of the day the company started an express arrived from Col Taylor the express brought by a young man named Hays[45] the brother of Col. Hays the Texian. There remained no doubt that Canales[46] knew that Col. Taylor ws going forward with specie his emissaries had told him $500000. Col. Taylor received satisfaction that Canales was looking out for him and young Hays remarked that for that much money they would fight hard. Genl. Patterson immediately ordered on 250 men from Col. Jackson's[47] Georgia Regt. They were fine looking men and I heard it said the choice companies of the regiment including the celebrated Jasper Greens[48] composed almost entirely of Irishmen. Of whom a

Georgian remarked in my presence "Give the Jasper Greens some whiskey and they will charge into Hell"—When the Missi Regiment left their camp on the opposite side of the River [Rio San Juan] on the 9th or 10th they left a great deal of property arms tents etc. Capt. Taylor[49] requested me to take care of his trunk. Col. McClung came over to the office a short time before he started and said Smith I shall leave my trunk and camp chest in the camp. Will you do me the favour to take care of them as well as you can. Certainly Sir said I. I will do all I can to preserve them for you precisely as I would to save my own property. I went over the 2nd day after they left. Lieutenant Bostwick[50] then in command of the sick (about a hundred were left behind) pointed me out McClung's two trunks and camp chest I got a cart and had them carried to Angel's tent the quartermaster's superintendent on the west side. I was unable to find Taylor's trunk no one could point it out. I told Angel he ought to get them all together he said he would try to do so. I urged the subject on Capt. Crossman's attention and he issued an order to gather all the property together and save it saying Col. Davis was his friend and he had promised him to save his articles and that all the property moved be saved. The day before Bostick had called at our office nearly dead it was from him I learned the Mississippians were certainly gone. He was nearly dead. He said he had about a hundred men with him all sick unable to help [one] another. That they had no rice tea coffee sugar or bread—nothing but pork—that everything had been turned over in the way of provision or carried off—that he had been trying to find Genl. Pillow—that he was utterly exhausted that he was in better health than any man in his detachment and that he was nearly dead. He begged me if possible to get him a horse. I represented his case to Capt. Crossman—and asked it as a favour to me to let him have one that I knew it would be returned. Capt. Crossman complied taking his receipt. He saw Genl. Pillow and returned and then begged me to put him in the way of getting provisions. I went with him to Lieut. Britton's the A. C. S. and stated to him Bostick's situation and that of his men. Lieutenant Britton[51] with a promptness that did him great credit immediately said it is irregular to issue as you know anything without a requisition but in such a case as this I will do any thing other than men shall suffer—he enquired where the men were across the river he immediately wrote to McBee his clerk across the river to furnish from the provision stores to Lieut. Bostick any thing he wanted taking an ordinary receipt for the same. The next day when I went over I found that Bostick had got for his men all they wanted as to provisions but that a man a Mr. Morehead[52] was laying dead in his tent and no one to bury him. I got Mr. Angel to promise me to bury him which he did—when the Mississippians finally left which was a day or two after I was with them I was told that they left a man James Boyd[53] formerly mayor of Jackson dead in the camp. I was greatly shocked at this. I never learned any explanation of this. I enquired about the dead man and learned that the quarter master's men had buried him also—another squad of sick Mississippians composed of men who had marched with the regiment but who had broken down on the march and had returned under the charge of Capt. Rogers[54] also applied to me. I was called on by a man named Rae or McRae[55] of Capt. Cooper's[56] company who represented that they had been attached 25 in number to Genl. Pillow's Brigade and were enrolled with Capt. McCowan's[57] company a company of Tennessee Volunteers. They were living on Capt. McCowan's men's rations which were short as they had drawn for some time and the day of drawing again was yet a few days off. [illegible scratched-out sentence] Genl. Pillow would at once straiten [sic] that I knew as soon as he heard of it. That Capt. McCowan could make a special requisition: then they had no clothes and stood in need of a great many things. I told them to go and bury [borrow] of Phelps their sutler. He said Phelps regarded them as detached from the Missi Regt. [and] would not trust [them]. Then they had no medicine or medical attendance. I told them all they had to do was see the govt. surgeon Dr. Wells. But thinking I could best serve the poor fellows by seeing Genl. Pillow in person I took my umbrella and walked with Rae up to Genl. Pillow's marquee. I represented the case to Genl. P. in the presence of Rae introduced Rae to him. Genl. Pillow at once said he would straiten every thing I then called on Phelps who after some discussion agreed to furnish the detachment with what they wanted as sutler to the Missi. Regt. and promised me to see the men and let them know. I inquired a few days afterward and found he had done so.

Wednesday the 23rd Capt. Crossman informed me that Capt. Sherman[58] was much dissatisfied with his position across the river and had applied to him to be relieved that he was sorry to part with me but matters had got into a snare on the other side and he heard he would be compelled to get me to go over and take Capt. Sherman's place: Angel the Superintendent on the other side whom I had known at Jackson Missi had been electioneering with me for two or three weeks to come over that everything would be done by him—I should have no trouble—I gave him no encouragement for the truth was I wished if I could not be sent to the army to remain where I was in my pleasant quarters. Capt. Crossman saying that he could not consistently with a sense of duty resist Capt. Sherman's application and that I would have to take his place. I promised with good graces to go when he wished. he said then I had better go over and see how Sherman was situated some time during the day and see what arrangements would be necessary for removal next day or such time as Capt. Sherman and myself could agree on. Just then Col. Riley entered the office and when about to leave he asked me to go with him to the camp of the 2d infantry (his command) that he had some good whiskey and would like it if I would go and get a drink. I complied and heard in his tent a good many fine anecdotes told by himself and the other officers. After a couple of glasses I returned and after dinner went across the river saw Capt. Sherman and made arrangement with him to exchange quarters with him the next day at 10 o'clock—he leaving his tent tables and chairs and I leaving mine.

Thursday 24th Sept moved across the River directly opposite Camargo. The superintendent and all the hands professed great pleasure the guard then stationed at my depot were regulars of the 2d infantry. After dinner which was helped along and augmented by a few good things sent me by Mr. Angel who rightly concluded that I had but a short time to stock my pantry. I was seated at the door of my tent when a soldier having a musket and fixed bayonet and some insignia of office marched directly up to me. Is this Capt. Smith Sir. Yes said I he then gave me a military salute. Capt. two Mexicans and a volunteer are fighting and a crowd is gathering threatening a great disturbance what must I do sir. "Take them under arrest" this I said with the most martial look and pronuncia-tion that I could command. I expected to see a dreadful affray in honor of my new command. I followed the Sergeant with my eyes he took an other of the guard. They marched to the combatants and such were the tones of authority with which he spoke and his military bearing that he marched off the combatants and dispersed the crowd without the least difficulty. I ate my supper in peace and slept soundly in my new quarters.

Friday Sept 25th My birth-day 39 years. Oh! Lord so old and I have done so little. I have been of but little benefit to myself or any one else, sacrificed pleasure in youth to ambition an ambition never gratified plunged myself into debt despite the persuasions of my wife her entreaties and her tears. Seven long years of toil and misery to myself of discontent to my wife compelled to live at a place she abhorred have been the bitter fruits of one improvident rash step. And again I took this step of coming here against my wife's entreaties and perhaps I shall never see her and the children again. From the moment I got out of my bunk I felt as if I had reached a crisis in my life. I never felt more mental agony. I was sure something dreadful was to happen to me. As Friday was an unlucky day I determined to stay in my tent and attempt no new thing. But taking up a novel and some friends calling to see towards evening I began to recover my composure. Looking off to the west of me I discovered tents going up ground staked out etc. for an encampment which threatened [to] approach within a few feet of me. Seeing Mr. Angel I beckoned to him we sought out the Commander who proved to be Major Wall[59] commanding (the 1st and 2d Cols. being both sick) one of the Ohio Regiments. After some argument and representation that his proposed camp would crowd the depot ground too much: He agreed surcease and to pitch the rest of his tents in a line with those already up on the other side of the road. I ate my supper and slept soundly. The next day

Saturday the 26th it was represented to me that there had been the 2 days preceding an unusual number of drunken volunteers about the depot and that danger was apprehended of serious brawls besides the volunteers were in the habit of shooting off their guns in such a careless manner that a man had been shot in the arm and that the lives of men were needlessly endangered by the practice. In the evening I stepped over to General Marshall's marquee and represented the grievances to him he treated me with great politeness and said he would issue orders to support the habits complained of and would see them enforced if possible. I then went to see Major Wall and he acted in an insulting manner throughout demanding my business cutting me short that he would take care of his men he commanded his regiment. I bowed to him and told him I had called on him as a gentleman and made a respectful representation to him and left him. I felt aggrieved by Major Wall's conduct and language and passed the river to get Capt. Crossman to carry him a note Capt. C. was out riding and had to wait until 8 o'clock when he came in I made known the facts to him, he would call in the morning and if the amende honourable was not made, he would place the matter in safe hands for a hostile meeting—I returned to my quarters and there it occurred to me that my forebodings of ill were expounded. I slept soundly rose early.

Sunday morning the 27th wrote a letter to my wife about such things as I deemed of importance to her in reference to my affairs without making however the slightest allusion to my difficulty. Just as I finished Capt. Crossman arrived. he called on Major Wall and he made the amende honourable. Declaring he did not mean the least offence regretting much the occurrence thought I came to insult him and intermeddle with his command and dictate to him that he did not know that I commanded at the depot nor had he the least idea that I was speaking to him in reference to the good order at the depot when I referred to riots but thought I was speaking to him as to good order in his regiment that he would call at my tent and make these apologies and statements with the greatest pleasure. Four young officers of the regular army called at my tent and I treated them to some brandy. After taking a couple of drinks they left and then some clerks from Capt. Crossman's office called and staid most of the day. In this way I passed all the day when it would have become me to have read the bible. About 8 o'clock that evening two of the quartermaster's men arrived from Monterey and also Capt. Eaton[60] of the army with despatches from Genl. Taylor on his way to Washington Capt. Eaton crossed the river for Capt. Crossman's quarters without a moment's delay. The men stopped at Col. Cumming's sutler's store to tell the news which came upon everybody like a clap of thunder in a clear sky no one expected for the letter previously received that there would be any fighting what then was our surprise to learn that the most desperate battle had been fought that it commenced Monday morning the 21st and continued day and night until Thursday evening. How fought the Mississippians I enquired with the greatest valor said one like damnation said another. How fought the Kentuckians enquired a

Kentuckian How fought the Tennesseans and so the questions went. Gentlemen said the tired messenger all the volunters fought well every man stood up there is no distinction. The volunteers fought as well as the regulars and they all fought alike but I tell you our losses have been very great the Mississippians the Tennesseans and 3d and 4th infantry are dreadfully cut up. Col. McClung is mortally wounded. Col. Watson[61] of the Baltimore Battalion Capt. Gillespie[62] and nearly all the officers of the 3d infantry are killed. Genl. Butler[63] is wounded. Is Genl. Taylor hit? I enquired. No he was wherever danger was but if there was a man to be killed or wounded behind him the Mexicans would rush their guns around so as not to hit him. In an hour all the quartermaster's hands on both sides of the river including carpenters and blacksmiths and clerks were hard at work unloading the Brownsville so as to have her ready to start by light in the morning to carry Capt. Eaton. About a hundred and 50 Ohioans to their honour be it spoken came down and offered their services to help at unloading the Brownsville. Those not engaged in unloading the Brownsville were variously occupied some crying and getting drunk, some rejoicing and getting drunk, some writing letters—few thought of sleep. About sunrise

Monday the 28th the Brownsville having on board Capt. Eaton with his dispatches and a large mail went booming down the San Juan under a tremendous head of steam. About 9 o'clock that night by order I suppose of Genl. Patterson there was a splendid exhibition of fireworks and at the interval of every 3 rockets that went up was played by the band a national air—Hail Columbia first Star Spangled Banner and so on until I heard Clear the Kitchen after that the tunes were not sufficiently national for me to recognize them. Being in town today I heard the greatest contrariety of opinions some said Genl. Taylor had needlessly sacrificed the lives of his men that he never ought to have let the Mexicans off but ought to have sent for his other troops and made the victory complete, that it was a drawn battle that Monterey was but of little importance that Ampudia had time to reinforce that there would be a still more desperate battle to fight before the road to the interior could be gained, that had we captured Ampudia and his forces the battle would have been decisive etc. About all which all I can say just now is *non nostrum tantus componere cites*—I want to hear more and see more but if the matter remains as it does now it would seem to me a hard fight to no advantage.

Tuesday 29th   Did nothing but mope and read a novel to-day it is said 2 Alabamians were found near their camp with their throats cut and that their regiment swears they will kill in revenge 10 Mexicans. About 2 o'clock A.M. morning of

30th Sept   I had just awoke I heard distinctly a gunfire near the river—almost immediately I heard a voice calling on the Ohio regiment camped about 50 yards from me to turn out then came the long roll beat most furiously by them then long roll in the Kentucky camp then the long roll in the Tennessee camp across the river— there was in every direction the clang of arms and the cries of the officers "fall in" and then the tide of human voices swelled and grew louder and deeper in all the camps. I heard no hostile shout or gun and I knew all was safe. I relapsed into my bunk and went to sleep knowing it was a groundless alarm originating doubtlessly from the fact that a great many Mexicans had passed down the day before from Monterey. Passed over the river today and enquired for letters. Still no mail from Orleans, there has not been one for a fortnight. Bustled about stirring up carpenters and blacksmiths etc. to have everything ready for the train—a very large one which is now preparing to carry ordnance stores subsistence etc. to Monterey. Rode out in the evening to a corn field which the superintendent had bought. found it full of cattle. The Mexicans had doubtless turned them in.

Thursday Octr 1st   very busy about the train passed over the river about 10 o'clock found Major Brower just on the eve of starting to go up the Rio Grande to ascertain whether it was navigable to Mier and Laredo so as to open a communication with Genl. Wool[64] and supply him with provisions etc. Genl. Shields[65] leaves with some troops this evening by land to join General Wool. In the evening Mr. Angel came to my tent to inquire if I would not like to take a ride with a party of gentlemen going to the rapids in the river [Rio Grande] about 4 or 5 miles off by land to see the steam boat "Major Brown"[66] attempt to ascend them. Glad of an opportunity to take exercise I had my horse got ready and joined the party which consisted of Genl. Marshall Genl. Shields Captain Lincoln[67] U. S. A. Lieut. Hamilton[68] U. S. A. [and] two or three non commissioned officers some steam boat Captains and a guide—an old man named

Jameson. We rode on merrily and gaily chatted about one thing or another. I was some fifty yards in advance with the guide and some others. Finding our friends did not come up we halted and soon afterwards a young man rode up with Genl. Shields who told us that Genl. Marshall's horse had been frightened and become fractious and unruly had kicked up and kicked Lieut. Hamilton on the leg and had given him a very bad hurt—that the Lieut., Capt. Lincoln and some others had returned to the camp. Now here is life for you Lieut. H. was just a day or so from Monterey where he had been in the thickest of the fight charging the enemy at their guns and had escaped unhurt and, while in a good humor laughing with his friends expecting no harm he is kicked by his friend's horse and his leg broken for I ascertained upon my return to the depot that the leg was broken the bone fractured etc. We reached the rapids the Major Brown had passed up 3 hours before without any difficulty. Genl. Shields and suite went on. Genl. Marshall and the rest of us returned to camp. I am very much pleased with General Shields. He preserves his dignity and commands respect although he is entirely sociable and communicative even familiar. To make every man feel at ease preserving at the same time self respect and securing the respect of others is the *omnitulit* function of intercourse among men. When I started I had no idea that Mr. Angel was going. When he still rode on with us I felt much concern the train was preparing some hundred wagons and 1500 pack mules for Monterey. I felt the awkwardness of the situation. The qr. mr. and the superintendent both absent. Mr. Angel rode by my side and said he would soon return that he knew every thing was going right that all had their appropriate share and business. At the earliest moment that I could after visiting the river I turned my horse on the backtrack Mr. A. joined and putting my horse in a long trot and Mr. A. his in a gallop we soon reached the depot. The sun was still an hour high and we found every thing right.

Friday October 2.   Great hurry scurry about getting off the train—The mules are being shod on the fore feet to do this they have to be thrown down. Wagons getting ready forage bacon and flour being packed ready for the pack mules. Looked around facilitated the business all I could. Took a ride in the evening with Mr. Twitchell, sutler to the Kentucky Troops. We rode to new Camargo[69]. Saw a great many new coverlets and blankets to wear richly wrought for

which they demanded from 20 to 30 dollars a piece. Returned after
dark. Sat at the door of my tent looking out on the moonlight—
thinking of home, wife and children. Shall I ever see them again?

Saturday October 3d   Learned to-day two Tennesseans had been
found not far from the camp just above Camargo on the East Bank
of the San Juan dead. They had been shot and their throats cut.
From the nature of the gunshot wounds they must have been
inflicted by men on horse back. In consequence of this I understood
that Genl. Patterson had issued an order to treat all armed Mexicans
as out laws—to take their arms and on the least resistance to shoot
them down. This was a busy day—orders and counter orders 1500
pack mules being loaded with provisions flour sugar etc. for the
army at Monterey—60 wagons with ordnance stores and pork and
pack mules with forage. Besides 50 pack mules to the use of the
military escort. Consisting of the five remaining companies of the
Georgia Regt. Lt. Col. Redd comdg. Such a scene clerks, agents,
contractors, dashing about on horseback—Mexicans packing the
mules—mules kicking up and running off—ale cider and wine dealt
out at the sutler's stores (spiritous liquors *eo nomine* being forbidden) underlings half drunk and insolent, superiors issuing orders—
oaths and profanity on all hands in all languages—one soldier being
drunk stabbed a mule with his bayonet from mere wantonness—I
was standing not a hundred yards off. I immediately sent for the
sergeant of the guard and ordered the man arrested—the sergeant a
fine Kentuckian took a couple of men as I ordered and marched on
the redoubtable volunteer mule stabber and carried him off to the
guard house to be taken before Genl. Marshall when sober. He
thought to make fight but to stab a mule and resist a Kentucky
sergeant armed with pistols and a saber and two tall fellows armed
with muskets and bayonets were distinct operations. He soon
yielded. In the evening Col. Redd[70] comdg. the Georgia Cos. called
at my tent and took supper with me. He is a young man about 23
gallant and brave as a lion. He said he had fought the Mexicans in
Texas that they are a brave people and all the difference between
them and us is that they can not shoot as well (never taking aim)
and are not animated by patriotism—there is an absence of motive
to protect a tyrannical government of which they have known
nothing but its tyranny, robberies, and oppressions. He thinks now
they are learning to shoot better and from late indications are

becoming united and patriotic, he thinks the fighting has just commenced. He says it is his intention not to trouble Genl. Patterson with prisoners—but hang all Mexicans who give him battle from here to Monterey or present themselves in hostile array. I told him I thought he ought not to hang but if he killed them that hanging would have a tendency to arouse the spirit of indignation and produce probably a rise en masse. That's it sir, said he we ought to be friends or enemies—It is a one sided game now—we furnish them the sinews of war, rent their horses pay them for every thing—they hoist the black flag, cut the throats of our men, and mutilate them within a hundred yards of our camps—It is time that this game should cease. We must kill too and I will do it. These sentiments prevail now among all classes. I told Col. Redd that I had noticed in the morning early two intelligent looking Mexicans traveling on fine horses towards Monterey. That it occurred to me from the travelling that way that he would be attacked—He said he would be on his guard, have a picket a quarter of a mile out and be ready for them.

Sunday Oct 4th The Lord's day. May the Lord have mercy on us and incline the hearts of the rulers of two nations calling themselves Christian to adopt the principles of the gospel and show themselves worthy of a name derived from the Prince of peace. I intended to read the bible to-day and write two friends. But some things were to be done—I had to see about the guard went to visit Capt. Lincoln, as he had company I did not like to make it a business visit so I sat hoping to sit out the company—Finally I had to call him out of his tent and tell him what I wanted. When I got to my tent So! a new trouble—a large quantity of subsistence it appeared had been left behind. Capt. Crossman had demanded to know the transportation necessary the Commissary Lieutenant Britton had stated the number of pack mules he would want. Capt. Crossman ordered the number required for subsistence and finding a surplus of mules of 278 over the number required from all sources gave an order to have them packed with forage so that they might carry something. The commissary contended that the number required had not been furnished after much ado the contractor Col. Kinny[71] was found. He would soon rectify matters and show that he had produced and if he had not produced would produce the number—He and Capt. Crossman went off together—I dont know yet how the matter has been or will be settled. I had preserved Capt. Crossman's written instructions and they had been complied with (so far as depended on me and my agents) to the letter. Bothered on this and other subjects all day. Had no chance to read but one chapter in the Bible—did not write any letters.

Monday Oct 5 Receiving clerk reported absent this morning while the "Rough and Ready" was being unloaded discharged the clerk which I hated to do. A fine brave magnanimous fellow very smart and competent but dissipated. One of the ten millions of cases showing that no genius no worth no ability can save a drunkard—If a man's a drunkard he is bound equally to fail however smart as if he were a born fool, unless like Luther Martin and others the habit is taken up later in life. Went across the river visited Capt. Crossman and Capt. Sherman advised with the latter as to making my quarterly returns. While in the latter's quarters an old Spaniard came in with slices of a half ripe water melon—and holding out a piece to Sherman and one to myself pressed us to take this offering exclaiming *mucho fresco—mucho* laying his hand on his stomach—I declined saying *mucho malo* laying my hand on my forehead—returning wrote a letter to Col. Claiborne—walked around the depot seeing whether all were at their posts when I returned. I heard a great hallooing and noise at the wagon yard a man whooping and crying out G. d. I dont care whoop hurrah for America—I dont care whoop—I sent for the wagon master not there—it was after sundown. I waited a while hoping the drunkard would get quiet but he grew worse—I sent for the officer of the day and ordered the man arrested and confined until he got sober which was done—This had a very good effect one of the drunkard's friends came to expostulate— saying he was a fine fellow good hearted fellow hoped I would relent. I told him it was impossible that it was useless to say any thing that it was very well in him to want to help his friend but that I had done nothing but what I was bound to do and I could hear nothing further on the subject, that the man had been whooping for an hour and I heard it all from my tent—the gentleman teamster who was himself half laid over then retired. The wagon master came this morning . . .

Tuesday Octr 6th to apologize, the thing should not happen again he would remove the wagon yard if I would say so. I told him no by no means but look to his men. General Marshall called this morning and held a long agreeable chat after making known his wishes in reference to the guard etc. He complains very bitterly of the bad conduct of the Ohio regiment and its officer Major Wall— that the troops violate his orders plunder and assault the Mexican families and Wall wont punish—That there was much jealousy springing up between the regiments all growing out of Genl. Taylor's arrangements in separating the commands having Genl. Hamer at Monterey with part Ohioans and Kentuckians and he here with two regiments, one Ohio the other Kentucky and the Ohio men not regarding him as their general. This morning arrived from Monterey an express from General Taylor on his way to Washington he reports Col. McClung as convalescent—out of danger. It is reported in camp that General Taylor let Ampudia off to go and assist Santa Anna who is in trouble and it was with a view to this and peace as a consequence that the capitulation was made. "All in my eye and Betty Martin", I dont believe a word of it. Rode out this evening wtih Dr. Matthews an intelligent physician of Lousiville Ky attached to the Louisville legion—we saw some seven or eight bald eagles[72]—two old the others young feeding on some offal. We rode up within 20 yards of them and stood and looked at them a few minutes before they flew. We saw a very large flock of tuft headed partridges[73] a bird between the size of the common partridge and pheasant. They did not fly but ran along leisurely into the chaparral. Doves and quails abound in the greatest abundance they all seem tame. None fly from you but run along like chickens. The Mexicans never shoot such game and very seldom ever take deer and then they dont shoot them but run them down on horseback. The Mexican can soon run down a fat deer—the deer runs until exhausted, falls down and dies—in the technical language of the prairie hunter—"he smothers". Only one gun I am told is allowed to ten Mexican families—the Mexicans depend on the Lasso the horse and the lance. This accounts for the tameness of common game and the bad aim of the Mexican soldier. I am told the armadilla [sic] is a common animal in the country. I have never seen one. They are represented to be about the size of an opposum—they are harmless and tame—said to be fine eating they borrough in the ground and when alarmed sink into the earth with incredible velocity—the red pepper[74] grows spontaneously all over the country. The balls are about the size of an ordinary rifle bullit [sic]—equally pungent if not more so than the

African cayenne. The Mexicans are very fond of it [and] use vast quantities in cooking. The Mexicans are generally very temperate— use no vinegar no spirits but tilla [herbal tea] no wine their dissipations consists in smoking and gambling—It turned out that the man who was put under arrest was the public ostler—I kept my horse at the wagon yard fearing he would be stolen if kept by himself at my tent. My horse had been so injured that he would scarcely travel at all—all his mettle gone and hobbling along as if he was crippled in all his legs—while the ostler was gone he had got kicked. It was then that he had got to a full trough of corn and was foundered—so much for doing one's duty every course in life has its inconveniences.

Wednesday October 7   An express arrived this morning about 2 o'clock A.M. on the steamer "Aid"—Lieutenant Armistead[75] only 14 days from Washington to this place—he left this morning for Monterey about day break escorted by 29 dragoons. The despatches to General Taylor were not more closely sealed than the express man kept his lips. All that is known or even remembered is that there was a long cabinet council held at Washington that upon its breaking up Lieutenant Armistead was despatched with packages to Genl. Taylor and the usual order to proceed with all possible despatch. When he got to some point on the Rio Grande finding no public boat he gave the "Aid" a thousand dollars to bring him to Camargo. Now every body asks every body what is the nature of the despatches. One says it means peace, another war—I conclude it is either an order to Genl. Taylor to march on Tampico or that it is an order to suspend hostilities pending negotiations opened—It cannot be a message that peace is declared because if so there could be no motive for concealment. It means then war to the knife, or that negotiations have been opened. Capt. Crossman says there will be peace. Genl. Patterson I am told shakes his head looks knowing and can only spare to the gratification of the curious the expression that we will soon have a plenty to do. I have the temerity to believe that they are no better informed than the rest of us. I would suppose that General Patterson ought to be but he delights in mystery and in giving importance to every thing—such is the habit of hucksters and chapmen of the small wares. Commenced making out returns.

Thursday Oct 8th   finished my returns as quarter master for the 3d quarter of 1846 ending 30 Septr—sealed up the papers inclosed to General Jesup and deposited the same at 3 o'clock this evening in the letter box at Camargo also deposited a letter to my wife. I went from the post office to Capt. Crossman's office. He gave me various orders as to having an account made out of property etc. on my side tents camp kettles etc. About to start home invited by Dr. Bass and Thompson to go to Trowbridge's sutler's store to get a glass of wine—as I returned by the office Capt. Sherman and Capt. Crossman invited me to ride with them which I did and crossed the river at sun down. When I got over I learned that Rector the interpreter and overseer of the Mexican labourers had got drunk and that a man named Hays a white labourer had insulted and refused to obey the orders of Mr. White the overseer over the white men. I found Rector he was not so drunk as I expected to find him told him I wished to see him at my tent in the morning investigated Hays' case and finding that his was a flagrant instance of contumacy and disobedience I directed his discharge. I should have mentioned that early this morning before I was dressed Genl. Marshall rode up to my tent and handed to my man for me—3 newspapers the National Intelligencer of the 17th Sept Maysville paper of the 8th—and the Picayune of the 25th—the papers were a great treat.

Friday Oct 9th   Very warm day. Hays discharged. Rector came to my tent. I told him in a very mild manner that it was bad enough for a labourer to get drunk and neglect his work but for those who oversee to do it was unpardonable and could not be submitted. That he had 34 Mexicans under his charge—that it was my duty to tell him if he got drunk again, he would be discharged at once—He made a proper apology said it should not occur again etc. Mr. Angel came in. I gave him information of what was required by Capt. Crossman handed him written instructions to make out complete lists of all property on hand and he said every thing was in its place could show every thing at once and could soon make out the list—he tells me the "Col. Cross" came up last night bringing an immense mail four heavy bags—Mr. Angel going over the river got him to inquire if there were any letters for me—there were none— this is truly disturbing—I left home the 2d of August and have not received a line yet from any one in the U.S.: My wife must have written and my letters miscarried—went to the Landing "Whiteville" just arrived "Col. Cross" just departing—Saw half a dozen Texians on their way home said Genl. Taylor told them if there was to be more fighting when the armistice expired he will let them know—I enquired about the Baltimore Battalion. They said there was no truth in the rumor circulated here to their disadvantage—They referred me to one of their company standing some distance off—Lieut. Owen[76]—I made myself known to him—He said he was on furlough going to Galveston to attend to some business that he had not heard a word of the rumor and seemed somewhat incredulous. I told him I was glad to hear his denial of the truth of what had been said as I was a native of Maryland. I asked him if when Col. Watson was killed if there was not some confusion he said as to that the whole division was necessarily in confusion at one time but there was no flinching any where and universally every man stood firm. The Texians told me that my cousin Stephen Smith[77], of Galveston Texas the son of my great benefactor Nathan Smith formerly of Washington city, was in the hottest of the fight and acted with great bravery and fought like a man—This is something at least—if I could not gain any laurels I am glad one of the universal name but of my own blood did. They also tell me that Stephen will be here to-morrow—I have requested Messrs. Angel, White and Winfield who know him to look out for him and conduct him to my tent. The Texians say McClung is certainly out of danger. Rode out in the evening by myself 3 miles—Met an armed Mexican—I had no arms. I believe we were both very badly Scared—he was a dark cut-throat looking fellow and had a very large sword and a carbine. The mocking bird abounds in this country and there is a species of black bird[78] about the size of a domestic pigeon which has a singular note—the first sound which strikes your ear when they sing resembles the breaking of the branch of a tree full of leaves—but soon the musick becomes as sweet as that of the canary bird.

Saturday Oct 10   Rose early beautiful morning the air is purer here than at any place I have ever been. The whiz of a bullit may be heard from the time it leaves the gun until it strikes—I am told by men from Monterey that as they advanced to the charge that the balls from the Mexican musquets made continual musick over their heads. That it appeared to them if they had shot lower there would have been left no American alive—If the Mexicans had been marksmen had they fired their small arms with the precision they did the artillery—the American army would have been inevitably destroyed—my cousin arrived to-day a fine modest young man—dressed in a red flannelshirt—cap—woolen pants and brogans which never were acquainted with blacking he spoke of his appearance. Sir said I think not of your dress—you are a boot taller in my estimation this day than any of our family—you have faced the enemy in one of the hardest fought battles ever known. He said a cannon ball raked a line of men[79] in two feet of him—he says had it not been for the cries of the wounded and the sight of the mangled bodies stretched upon the plain his sensations would have been far more agreeable than painful—That the excitement was pleasant decidedly while marching to the charge until he heard the cries of the wounded and saw the horrid ghastly sights the cannon balls made—that he never for a moment thought of personal peril and as for going back that never occurred to him as a course even to be supposed much less entertained. He dined with me. The true story of his going on is this when the Texian Regiment under Genl. Johnston[80] arrived here on their way to Monterey—they found they could disband if they thought proper as Genl. Taylor had no authority to hold them— their time was out. Well the whole Regiment disbanded and went home or somewhere else except 55 men. these 55 men constituted a company under Capt. Shivers[81] and my cousin was one of the number. It appears that General Worth[82] is the great favourite at present. He did good service and saved his men. Some of those not under his command insist however that he had the easiest task to execute. That the bishop's castle could be taken without danger until within a very short distance. All represent Genl. Taylor as one of the bravest coolest men in battle ever known. At whatever point that he saw the men falling fastest there he galloped and stood amidst the hottest of the fire. In the charge on the batteries on our part was dead silence. Genl. Taylor rode up and announced to the men that Genl. Worth had taken the town on his side then went up an earthquake shout. Three cheers were proposed and given for Genl. Worth at the second cheer the Mexicans gave them a fire from their heavy ordnance but it did not interrupt the ceremony—the 3rd cheer being louder than the rest. Nothing can surpass the beauty of Monterey and the surrounding scenery—Mountains piled up to the Heavens—the orange and pomegranate trees are in the greatest abundance—the fruit are just now ripe—the finest my cousin says especially the pomegranates he ever saw. The whole army has been living on these delicious fruits ever since the battle and there are more than an army can eat or destroy. My sergeant has just brought me a couple of fine oranges which a Texian friend on his way from Monterey gave him this morning. Nothing can exceed the beauty of some of their gardens—orange pomegranate and fig groves—interspersed with bubbling fountains of chrystal water led off in every direction in canals of white stone. The town is represented to contain about 20,000 inhabitants—the houses are palaces of stone with flat roofs—except in the suburbs where as in all Mexican Towns are hacals [*sic*] or thatched huts. Now two things I regard from all I have heard as reduced to a certainty—1st That when General Taylor allowed the Mexicans to capitulate the hard fighting was over on our side, our cannon bearing on the plaza and street the Texians on the top of the houses dealing death at every shot, all the forts taken but one and that it was then easy to compel a surrender at discretion. 2d That unless his policy can be explained by the nature of his orders from Washington or assurances upon which he could rely from the Mexican Authorities his conduct as a General in first exposing his men to almost certain death and then treating with the Mexicans when he could have destroyed or captured them deserves the severest reprehension. It is charitable at present to conclude (*omnia presumuntur rite acta*) that a general at the head of such an army surrounded by the patriotic the wise and the brave of the land—adopting his course for causes hereafter to be explained which when known will entirely justify him in the eyes of his countrymen and the whole world—Having business across the river I went over about 11 o'clock in the steam ferry boat Troy—just as I was about to go aboard—I noticed a little delicate boyish looking man with a sword by his side and an eye of fire endeavouring to pull aboard a Mexican poney from which he had just dismounted—I helped to get him aboard and finally ordered one of the men to push him aboard—as soon as I stepped aboard Capt. Lincoln introduced me to the owner of the poney as—Capt. Shivers I had heard from the Texians that morning and several days before a great deal of Capt. Shivers and *presto video*—there he was cool, collected, with the eye of the grey eagle. He went with me to the pay office and handed to one of the clerks a rouleau of gold which he said contained a thousand dollars—sent down by him he said by order of General Taylor to pay his company with—so that there might be no disappointment. I then went with him to Capt. Crossman's office and introduced him. He then accompanied me [to] Col. Cummings' store where we took a small glass of porter together we then parted—Returned to my tent sent for my cousin—he dined with me after dinner Mr. Winfield called to see Stephen and we sat chatting together until 4 o'clock when they left. Heavy train of some 50 wagons just arrived from Monterey—orders to shoe the mules and to despatch the train as early as possible. In anticipation of the train force new forges were built this week making six on this side. Blacksmith's being scarce Genl. Patterson on application from Capt. Crossman ordered twenty blacksmith's to be detached from the regiments—to commence work this morning seven reported to me about 9 o'clock—One of them said that he had understood they were to get only 15 cents and asked me what they were to get "Sir I said I can not inform you what you are to get all I can tell you is that you have to obey orders, you have been ordered by your commander to report to me to work in the blacksmith's shop. I now order you to go to the blacksmith's and report yourselves to Stewart the head blacksmith and go to work." They went off but as they went one of them said sotto voce, "I will never strike a lick for 15 cents." This evening Mr. Angel reported the blacksmiths would not work. I reported the facts to Capt. Crossman about night I got an answer to arrest those who refused to work and report their names and regiment for further orders. I sent to Mr. Angel a written order to arrest the men—Mr. Angel went to their commanding officers and while seeing them night came on. My man Gaines comes in and says he had just seen a fight or an affray between Capt. Shivers and one whom he took to be another officer of the line that there was no doubt with any one but that a duel would be the result. The circumstances were these the strange officer came along the river shore on an old Mexican horse which he was spurring violently— Capt. Shivers' company were just landing from the steam ferry boat Troy—The horse splashed in among them—One of the company remarked "you dont intend to ride on a man do you" or something of that sort to which the officer made some very short answer. Capt. Shivers spoke up and said "These men are under my command and I dont wish my men insulted" "D———n you and your men" was the rejoinder. Swift as lightning Capt. Shivers struck him with his sword in the scabbard and drawing immediately was about to cleave him down when the blow was warded off by a third person then Shivers struck him with his fist and knocked the officer off of his horse. There will be a duel of course if the strange man be an officer, but this I doubt. Angel comes in after supper and relates pretty much the same story and says that two duels are now on the tapis General Marshall and Bayley Peyton[83] and Capt. Shivers and the strange officer duels likely to come off in the morning etc.

Sunday October 11th   Heard this morning that the strange officer had made friends with Shivers—I also heard his name and regiment but as he has made himself amiable under such discouraging circumstances I will not mention his name. Heard that General Marshall and Baylie Peyton were to fight this evening. This must have been given out to mislead, men do not fight duels of an evening—not generally. Blacksmiths detailed refuse to work for 15 cents per day. Say they it took a long time to get their trade they left their shops to come and fight that the clothes they would destroy in two or 3 days would cost them 2 dols to replace. The Alabamians withdrew without saying anything. The Kentuckians said be d———d if they would work. They would see all the generals in Hell—Told Angel he was bound to execute the order—5 Kentuckians who were at the shop using this language were taken into custody. Col. McKee[84] called on me. I told him my orders were positive that I thought it a very narrow minded policy to compel men to work and to raise cain for nothing especially on Sunday that the public good required that this blacksmithing should be done without delay but that neither he or I could do any thing but it was for Genl. Patterson the commander to decide that he had better see him said he would. The Kentuckians acted nobly at least. They would not skulk but went to the place where ordered and there refused to work knowing well the consequence of refusal—I reported to Capt. Crossman that five men were in custody and that I awaited further orders also reported the names of those belonging to the other regts. who had reported and then gone off or not reported at all—At ½ past 4 having received no further orders I got on my horse to ride—fell in with a party going to a fandango about 9 miles off—with them was Mendiola[85] who was formerly guide and interpreter to Genl. Worth in Texas. It is said that he was formerly one of Canales' corps of Rancheros alias robbers that falling out with Canales he went among the Texians who are said to be much attached to him. He is now employed or rather taken care of by Col. Cummings the quarter

Master's sutler—a brave generous man. The Mexicans hate Mendiola and have repeatedly tried to take his life. Mendiola amused us greatly—he was on a Mexican horse armed with a knife pistols and a lasso and had a bottle of ale stuffed in his breeches pocket. When he saw a Mexican he would charge down on him as if to attack. Sometimes the Mexican would take to the chaparral—sometimes he would stand in wonder seeing it was a Mexican but most generally they would know him. When they found out his object was sport they would enjoy the fun greatly. Mendiola showed how they ran and caught cattle—throwing his lasso over the horns and never once missing—we rode the nine miles and came to the ranches where the fandango was to be held—men women and children collected dressed very cleanly in white—I determined not to remain seeing there were a large crowd of white men and concluding there would be more Americanism than Mexicanism and my only curiosity being to see a fandango. One of the party wishing to return we turned our horses—But riding around a ranch to bid our friends farewell we got into a wrong road and after riding two miles or more came out at the river where there were fifty large roads crossing each other in every direction and signs of many camps we concluded that this was where the different trains encamped for water—we struck into one road which looked like losing us in the chaparral. We saw some Mexicans I hailed to them thinking they were Americans being near sighted. My friend corrected me—the wind was high the Mexicans did not hear us and being behind some bushes—They passed on without seeing [us]—we returned to the camps and the next time were more fortunate taking a road which soon led us to the big highway between Camargo and Monterey—We rode fast overtook a party of Texians coming down from Monterey and reached the camp about 8 o'clock.

Monday October 12th The officer of the day released the Kentuckians without orders—They having been in confinement since yesterday— many blacksmiths applied to work this morning having got furloughs— went over to see Capt. Crosman what could be done. I stated the facts and told him that Stewart, the head blacksmith said he could get along with six and that there were enough who had furlough and that if he would allow me that I would suggest that it would be proper to employ them at the usual rates—He said no he would take no further responsibility in the matter but would leave it to

Genl. Patterson to act as he thought proper—Soon after I got back Capt. Caswell[86] Genl. Pillow's aid came to me and wished to know if the Alabamians had reported. I told him some had reported but they had all gone off—none were at work this day I was assured by Angel was the truth. I went to the blacksmith's shop with Capt. Caswell—the smithy said the same thing—left word for Stewart to come see me—he did so now 2 Alabamians had reported to him Saturday Collamer and James Bennet. Collamer worked half a day Saturday—Bennet not at all. Bennet soon left—Collamer (left) at night—and neither of them ever returned. Col. McKee told me today that Genl. Marshall and Col. Peyton had settled their difficulties. As I was leaving Camargo I came across Capt. Shivers in the street—I told him I had heard of his difficulty and was glad to find it was to go no further—he said it was not yet settled—why said I I heard it was—no—I will tell you in confidence of course. certainly said I, so regard our conversation. Then said he, I am challenged. I have accepted—I was asked by my friends if I could not make an apology I told them all I could say was that "I *regret* that your conduct was such as to require my treating you in the manner I did on Saturday"—Well said I, we are from the same state. I would like to witness the affair if it must be not as a *party* but as a friend—He said he would try and let me know through Stephen. Here is a hard case a man just from a hard fought field of three days blood and battle—covered with laurels and on his way home to join those who love him and await his arrival with hope and gladness—to get into a difficulty and be destined to perhaps to die by the hand of his countryman! but I hope not I hope neither will be killed! Such is life we are always in danger! *coelum non animum mutant qui trans mare currunt* which translated to suit my purpose means we may escape the dangers of the gulf, fight 3 days at Monterey and yet die at Camargo just when we are about being paid off and mustered out of service. There is no more security for a hero fresh from a hard foughten field than there is for an inglorious woodsman in the swamps of Yazoo. Just heard that the duel is to be fought 5 o'clock this evening with place one mile below Camargo—terms rifles at 40 yards—There will be no harm done but the disfiguring of this veracious history with trite morality. There will be no fight—For all the harm that any rifle is to do him this evening Shivers is just as safe for a sight of his native Port Gibson in the goodly county of

Claiborne state of Mississippi as I am for bad coffee and clammy biscuits for supper. By the bye I have lost a good cook and got in his place a good man but a very bad cook—my old soldier saw a chance of promotion as guard to the ferry over the San Juan. He electioneered with me to speak to Capt. Crossman and get him the place. I told him that I knew that I should be greatly the loser—But he spoke of his three orphan children—I told him to say no more I would do my best for him and immediately I gave him a note to the Captain recommending him—He was immediately installed. This may look to the proud and prosperous like the Irish man's promotion "to carry the hod" but poor men know the difference between $25 and 40 per month. Especially when there are motherless children to take care of. Shakespeare says "first to thine own self be true!" I leave on record for debating societies or Casuists fools or philosophers (who ever may choose to argue it) this question was I true to myself in doing this generous action at the expense of my stomach and the digestive organs? Heard a good anecdote of General Sam Houston. When he was President of Texas three men called at his tent whom he had employed to go after some money and to whom he wished to give some secret instructions—his tent was crowded—Gentlemen said he I wish to give you some private talk in relation to a matter of great importance to the government wait a few minutes until I can have an opportunity to talk to you. The company did not take the hint—presently said he gentlemen call again after an hour. The three men went away and returned as directed—the tent was still crowded—Gentlemen said Houston hold. I will certainly have an opportunity to talk to you in private before long as the business you are to attend to is of a delicate nature and vast importance. Nobody moved. After a short time gentlemen said Houston taking up his hat follow me into the middle of that lake and I will talk to you there. There was a beautiful little lake about a hundred yards from his tent about waist deep. Off he strode plumb into the lake—the 3 men followed—The crowd all holloing stop general we will leave general we are gone oh no said Genl. Houston waving his hand I pray you by no means— make yourselves *entirely comfortable* gentlemen there is not the least necessity for your going. The Sergeant of the guard comes in and says he has in custody an Ohio volunteer who does not regard confinement as any punishment. The said McConnel boasting every day after he has passed a night in the guard house of the honor—ordered (the Sgt. of the guard) to report the facts to the Adjt. of the Ohio Regt. with my request that some additional punishment may be inflicted that if his riotous conduct can not be stopped otherwise a ball and chain might bring him to his senses. Reports also that he has taken an armed Mexican with a cloak marked Paredes no [number] 64. ordered to report the case to the adjt. of the Ky Regt. for Genl. Marshall's action—9 o'clock heavy rain every appearance of a Norther.

Tuesday October 13th It turned quite cold in the night after the rain but there was no Norther—this morning I had to put on my blanket coat and warm myself by the cook's fire. Four men reported to me as blacksmiths from the Ala. Regt.—ordered them to go in charge of the officers and the Superintendent to the shop to work—afterwards they said they would not work and going by the smith's shop I saw them going away—I inquired the cause—said they would not work called the officer of the day and ordered them to the guard house—two of them had furloughs signed yesterday but they were reported as *detailed* men of to-day—so expressed in the Col.'s written order which the officer showed me immediately reported what I had done to Capt. Crosman stating in the note that I awaited further orders—Now I have not heard [if] the Kentuckians were punished what will be done with these men? It appears that Capt. Shivers and his antagonist took their positions on the field yesterday evening rifles in hand—But they did not fight, the affair was settled on the ground—as I expected. Wolves abound in this country on three several occasions I have heard a gang of them howling since I have been here. I am told they are all through this country and in Texas thousands upon thousands of these animals. Speaking of them a week or two ago Lieut. Brereton[87] informed me that it is well ascertained that they hunt in this way—They go to a place which they select to hunt in—They then start severally in different directions like radii to a focus—keeping sufficiently close to hear each other—as soon as one starts game and barks the others rally to him—if the wolf that barks has made a false alarm or the others can not be satisfied that there was something to justify the call—they all fall on the delinquent and tear him to pieces—a gentleman in western Texas saw this operation performed—the wolf had barked at him and knowing their habit he hid him self in a tree—The other wolves searched around for a time but finding nothing they fell to devouring the alarmist. Capt. Crosman sent my report to General Patterson endorsed "respectfully referred to the Comdg General"

G. H. Crosman

12 O'clock '46   a. q. m.

About 5 O'clock going over to Capt. Crosman's office in the business to wit to see if I could not be spared to accompany Capt. Gholson[88] and others to Monterey on a visit to our friends (which request was refused me) Capt. Crosman handed me my report on which were endorsed these words "It is the desire of the comg Genl. that these men be kept in confinement—on bread and water" signed "Geo A. McCall[89]

A. A. G."

My report was in these words

"Opposite Camargo
9 O'clock A. M. Oct 13, 1846
Captain Crosman
    Four men were brought to me by an officer of the Ala. Regt. to work as blacksmiths—I ordered Mr. Angel and the officer to take them to Stewart to go to work. Walking down by the shop a few minutes afterwards I saw the men walking off—I enquired of them where they were going—They said they would not work—I sent for the guard and ordered them to the guard house—The names of the men are Wm. Robertson George Adams Co. I, J. Bennett Co. C, J. Bird Co. K.—The two first Robertson and Adams pulled out written leaves of absence on furloughs for a week dated October 12.—but I disregarded them deeming it my duty to consider them as detailed men and as so reported to me. The 4 are under arrest what shall I do with them? Bird is a very young man—he says he is no blacksmith. How many shall I release or retain in custody?   Respectfully
F. Smith a. q. m."

As soon as I could get over and could write I sent to the Adjutant 2d Regt. Ohio Vols a note copying the General's order as the quarter guard was taken from the Ohio Regt.—As soon as I could procure Mr. Angel about sunset I sent off the note to the adjutant—I have learned from Mr. Angel that the Kentuckians were rearrested this morning and confined—Now this is a little business and considering who these men are the brave and proud of the land who have left their homes to fight—and considering all the waste and extravagance going on all around us this is a hard case—It is painful—Mr. Angel returned in a few minutes and reported that the Alabamians had been confined an hour or two and then released and sent to their regiment by order of Col. Morgan[90] who I am told has come in now from Matamoras (where he was confined by sickness) and is now in command of his regiment.—Captain Gholson of Kentucky asst. Commissary a good fellow what Kentuckian is not? called on me this evening and said he and Major Boyd and others were going to Monterey on a visit—expressed a wish that I would. I went over the river to see Capt. C. but he said he could not spare me impossible. He first said I could get another quarter master to act while I was gone, I could, but [he] soon retracted saying Captain things have gone on smoothly since you have been across the river. There is a heavy train coming from below, the steamer Mercer sunk and there is much transportation yet to be furnished. I would like to accommodate you. I would like to go myself. I assure [you] I am so harassed and oppressed that I feel sometimes like giving up and going overboard.

Wednesday October 14. A carpenter named Smith (confound the name) becoming toploftical [?] struck for higher wages declaiming he would not work unless he got $45 per month. Now $40 and a ration and a half certain payment ought to be *rational* satisfaction. A man named Kirby as good a workman being ready to take Smith's place at the old rates—Smith discharged, Kirby employed. Reported in writing today this morning to Capt. Crosman the release of the Alabamians yesterday. A young cadet now a Lieutenant in the army, graduated in June—Marcy—with a long sword well mounted—young fresh and of a good deportment applied to me to have his horse shod—certainly he is to form a part of the military escort to the train—What a thing it is to be young who does not feel a lively interest in any young man just commencing his professional career. The heart that does not is seared as with a hot iron. "Sir" said I while writing the order to the blacksmith "had you come a little sooner you would have entered upon your profession at a glorious time"—"Ah! sir could I have only known it!"—Poor fellow what will become of him perhaps be killed at Saltillo perhaps live a Lieutenant for 10 years grow weary and disgusted, find that there is no

certainty in promotion as there was in good marks at West Point
according to good conduct—take a drink, fight a duel, go the usual
round of dissipation and drop beneath the sod unpitied and unknown—
perhaps not—and if there be any thing in faces he will rise to be an
ornament to the army. Steamer Mercer sunk yesterday Troy sent to
her relief. Heard a good anecdote to-day—An officer in one of the
vol. regiments while stationed at Burita went round to look to the
sentinels—the night was very dark and raining and the mud deep.
Coming along cautiously he heard a sentinel soliloquizing thus—
"Well this is the G——d damnest shot of work I ever saw yet. I
voted for old Polk G——d d——n him and here I am in mud and
rain and misery. I came out here to fight and instead of fighting I
have to tread this mud for four hours what a d——d fool I was—I
ought to be in Hell for a d——d fool. Who comes there?" "James
K. Polk" was the officer's reply "Well" bringing his gun down and
taking aim "Stand James K. Polk for I'll be d——d if I dont shoot
you if you give me the least chance". Went to see Capt. Gholson to
tell him I could not go with him and give some messages to Missi
friends—As soon as I saw him he told me that his trip was knocked
in the head—he had learned late last evening that it was necessary to
get the permission of the Commdg. General in addition to the leave
of absence of his Col. Col. McKee and his General Genl. Marshall.
He got the written permit from Col. McKee repaired to General
Marshall's tent who happened to be absent but knowing he would
give it having already had it verbally and as it was late in the evening
and had some arrangements to make preparatory to his departure—
he took the Col.'s permit and went over to see Genl. Patterson. He
was asked by an officer at the door whom he should report to Genl.
Patterson as wishing to see him. He told him then he was ushered
into the august presence. He stated his business Sir said his High-
ness your application is irregular and in violation of military courtesy. He would hear no excuse or apology—"Sir you should get your
General's signature and it should then come to me through his
sergeant. Don't you ever approach me again in person on any such
application"—The captain retired got Genl. Marshall's signature and
it being suggested to him by his friends that if he sent it the answer
would be too slow in coming if at all he had the temerity to venture
a second time into the (presence of the) Great Man. He seemed says
Capt. G. offended as soon as he said used still more pointed

language than before would listen to no excuse and treated him so imperiously that he left his paper and withdrew. It is well says Capt. G. that my hands were tied. He says the August Personage treated Genl. Shields with equal indignity—so much so that the General is bent on personal satisfaction whenever the army is disbanded—that Genl. Patterson hearing of Genl. Shields' dissatisfaction endeavoured to reconcile him—granting him the escort to join Genl. Wool for asking which he had been insulted and urging through his friends reconciliation that Shields declined all reconciliation refused to drink with his Mightiness and left Camargo in the language of Solicitors "reserving to himself the benefit of all manner of excepting to many manifest errors insufficiencies and mistakes" of the said Major General. So goes the world. "uneasy lies the head that wears the crown" to wit the head of a salesman of pack thread and quick lime converted into a Major General of the U. S. Army in actual service. Rode out this evening—Prickly pear grows every where. Sometimes it is as large as a man's body and ten or 15 feet high branching out with its elbow limbs in every direction. A wound from its pricks is incurable is the thorn is left in the flesh—the only cure is to cut down in the flesh as if cutting out a bullet—this thorn being barbed it cannot be pulled out. The Mexicans might well make it their coat of arms. It is a much better emblem than the Scotch thistle and much more deserving the motto *Nolli me tangere.* The Mexicans have vassals or slaves called Peons—in legal contemplation the Peon can redeem himself by paying the debt which he owes his Lord—But such is the usurious interest charge and the constant accumulation of the debt—the Lord fixing what price he pleases on the articles required by the Peon to support himself and family that practically it is slavery—slavery from father to son—the son being bound for the debt when the father dies—A man's wealth in this part of the country is not estimated by lands and houses gold or precious stones but as in the days of the partiarchs by his blankets robes shawls herds and flocks. In the town when they say a man is rich they denominate him a man of *mucha* plata. Train got off yet though, all the mules shod and wagons loaded at 9 o'clock this morning delays occasioned by some of the volunteer officers and their quartermasters going forward not knowing what they wanted nor how they wanted—one single officer has had five sets of papers made and signed to-day—Well everybody must learn. The wagoners finding that they were not ordered forward at the usual hour this evening took the privilege of a regular set too at drinking—and now 8 o'clock at night I am just informed that the Wagon Master and Teamsters are all drunk. This too is perfectly natural sailors and soldiers expecting death at every turn and kept from liquor by their officers—when they get at it they will get drunk—how they get it is more than I can find out—some say it is musceal [mescal] brought down in the wagons some say whiskey brought in the steam boats and smuggled ashore below the camp. A company of regulars—a company of dragoons—Remainder of the Louisville Legion and some Ohio troops I am told go forward as the escort—a large sum of specie some say $150,000 some $500,000 goes up to Monterey in the wagons.

CHAPTER 2

October 15–November 7, 1846

This is always the case with your great men in small things
and your small men in great things and if there ever was a
man *magnus in parvis parvuis in magnis* that man is his
excellency Major General Patterson.

*Supplies were being transported overland on a more or less regular basis
from Camargo to Taylor's army in Monterrey by means of wagons and
pack mules. A single wagon train might be made up of as many as 150
wagons and over 1,000 pack mules. The route of the wagon train from
Camargo south to Monterrey wound through enemy country, and raids
occurred often. Mexican irregular troops known as "rancheros" threatened
all supply and communication routes. The rancheros, under the leadership
of Gen. Antonio Canales, the so-called "Chaparral Fox," frequently
attacked travelers and gave no quarter to any captives taken from the
roads. Guerilla warfare was waged in the countryside of northern
Mexico from 1846 to 1848. Civilians and neutral parties were often
targets in this struggle. Any hacienda refusing to supply the needs of the
rancheros was burned by them for being "unpatriotic." On the other
hand, when word was received by the American army that a hacienda
had accommodated the rancheros, a retaliatory raiding party was sent to
burn this "partisan" hacienda. Many Mexican citizens were forced to
abandon their farms and ranches and take refuge in the mountains or
risk being murdered by the opposing sides. By 1848, one traveller through
this region reported that "all the haciendas are blackened shells, . . . abandoned
by their residents." This type of warfare is all too familiar to the
modern-day farmers and country folk of Central American countries such
as Nicaragua and El Salvador.*

The flow of supplies to Taylor's forces in Monterrey was likewise threatened by seasonal drops in the water level of the Rio Grande. The river generally was the lowest in the months of November, December, and January. By that time of the year, steamboats loaded with supplies en route to Camargo began to stick on the many sandbars that were protruding into the shallow river channels. Anxious steamboat captains wondered how much longer the river would remain open to navigation.

The daily rumors about the war that were faithfully recorded in Franklin Smith's diary turned out to be, for the most part, quite accurate. The Mexican government was beginning to organize resistance to the American invasion. The United States had unwittingly helped furnish the Mexicans with their most able leader and organizer, General Santa Anna. As late as May 1846, this exiled former president of Mexico resided in Havana, Cuba, and monitored the political climates on the mainland, awaiting the right opportunity to re-enter Mexico. In secret dispatches between Santa Anna and President Polk, Santa Anna expressed his opposition to the war and offered treasonous advice to Polk on topics that included the best routes for the invasion of Mexico. Santa Anna maintained that if he were to return to power in Mexico an immediate end to hostilities between the two countries would be negotiated. The terms of this negotiation, according to Santa Anna, would allow the United States to annex liberal portions of Mexican territory. President Polk, apparently acting on good faith, dispatched orders to United States naval ships blockading the eastern coast of Mexico to permit Santa Anna to return, if he so desired. Polk hoped that Santa Anna was sincere in his statements but also reckoned that the general's presence in Mexico would cause the fall of the current government, which was teetering on the brink of revolution. On the night of August 16, 1846, the United States Home Fleet intercepted the British ship Arab *bound for Vera Cruz from Havana. Knowing that Santa Anna was on board, the ship was not searched but was signalled to resume her original course.*

Santa Anna arrived in Vera Cruz to find a country torn by political dissention and dismayed by their army's lack of leadership. He immediately assumed the posture of a great patriot and offered to lead the Mexican army that "will drive the Yankee invaders to the banks of the Sabine River." In the meantime, Santa Anna's followers engineered a coup and took control of the Mexican government. Santa Anna assumed command of the army by October 1846 and moved his headquarters to San Luis Potosi. From there the Mexican army was ideally situated to repulse the army of General Taylor in the north or to check any anticipated invasion attempt that might be launched against Vera Cruz. Santa Anna was a very able organizer, and his army quickly grew in strength, soon posing a threat to Taylor's army.

By early November, President Polk's reply to the terms of the treaty for the surrender of Monterrey was received by Taylor, who was quartered in that city (see the diary entry for November 2). Polk was extremely unhappy with the terms of the surrender, feeling that the Mexican army should not have been allowed to march out of Monterrey retaining their arms but should have surrendered and been paroled. He further felt that Taylor had exceeded his authority by approving an eight-week armistice between the belligerent parties. Polk ordered Taylor to declare an immediate end to the armistice. Taylor angrily followed the president's orders and dutifully notified the Mexican army at San Luis Potosi that a cessation had been declared in the armistice.

The American army quickly renewed offensive operations by dispatching a force led by Gen. William Worth to capture the Mexican city of Saltillo, about eighty miles southeast of Monterrey. Secretary of War William L. Marcy directly ordered General Patterson at Camargo to prepare a force to advance overland and capture Tampico. American forces were consolidating their hold on northern Mexico and preparing for an anticipated advance against central Mexico.

Thursday October 15th The military escort left yesterday evening and camped out a few miles from the depot. The train took up the line of march this morning from their park beyond the Ky camp at daybreak. Passing along the river bank and through the depot grounds they came by my tent which is near the Monterey road a little before sunrise. They were joined by some wagons loaded at the depot numbering in all about 70. I heard while in bed the word "Forward" pronounced in a loud voice. I got up drew on my pantaloons and stepped to the door of my tent. It was quite an imposing sight. Each wagon was covered and had five mules, the teamster mounted on the off hind mule. The wagon master and other agents galloping up and down the line seeing all right. At the word "Forward" they stretched out on their toilsome journey one directly after the other forming a line I suppose a mile in length. All this trouble and expense thought I to enable our race of men to destroy another and yet we complain of the shortness of human life!

But what are we in fact doing? We are now eating up our provisions and bankrupting the treasury while the enemy are fortifying their strongholds and recruiting their energies. When the armistice expires we should be short of provisions the Mexicans will have pocketed all our gold and silver and double the quantity of blood will have to be shed and triple the expense incurred had it not been for our mistaken humanity and had not our President believed in Santa Anna and our General in Ampudia. This I fear will prove to be true but it is easy to croak and find fault. No man can or should pronounce with confidence on the conduct of either excellency until the General's despatches and the President's messages are published. When that is done we shall then see "who's the dupe" and who the great man. Mr. Raybord, Col. Cumming's clerk called after breakfast telling me he wanted a bundle sent on by the train. I told him he was too late he said he would ride and overtake the train. I told him I would ride with him to see if any accidents had occurred or any thing forgotten. We rode on slowly two or 3 miles without overtaking the wagons and the young man said his business would not admit of his going further—he would select some other conveyance. Saw this morning a vast number of wild geese flying from Northwest to S. E. that is from the upper Rio Grande and the mountains to the lower Rio Grande and the gulf coast—Cold weather I suppose is at hand—We also saw myriads of crows[1] darkening the chaparral. They were larger than the crow in the U. States—the noise they make is different from our crow. Their note is more like the croak of a frog than a crow. Instead of "caw caw caw" it is "carack carack". When I returned I found Capt. Sherman at my tent—He had called to see me not on business but as a friend. After some time he rose to go. I invited him to dine with me no would come some other time. Walked around and looked at the grounds and public stores—he made me some valuable suggestions. When we were about to part he insisted upon my going with him and dining with his mess. (He and Capt. Crosman and Veitch the forage master eat together) Wishing to see the Captain and get some papers and perhaps a letter I went with him. Ascending the bank on the other side proposed to stop in a moment at Lieutenant Britton's the Commissary's—soon after we got there: Two Texians lighted from their horses just from Monterey. They were pregnant with news—the news pregnant too. They said Santa Anna had issued a proclamation calling on the people to fight for their altars and their firesides, declaiming that in 60 days he could have at San Louis [Luis] Potosi seventy five thousand men. That he would never rest satisfied until he planted the Mexican banner on the banks of the Sabine etc. That the nature of the express from Washington brought by Lieut. Armistead was that all hope of peace was at an end and to prosecute war with the utmost vigor. They further said that Santa Anna had repudiated Ampudia's armistice that Genl. Taylor had suffered himself to be overreached by the latter, that there was great dissatisfaction in the camp (every body that comes from Monterey says this) that men ask in vain why was it after the loss of so many valuable lives and they had the Mexicans hemmed up and could have captured or destroyed them why was it that General Taylor, at the moment that Genl. Worth and the Texians were dealing a deadly and triumphant fire that Genl. Taylor should have permitted them to capitulate. They said further that Ampudia and his troops were seven days in leaving the city taking six of their best pieces of cannon and everything that was valuable. That they went out in great spirits drums beating flags flying and displaying every evidence of triumph. That they were fortifying near Saltillo. Dined with Capt. S. and Capt. Crosman. Genl. Patterson came in after dinner. He had a slip of paper which he read through a quizzing glass. The Alabama blacksmiths—they were discharged said Capt. S. before your order reached the Ohio Commdr. I had Capt. Smith's report to that effect which I intended sending you—"by whose order" by your order it was reported "to me" said I of the Col. of the Ohio Vols. He seemed glad to pass the subject I thought evidently to my mind regarding it as very well disposed of—No doubt he felt relieved—"Everybody gets whiskey, where do they get it from" again quizzing his paper. "I am told it is brought by the pilots and engineers of steam boats, is that so" Capt. C. "Very likely and landed below the camps" Genl. P. "I have an idea of swearing them off as well as the captains as to what they bring up! Your mules are not regularly watered Captain, they rush into the river at times as if they were famished". Capt. C. "Very likely I can not attend to the mules in person and if gentlemen who see the neglects you speak of would come to me as they saw the offence so that I could fasten the offence on the right person and discharge him it would do good but out of the variety of agents and the number of horses and mules on

hand a general charge amounts to nothing as I have no particular
person to fasten the charge on. I can only do what I have already
done renew my strict injunctions as to a proper care of the mules
and horses"—Genl. P. "by the by I may be ordered on soon you
must pick out the four best mules for my wagon"—Capt. C.—"I
dont know about that you will have to look to that." "Ah But Capt."
smiling as if to do away any unpleasant reflection "You will please
manage it so that I can get a *crack team*, I want a *crack team*." Capt.
C. smiling "A crack team" then some evasive answer and a laugh
"the crack team" like the postscript to a lady's letter the last put in
but in fact containing the whole gist of the correspondence. After
some other remarks about the law as to Peons and Masters in which
the general defined his views I thought very properly—that the
master should have the money earned by the peon while in government employ until the debt was extinguished but not the person.
(The reason I think this a good view is that by the Mexican law the
personal servitude is the only mortgage or lien for the liquidation of
the debt—the debt being the principal—the servitude the incidence—
the debt redeemed the servitude ends in contemplation of their own
laws.) After making these grave comments and inquiries—the great
personage with such an air of dignity as a charley exhibits when he
makes a call "stand"—accompanied by a constrained smile such as a
counting house merchant may be supposed to give his clerks of a
Monday morning being *tout ensemble* a desperate effort at the
blending of the *fortiter in re* with the *suaviter in modo*—The Great
Personage I say took his leave from the company above said on the
day and year aforesaid at the place aforesaid. The news from
Monterey spread over the town and surrounding camps and the
officers began to pour in to see Capt. C. to know if it was official or
only rumor. I took my leave I felt in a very good humor—I had
gathered up a bundle of fresh newspapers by the Captain's leave at
his quarters and leisurely strolled along the river bank innocent of
harm and dreading no ill. When I got across the river about four
o'clock I found Stewart the blacksmith Dinsworth the wagon
master and Cornel the receiving clerk with these exceptions it
appeared to me the whole concern was drunk—Interpreters, bosses,
overseers of labourers—the labourers themselves, journeymen,
mechanics—all as if by common consent and common right—drunk—
the whole depot swimming in a sea of glorious intoxication—They

had eaten of the Lotus tree and drank deep of Letha—suffering friends home country wives children all forgot—Like Tam O'Shanter.

They were glorious
O'er all the ills of life victorious.

The interpreter having under his charge thirty four Mexicans crosses my wrath first—He has something to tell me but the liquor has washed out of him the little English he ever knew—I leave him—An underblacksmither comes next—"Captain Lincoln wants his horse shod and he has a better pair of shoes on already than he can make and Devil d——n it if he will shoe him unless it be my order" —Found from the Captain's servant that mister Smith (the black smith I mean) has mistaken the Captain's wishes which were that the shoes might be removed the hoofs trimmed and the same shoes put on—I ordered it to be done accordingly—the overseer over some 16 or 20 hands a most worthy man when sober, Mr. White, he next accosted me with his hand under his chin by way of prop—"He is ordered to do every thing by men work night and day." "Sir" said I "I can not talk to you now call in the morning at my tent and then I think we can better understand the matter." I thought then I might reach my tent safely, but no Col. Cummings tells me his store is overrun with drunken men that he could not stand it—"The guard has orders" said I "to seize and take to the guard house all drunken men." "Sir, I make no report to you or formal complaint but as to the guard, they are good for nothing." I reach my tent. In a little shanty not far off where some of the men mess, two of them are defying each other to mortal combat. From down at the wagon yard comes up an uproarious shout—I rush from my tent in distraction. I meet Mr. Angel with papers in his hand—one a report of two drunken men the other a report of a guard asleep at his post. We retire to my tent I write a complaint to the Col. of the Ohio Regt. as to the guard and ask that he be punished. I discharge the drunkards and told Mr. A. the matter must not stop there. Some of our men were very good men, but high and low all must go by the board who were *so drunk to-day that they could not do duty*—That it was necessary to strike and without remorse. That over and over all these men had been admonished and had promised amendment. Mr. A. will bring in his report in the morning. After supper Mr. A. and Mr. Cornell called at my tent and while we were talking about our drifting—Captain Superintendent Overseers, guard labourer and all to the devil unless stern measures were adopted up come two men—apparently officers with hurried steps and clattering swords—"Sir said one did you not order two of your men to the guard house"—"yes" said Mr. A. they were drinking and fighting and I ordered the guard to take them to the guard house. Well sir here is a man who has ordered the men to be released. I would not do so unless I knew his authority to issue this order. Who is this man I asked. Why said Angel he is one of our labourers and had no authority to give any such order! "So I thought" said the Sergeant of the guard for his was the first speaker—"I thought no one as intoxicated as this man seems to be could have any authority and the next time he comes about me in the way he has done I will put him in the guard house"—Said I "You can do that now, take him to the guard house"—Said Angel I had better disarm him—certainly said I by all means and our self constituted officer was marched off to the guard house, stripped of his long sword. This was decidedly the richest scene I have witnessed yet. The labourer a six footer had buckled on one of these long dragoon swords. He strode boldly forth and made quite a martial clattering—and said in his defence "Yes I ordered the men released—they have been in long enough they are my mess mates they are now very sick and they are sorry for what they did and I thought I would get them out"—He had put on the sword to impose himself on the guard as an officer—I need not say that this man was an Irish man. None but an Irish man would have had the wit except a Yankee—The Yankee would have done it effectually personating the officer in every particular but none but an Irish man would have thought of going hurly burly drunk and with a dragoon sword. Every body had been hard at work for 4 or 5 days getting the train ready etc. and the train having got fairly *extra territorium* to wit beyond the chance of further annoyance. There seemed as I have said a set to at drunkenness by common consent and as of common right. Well if it had not come before me "in a shape so questionable" that I was bound to "speak" to it—the actors might have had a long lease—but they had no "method in their madness" it was broad daylight in business hours and almost universal. To have yielded would have been to write myself down—a poor spirited cowardly sneak, and to bring on me an order from headquarters not at Monterey not at Washington but at Camargo. When the blue laws of Connecticut set off with the ceremonies of royal courts are being administered in all their varieties to keep a boarding house to sit on the basement wall of the General's palace to commit fornication or to buy a plug of tobacco from a Mexican being all alike positively forbidden.

Friday October 16 (Dies Infastus) —discharged seven men this morning for drunkenness—the depot to-day is a grave a perfect solitude. The expression of Tacitus, *Solitudinem facuint quan appellant pacem*—has occurred to me several times to-day. Instead of wreathed smiles and "How are you Captain" with an air of easy satisfaction, which seemed to say the Captain is "a clever good sort of a fellow every body likes him." I have met to-day looks of faces hard as adamant—bronze cast faces. Three or four of the men discharged were getting large salaries and had come to the pleasant conclusion that *the public service* could not get along without them. This is a false error in public or private life. Many an insulting overbearing man has lost a good friend son or brother acting on the idea that his dependent could not get along without his aid. And as for public men or politicians taking into their heads the foolish fancy that their party or country could not do without them with such the shores of oblivion "are heaped like pebbles". The expression often occurs in the Bible that "God hates a proud look"—and how must He hate the proud fool who conceives that his services or the services of any one man are indispensable to his country or friends—The very idea is insulting to God and man—and the wright who gets it well fixed in his heart—I have ever noticed is partially or finally ruined according to his reformation or perseverance in his delusion. There is a stillness to-day vault like—The discharged and their friends are stunned—I suppose they will adopt some course in concert. Let them. Now this is the way the few plunder the many—first usurp one privilege and then another until the usurpation settles into precedent and they go on plundering and increasing in usurpation until at last—the many roused from their supinings like the harpooned whale snaps the chords of tyranny. Captain Arnold[2] reached Camargo to-day with one hundred fifty wagons on their way to Monterey to carry subsistence to the army and some other stores but principally subsistence—500,000 rations are required—a good many troops came with this train of wagons I understand Col. Baker's[3] regt of Illinois vols. About 3 O'clock I heard a voice (I took to be Britton's) call out from the other side of the river to the Capt of the Troy to "Stay and take over General Taylor and his party"—everybody was immediately on the *qui vive*—"General Taylor is coming"—etc. Soon Col. Taylor General of the Subsistence department and some dozen gentlemen arrived. The crowd did not know but that it was the general—the crowd stared in silence no one gave a shout or uttered a God speed you. They thought of Monterey but they thought also of the noble dead slaughtered to no purpose and of the escape of the Mexicans—This what *I thought they thought*. Soon afterwards Captain Taylor and 29 Dragoons arrived—turned back to bring on the artillery—The two eighteen pounders which have lied idle here since General Taylor's departure *and which should have been at Monterey but were not*. Bring on the cannon now bring on the stores—the fighting has just commenced, blood will now flow in earnest. But the Mexicans have got our spare cash—Treasury notes have made their appearance just as the order comes to begin the war—paper money—the harbinger of woe

Saturday October 17th   I have been applying in vain for 3 weeks at the pay office to get some money to pay my scores. Today I heard that Major Burns had returned from Matamoros with a plenty of money—I applied again with Dr. Patton—Major Burns said he had some treasury notes—that he had a large muster roll to look over and settle. "When shall I call said I" "dont know Captain" was the reply—"Major Hammond[4] is sick, my clerk is gone home sick. Major Coffee[5] is in New Orleans and I have not much money." Dr. Patton also accorded no satisfaction. Dr. Patton came out a private in Capt. Downing's[6] Company—Hinds County Missi—It devolved on him to act as surgeon to the Missi Regt before the arrival of Dr. Halsey—Coming up from the Mouth of the Rio Grande in the same boat with Dr. Wells, the latter noticed his treatment of his cases and formed a good opinion of him and got him appointed at Camargo a Surgeon in the army. He was ordered to Matamoros and having there faithfully and successfully discharged his duties he has been relieved and is now on his way under orders to Head Quarters at Monterey. He called on me this morning and after paying a short visit to Camargo he returned and dined with me—I told my new cook that I wanted him to get as good dinner as he could. The consequence was that he got some fresh pork as better meat than nice fat mutton which he had bought in the morning. The dinner was delayed till two o'clock—which consisted of pork—a plumb pudding which might have been mistaken for sandstone—sauce made of vinegar milk and brown sugar—the vinegar the predominating ingredient—coffee and pickled onions and biscuits—the poor fellow did his best and Dr. Patton praised his dinner and ate with a good relish. I said neer a word but did likewise. Dr. Patton a sober man like Lt. Johns the Baptist, he drinks neither wine nor strong drink—Ah there is the secret what man of talents ever imbibes. Went over this evening to see Capt. Crosman my mentor to know if there was any way to raise money—he informed me that he had applied to Major Burns but could get nothing—that he was about to send his pay account to his wife to be paid to her order by the paymaster at Philadelphia—I told him I would do the same thing but after making out one account he said I could get the money he expected on it from Col. Cummings so that I might if it suited my purposes retain what I pleased and send the balance to my wife—for which he would give me a check. Saw Col. Cummings he said he would do it with pleasure. Took supper with him and Major Allen[7] of the 4th Infantry who was in the battles there at the head of the gallant 4th. He is a weather beaten looking old soldier—Been in many battles battles of the 8th and 9th of May and at Monterey and God knows how many other places. He says Morris[8] poor fellow had a wife and children and was killed but he an old bachelor escaped unhurt. A Mexican was taken up this evening for having stolen one of Col. Taylor's mules while at Monterey—I was sitting in my tent this morning—in my shirt and pants and barefooted writing—an uncommonly warm morning—some Mexican labourers had just brought me a barrel of water—I got a bucket of it and observed to the Mexicans *Manianna mucho calor Si Si senior*. I returned to my writing I noticed that the wind was rising but thought I would finish my writing—but soon my fingers became numb and I was compelled to haul on my great coat—"A Norther had come on"—whistle came the wind—flap went the tent cold cold cold all in a minute—I thrust my feet in the water my wont of every morning—the water felt milk warm. From this some idea may be formed of the sudden transition from heat to cold here when there is a norther. J. E. Roberts came up yesterday evening—very hard now the captain says to get up the river it is so low. The "Mercer" is a total loss there are suspicions that as the insurance on the Mercer would expire in 3 days she [was] run aground on purpose—80 [tons?] is a large vessel from New Orleans to Brazos with all the Govt. stores including the medical stores for the army—Misfortunes seem thickening around us—The Treasury empty—The river almost unnavigable the foe haughty and inspirited—I would not be surprised yet if the army found a *Moscow in Mexico* instead of the "Halls of Montezumas." God delights in humbling the proud and exalting the weak—and never was there a prouder more confident and vain glorious army than this—or one that looks less to God and more to themselves—*Feriunt summos fulmina montes*—What if there should arise among the Mexicans some William Tell or Bruce or Washington to stir his countrymen up with words of fire and give to history and the world another Bannockburn! "The battle is not to the strong nor the race to the swift"—The issue is with God. This army should stop still in its tracks—defend what it has and attempt no more—While an other army under Worth or Scott should take Tampico and rush upon the Mexican Capitol. Col. Riley's splendid band played as usual this night just before tatto—Col. Taylor and suite go down in the J. E. Roberts tomorrow.

Sunday October 18th   Dies Dominicus non juridicus but there are no Sabbaths in war—war like the grave levels everything—Christian people fight each other on that day which the founder of their faith consecrated to the reign of peace and universal love! Oh! blessed day how many recollections hallow thee. The great day in seven of joy and gladness to the school boy and the lover! The cleanly dress fastened on little limbs by maternal hands The new suit, The shining hearth the well swept house. The smiling salutations of servants collected at the Great House with presents of fruits etc. and getting old dresses or a dram in return—The horses standing at the rack— ready to be mounted—Off the party goes to church, the anxious mother sending her injunctions to them as far as they can be heard "Take care of yourselves my children". Or change the scene to the city. The father and mother are seated in the parlor the happy urchins running up and down the steps and gallery or passages of the house—The girls are dressing upstairs in their chambers the youth are decked in their best are sporting a cane and sauntering up along the streets leisurely toward some news room as a walk before church—The first bells are ringing—And so they are here! There

being a great ringing going on across the river just now at the old
Catholic Church. The weather is bitter cold this morning. I am
writing from my bunk! One of the volunteers has just thrust his
head into my tent saying that his Captain requested him to ask me
to have a coffin made a soldier died last night. (By the bye they are
always dying here—It appears to me there has been no day scarcely
that I have not heard of a death or heard the firing of a platoon over
some dead man) I told him that since the 9th of September there
had been no coffins made at the quarter master's department on
either side of the river—that the only way was to give his comrade a
soldier's grave—that that was the only kind of grave that any of the
rest had got since that time—But if he still desired it I could not
resist him and to go to the head carpenter and tell him to make one
if he had the lumber—The generous Kentuckian said no he preferred reporting what I said to his captain. He reported that they
would bury him as others had been buried—I learn that two days
ago there were some of a strange tribe of Indians who camped near
this place, the name I could not learn—They were not *Comanches.*
While encamped in this neighborhood—they had a marriage—a
young chief to a chief's daughter. I learn that as a part of the
ceremony the young man's arms and legs were horribly gashed—
which gashing he had to stand without wincing—that after some
other ceremonies and a day or two elapsed they were finally made
man and wife—that the young chief being very ardent in his
affections deported himself towards his bride in a manner unbecom-
ing the gravity of the Indian character—and for so doing the old
chief made him lie on his back 24 hours without moving hand foot
or muscle—(I learned these things from Twitchell the sutler) Went
across the river to see Col. Cummings. I had promised I would call
this morning and get the money on my pay account. I did not
reflect on its being Sunday but I deemed it a matter of prime
necessity and did not feel disposed to let the opportunity slip.
Called and got the money and handed him my pay account in
duplicates receipted—carried the money in a bag to Capt. Crosman's
office—Express just in from Monterey—returned and found Dr.
Patton whom I had invited to dine with me at my tent—We had a
fine dinner on the neglected mutton of yesterday. Rode out with
Angel on the heights two miles South West where we had a fine
view: Town Camps river and surrounding country for miles lay in

view—Came around by new Camargo—great improvement there in the last 3 weeks a great many thatched houses built. We lighted at the house where there was a brass or copper kettle over a fire in the yard which I suppose would hold three barrels—One woman was pounding stone with an iron mallet—They said they were making soap. General Marshall, Col. McKee and several other Kentucky officers who had been up the river to see the falls rode up—The Mexicans brought out a large cake of soap to show the General. The General soon turned to go and addressing Angel and myself said "Gentlemen if you have no further business we will take you along—but if you have any we will not interrupt you".—All of us enjoyed the joke and came off together—very cold tonight—Took up Bible to read preparatory to going to sleep and in respect for the day. Angel came in with a report that a barrel of molasses and a sack of flour had been robbed within 6 yards off a sentry's post—He suspects the guard as having done the robbery—very likely—most likely. Sent the report to Col. Morgan at 9 o'clock P. M. with the request that the facts be investigated and the delinquent be punished— Now nothing of this kind happened when the Kentuckians stood guard—

Monday October 19th 1846 Winfield Commissary's clerk called this morning and upon my asking him the news he said he would tell me what he had gathered from reliable sources though he did not wish his name mentioned. That the armistice was founded upon a base lie told by Ampudia to Genl. Taylor that there were two commissioners in Mexico at the time of the capitulation negotiating a final peace. That our policy now is to fortify within the line agreed on and stretch the lines of the army from Rinconada to Tampico— There Gen. Scott would soon be with a fresh army and then we would act on the defensive from Tampico to Chiwawa [Chihuahua] and Santa Fe—That then possessing all upper Mexico and the Californias—our government will say to the Mexican government it will be your turn to invade—pay us what you owe us and the expenses of the war and agree on a fair and just boundary or here our flag waves forever. If you come within our lines we shoot you if you do not choose to pay and be friendly we hold what we have conquered—Paying for forage etc. is to cease also—To hear these things is a great relief—For nothing but disaster ruin and disgrace could have attended us if we were to go on stretching our lines weakening our force and draining the treasury by transporting provisions over the mountains and wastes between this and Mexico! I pray God those things are true. Crossed the river paid Capt. C. $49.50 which he had loaned me—Inclosed a check drawn by Capt. Crosman on the Canal and Banking Co. N. O. payable to Mrs. A. J. S. or order to my wife in a letter of this date for eighty dollars— went round to the post office mail closed and the mail bag sent down to the steam boat "Warren" some half hour before I got there. Now I had lost an hour in this way. I had gone by Col. McKee's tent—which happened to be in my way after examining the place where the molasses had been stolen not expecting to stop, but did so. Some officers had been on a visit to the Col. and he had some of the best London Brown Stout I ever drank—Well I must take a glass—Well that being done I stopped to talk awhile as good manners required. After talking a while the Col. (who is one of the noblest of noble Kentuckians) got to telling a long anecdote about a member of the Kentucky Legislature—I staid an hour—Lost there-by an opportunity to send my letter and the Rio Grande being very low God only knows when there will be another boat. I look on my fate as worse than Tam O'Shanter's I had rather lost fifty horse-tails and rode a mighty race pursued by fifty devils than have missed the opportunity to send my letter—Left the letter containing the check with Capt. Crosman he promised to send it by the first mail. Paid $2.50—Saw Col. May[9]—his hair is as long as Absalom's ever was but he is too smart ever to meet the similar fate—He had just bought Capt. Crossman's horse the horse which had thrown the Capt.—Capt. C. told him that he had better mind how he used the spur—May drove the spurs into the animal and commanded him with the utmost ease. "Troy" returned to-day from Clay Davis'[10] wood yard where it was sent by order of Genl. Patterson to seize all spiritous liquors. I am told she brought up some 20 or 30 barrels of whiskey and 8 or 10 tierces of Brandy—I learn that a good deal of the barrels were directed to a commissioned officer—And the Capt. told me it was thought that a commission might be in danger—Did not hear the officer's name. I learned from the Capt. that rumors are afloat to the disadvantage of the integrity of some whom I never would have suspected nor do I yet suspect—I await proof—But if proof comes *"fiat justitia ruat coelum"*—so hot in the middle of the day to-day that I felt when I got to my tent as if I had been struck with a sun pain—I learned to-day that the Mexican liquor Poulkie [pulque] when in its natural state—Muscal [mescal] when distilled— is extracted from a tree or plant called the Magae [magay] plant. It is said that a man may get drunk on it and be beastly drunk—but never vomit or have the headache—a pint of muscal will make ten men drunk. Heard a Texian say a few days ago that General Taylor when he marched up to Monterey knew so little of its fortresses and condition (so entirely confident was he that the enemy had or would retreat) that he and his staff were riding up within reach of the enemies guns designing to pitch his camp close up to a strongly fortified fort. The first intimation he had that his camp would be placed in a dangerous place and that the foe designed to fight was a discharge of artillery at him and his party—He halted coolly gave directions that the camp should be pitched at some springs two miles back—saying that he thought it would be a more eligible position and more convenient to water. Adjutant Joline[11] of the 2nd Regt Ohio volunteers called on me this evening with a request that I would give the blacksmith an order to have his horse shod. After writing the order I enquired whether they had been able to detect the guard that stole or allowed the molasses and flour to be stolen. The adjutant promptly replied that they had succeeded in detecting the thief—Allen 1st (there being two Allens in the guard) a red-haired villain—He had been seen with the molasses and flour and upon one of his comrades enquiring where he got such things—He said any man who stood guard over the Commissary's stores as he had was a fool not to get what he wanted. But said the comrade how? Oh said he, if you are such a d——d fool as not to take a hint, I bought of the sutler. All the sutlers were applied to none of them had sold him the articles. In this way he was found out and he and two of the guards heretofore reported are now in the guard house awaiting their trial by court martial. The adjutant said that the men had got out here—many honourable men at home—a strange sort of morality—they do not consider that the quarter master and commissary have to receipt for and account for property—they look on it as Uncle Sam's and that they are as much entitled to it as any body else. I know that such a feeling exists but when it comes to a *guard* placed to watch goods setting up such an excuse for breaking into a barrel with staves a half inch thick and that too with the butt of his musket and lugging off twenty five gallons—the blanket of this new morality can not stretch over so dark an act. This man must have been a rogue always—Besides the adjutant denounced him as a vile man every way—"See with a spot I damn him". As the fly has sometimes the honor to be preserved in a bottle of pure wine, so this rogue's name is handed down to posterity in this veracious history. Capt. C. sent over his old receiving clerk to-day to see if some harness and saddlery is all right. Some one has carried him a story (one of the discharged men I suspect) that one of the sutlers furnished himself with a wagon harness out of the public property here with the connivance of the superintendent. I dont believe a word of it I think it a vile slander and yet the investigation will be of much service to confirm my good opinion or stop abuse before it goes too far. I wish the same examination would run through all the offices departments and stores here. The only suspicion I have has been as to the forage—yet it is a mere suspicion for though I have tried to find out if there be anything wrong I have been unable to do so. *Nous verrons* It is just reported to me that the keeper of the forage is drunk to-night. I am told he is about to leave, he is a shrewd fellow—what if he has got drunk by design so as to be discharged and then get off without closing his accounts or showing his hand. I must see to this first thing in the morning. Rode out about two miles with Capt. Gholson a warm hearted most worthy man he is distressed to death at not hearing from his family. He has received no letter yet. I thought I was the only officer so unfortunate— but it appears not—he left home before I did. He says he knows his wife has written once a week that he has cause to be as much attached to his wife as ever man had—Married her against the will of her father—and they have had to struggle from the start—that they now have 8 children are in comfortable circumstances that his wife never for a moment repined or complained at any thing since their marriage until he took this step—and that during their lives he never crossed or opposed her wishes in any thing of any moment until he came on this expedition—And when he left her weeping and prognosticating evil it almost broke his heart—But that he felt bound in honor, bound as a man to come. That he was one of the first to declare himself in his county in favour of the annexation of Texas and to pledge himself if war came to step forward in the service of the country and if need be to offer up his life and humble fortunes in defense of her rights. That he endeavoured to impress this view of the subject on his wife's mind but to no purpose. This story is in the main applicable to hundreds now in Mexico—Such are the scenes produced by war—well may wars be denounced as horrid—*Bella—horrida bella*—I have encouraged the Captain—Told him I have been very miserable for 3 or 4 weeks about not hearing from home—but that I had a convenient sort of philosophy one of the canons of which was that the ills of life hardly ever spring from the quarter we expect them—that he would see his wife in safety and peace etc.

Tuesday October 20th   Went over to Capt. Crosman to know if his clerk who had been counting the wagon harnesses and saddlery on this side had reported all right—and to know whether the charges brought were intended to reflect on me in any way. At the mere suggestion of the latter query, no no Captain not the shade of a shadow—these things reach back before you went to the depot. I told him I had the utmost confidence in his friendship and sense of justice that I took a much greater interest in protecting the property than if I were in sole charge—that if anything was said any suspicion whispered any idea of things going wrong I would expect him to come immediately to me and in person go with me and examine every thing that I would at all times rejoice at an investigation, so that abuses might be detected the guilty punished the slandered vindicated. But that it was in the power of any vile wretch smarting under the sting of disgrace at being discharged to whisper slander on the fairest names—Was the harness all right—all right— Well I have said from the beginning that this charge came from a discharged man, who was the informant? I should like to know him. Immediately the Captain sent for O'Neil the wagon master that had been discharged from this side—While he was coming he asked two of his clerks what O'Neil had told them—one said he said that Mr. Angel had sold or exchanged quarter master's property for whiskey etc. What property—axe helves said one and other property—and that a sutler's wagon had been furnished out of quarter master's property. Harness did he say no—that was our inference—but over and over again he charged that quartermaster's property had been exchanged for liquor and other things. Capt. C. Well did he specify—no only axe helves—and the fitting out of a sutler's wagon— soon O'Neil arrived—face to face—the whole party including myself went into a back room. Capt. C. to O'N. what did you tell these men looking at him with a searching look what did you tell them the exact language. I told them said O'Neil that Mr. Angel had let Mr. Baker the sutler have a wagon tongue. Is that all? Said Capt. C. That is all I told them—the clerks with great indignation "You did not say axe helves—the exchange or sale of property for whiskey repeatedly—No said O'N. there must be some mistake! I did not say these things. Capt. C. dismissed the whole party saying I see how it is drunkenness and anger—I understand it all. Immediately I came over I told Mr. Angel what had passed. He explained about the wagon tongue—Baker's wagon had broken down in the night at a deep ravine a mile from the camp—A government wagon containing a forge could not pass so as to join the train all important that the forge should go on. The teamster of the government wagon could not speak but a few words of English—He spoke of the broke wagon—I told Mr. Angel to take out to the wagon all things necessary to get on the forge immediately. It appeared he took out an entire wagon tongue—Baker was allowed to carry it on because there were no ropes or convenient place to carry it in the govt wagon. The govt. wagon taking some tobacco—Baker furnished his own wagon tongue—and the superintendent thought it best that the extra one should go on not for Baker's use and so expressly understood but for the use of the govt wagon should it be needed. Now all this if so and I dont doubt it a moment was praise worthy rather than blamable. Then the charges as to the forage—originated so far as I could learn in the same way. I am satisfied my suspicions of the forage keeper were unjust—he got drunk it is true—he is discharged—He is greatly distressed—he has given in his written statement and vouching correct I am sure that on a count from all I can learn there would be found forage to exceed rather than to fall short. I told Capt. Crosman that I was satisfied the discharged men were ready for any thing and that I should deem it proper to issue an order that they and all suspicious persons out of govt. employ should leave our depot in 24 hours—No said Capt. C. "Capt. issue an order they be thrown at once in the guard house to remain there until a govt. boat arrives on which they are to leave, they have been warned over and over again that immediately out of govt. employ they are to leave here and they have all suffered several boats to come and go without obeying orders." I then drew the following order and submitted it to him.

"To A. Angel superintendent opposite Camargo October 20, '46
      You are hereby instructed to seize and secure in the guard
house all men discharged from the quarter master's department
idlers and suspicious persons not in the employ of the government or having a permission from some officer to remain here
and keep such persons in the guard house until a public boat
leaves, on board of which they are to be sent away.
                                              Franklin Smith
                                              a. q. m."

That's it said Capt. C. reading it—Yes yes sir have it enforced and if
necessary call on Genl. Marshall for the military arm if necessary. He
then told me it was Genl. Patterson's order that when a train arrives
from Monterey for me to apply to Genl. Marshall for a company of
infantry to meet the train and search for liquor muscal etc. I want
Genl. P's order said in writing—"He did not give it in writing—but
verbally—that will do. I felt very certain it would not do—and on
application starting this evening for the company of infantry—150
wagons arriving from Monterey—the application was rejected by
Genl. Marshall (and most properly too) unless Genl. P's order was
addressed to him from Genl. P. direct in writing. Now Genl. P. is a
great stickler for courtesy and etiquette—ready to insult and blaze
out against any one who does not pursue the strict military rule and
he could commit so great an outrage against military propriety as to
have a verbal order transmitted to a Brigadier Genl. through an
inferior officer not of his staff or regiment or of the staff of the
Major General—This is always the case with your great men in
small things and your small men in great things and if there ever
was a man *magnus in parvis parvuis in magnis* that man is his
excellency Major General Patterson. There is an excuse for him
however in this instance it has been for five or six days exceedingly
dry and dusty—The General issued an order that no wagons or
horsemen should pass the street facing his palace door—It is the
principal street leading to the landing and on one side at least very
inconvenient to go round—Twenty times a day he and his orderly
and the sentry on his pavement have been thrown into spasms at
ignorant teamsters and horsemen endeavouring to pass—He has
consequently lost a great deal of sleep, had to swallow much
unmilitary dust, and he's doubtless had a fit of indigestion. Besides

horrible dictu—Col. May and Lieutenant Britton affecting not to understand the order or to forget it gallop past the palace door a dozen times a day with lightning speed and raising a devil of a dust lost in the clouds of their own creation before the sentinel has time to call a halt. Now to send Britton to the guard house would be an easy matter but to imprison the gallant May now the darling son of America and dear to all hearts for galloping down in a public street in a town which he helped to conquer must give the Comdg. Genl. pause this along with the other causes will plead the Major Genl.'s excuse for failing to send a written order to a Brigadier General. I reported to Capt. C. Genl. M.'s refusal to order out a company to examine the wagons without his getting Genl. P.'s written order— This evening the written order came in due form—but in the mean time all the wagons had arrived and were parked at their usual ground now what if they brought whiskey or brandy and hearing the devil was to play here about liquor should secrete and await the covering of night before they began their diabolical work of dealing out their liquors. What a heavy sin will rest on the Commdg. General's soul. All owing to his neglect of military etiquette and duty. Oh how will he stand on the day of his final account before our great spiritual commander after having passed through the dark valley where the fate of all men is written "Dust thou art and to dust thou shall return?" Suppose on that dread day a thousand d——d souls should cry out to him "Here we are because you suffered liquor to be brought to us from Monterey when if you had done your [duty] we would have now been among the blessed"—I tremble for you genl. instead of thinking of dust in the streets of Camargo I tell you you had better be thinking of "the road to dusty death and your immortal soul"—Genl. Henderson[12] and his party arrived this evening from Monterey en route for Austin, Texas. In a short conversation with him on the bank of the river while he was waiting for the Troy he said that he was satisfied that if it had been insisted on Ampudia would have surrendered at discretion, that he is a d——d coward and he saw from his whole deportment that he was scared—"That the responsibility for the capitulation entirely rests with Genl. Taylor and that his course whether justifiable or not depends on the orders from Washington and the policy of our government of which he supposes Genl. Taylor was well informed." —He confirms the reports that and the opinion is universal that the Mexicans could have been forced in a short time to surrender at discretion. He was very guarded as he should be and used no strong language any way. One of Captain Cooper's [men], Copy Wilkinson[13] Corinth Mississippi dined with me. After dinner young Durham[14] from Madison County Mississippi—a youth about 18. Called on me—poor brave young man his fate was a hard one taken sick on board the Col. Cross partially recovered—relapsed at Seralvo [Cerralvo] —still went on—ill during the fight all the hardships without any of the glory of war. He wanted medicines and brandy: I gave him a note to Dr. Wells—the surgeon asking it as a favour to me to inform him where Dr. Patton could be found etc. He promised to call for letters to-morrow and carry them if I wished it and put them in my wife's hands—I immediately commenced writing to my wife. Thinking I should like to send her a present went out and the best thing I could find was a red Mexican bag—which was wrought by some Mexican woman—worth three dollars—Mr. Bartlet Col. Cummings' clerk upon my saying what I wanted with it with the politeness of Southern men said "Ah no Captain, you shall not have it for three dollars you shall have it for what it cost me 12 bits" ($1.50) he would receive no more but I told him if he had to supply himself at a greater price he must consider the over plus any debit—He would not hear to it—wrote a long letter to my wife and one to Wm. Smith, my brother.

Wednesday October 21.   Writing letters so late last night (it must have been 2 o'clock when I went to rest) cost me dearly. Headache this morning did not get up till ½ past 8—It turned very warm before day—I had drawn my tent close. I got into one of those feverish disturbed sleeps without being able to arouse myself sufficiently to know the cause—heat—My cook thinking that it would not do to disturb "the Captain" and being a soldier and receiving no orders, let me sleep on until a gentleman came on business. Now it is, I believe, one of Lord Chesterfield's maxim's "never to be in a hurry"—And it is a maxim received from the Romans "*festina lente*" I ought to have remembered these maxims—For as generally happens to hurried men I had done things out of place, written all night and now at 3 o'clock to-day no one has called for the letters and probably will not for a day or two—I might have preserved my health and done as much at my leisure if I had remembered the Maxim *festina lente*—I believe it may be safely laid down as a rule that nothing is gained by being in a hurry—To be active industrious energetic are different things—Col. McLane[15] Lieutenant Col. to Col. Johnston's disbanded regt. and volunteer private at Monterey in Capt. McCullough's company of Rangers came to my tent after dinner. He says the Mexicans were four days leaving Monterey—That they did not shout as I had learned—that they went in order however with banners flying and bands of musick playing—That there was about 10,000 regulars—6,000 vol. Mexican troops. The latter went off as they pleased the former marched out in order. That they were allowed 6 cannon and they took off 9—stealing away 3—that there were some ten or twelve deserters from our ranks among them foreigners—That the first gun fired at General Taylor was aimed by one of them. He says I was misinformed about Genl. Taylor being about to pitch his camp near the fort when fired on—*that he had already ordered his camp* to be established about a mile and a half or two miles from Monterey after giving the order as to the camp—He confirmed the account as to dissatisfaction in the army at the result etc.—A new trouble this evening some of the clerks and others have been keeping ponies. Ordered that all private horses be sold immediately or sent from the depot. Col. Jacob F. Foutes' youngest son[16] a handsome youth not quite 18—a volunteer in Capt. McManus' Company from Jackson Mississippi called on me. Poor young man. He fell down the hatchway of the steam ship Massachusetts when coming over from New Orleans to Brazos—laid insensible for four hours and waked up to find himself a cripple for life—but he concealed his injury as much as possible so that he might keep with his company and go on. When he got to Seralvo he sunk under his affliction but still protested against being left there. But he was compelled to remain. After a day or two he left with some others for Monterey and to use his own expressive language "he arrived in time to witness all the horrors of the battle but too late to share in its glory". He declares that he should have much preferred being at Monterey even if he had been killed to his present hard fate—to have been within a day of sharing in the dangers and honors of a glorious field and to have missed it, to find himself a cripple for life, in this I hope he is mistaken as he certainly is in his estimate of his misfortune at missing the fight. But it is a good sign to see such noble enthusiasm—I predict that if this young man lives he will be an ornament to his family and his country.

Thursday October 22. Rose early. Mr. W. T. T. Durham my Madison County young friend called to get my letters. Poor fellow he looks worse than he did the day before—He is almost deaf from the excessive use of quinine. He took breakfast with me. He helped me to fold up the bag and cushion cover. I put them in an envelope of newspaper first. Then placed the letter between the newspaper envelope and another one of wrapping paper. Sealed the outer envelope and carefully secured the bundle with a string and directed it to my wife. He promised me that as sure as he lives he will deliver the bundle to my wife. He will do it I know—Nothing but death will prevent him. Wagons loading up for Monterey Capt. Arnold's big train starts this evening or tomorrow. Capt. Waite's[17] Co. 2d Infantry (Col. Riley's Regt.) goes as part of the escort. Met Capt. Waite on the other side he asked me if I knew what other troops were going. I told him I did not. He said he had been trying to find out but could not. Some more of Genl. P.'s confusion where order and precision are required in things of movement. He is to be excused I learned this morning that his anti-dust paroxysms are becoming more and more violent. The clouds lower but there is still no rain. To become poetic: Oh! protecting Heaven favor Genl. Patterson with a shower and lay the dust of the streets of Camargo, lest the under officers mock at a Major General and the daughters of Mexico rejoice!—I gave Durham a letter also for William Smith to deliver to Foutes care—Foutes got the letter but called to see me and know if he could do anything else for me. "Hatchee Eagle", "Whiteville", and "Corvette" just up and one or the other will take these boys down Whiteville reports the river very low. Navigation very difficult—Foutes, Durham and the Mississippians generally including Col. Davis[18] and Capt. Willis[19] left about three o'clock in the "Hatchee Eagle". I saw and conversed with Col. Davis told him that it was universally admitted that his regt. had covered themselves with glory—That I had heard of him personally that he had walked as coolly in battle at the head of his men as if on parade but that when ordered to stop when about to take a battery that he had wept. He laughed and said that he had not wept as he knew of but was excessively mortified "Sir said I [I] understand had you not been called off the Mississippians would have taken another battery[20] in five minutes". "Yes sir that is true I feel confident that we would have done it". He dont know whether he is a member of Congress or not if his resignation has been presented and accepted he is not if withheld he is and goes on to his seat. He says he has no evidence as yet that another election has been ordered. Parker mailed my letter to my wife containing the check for $80—the mail however did not go by the "Hatchee Eagle". It is to go by the "Whiteville". So it goes safe is all I care for—and as the Whiteville draws less water she will probably be safer than the Hatchee Eagle. From the despatch with which the "Hatchee Eagle" was sent off Capt. Crosman forgetting to order the mail aboard or not caring to do so—and from the fact that one of the Commissioners Col. Davis was going on I suspect there is some grave matters of state pending and requiring despatch—The everlasting train inquiries for Capt. Arnold Capt. every body—dray wagon and five horses just run away down the river bank through the Ohio Regt. on with fury. Down again towards the river—Turned by sticks and shouts here they come full tilt towards my tent they are turned suddenly in a different direction by a brave skillful man seizing the largest and most furious horse— the right wheel horse by the bridle and jerking him down—I tried to learn this brave man's name but could not. It was a most perilous undertaking and I expected to see him killed. This evening got drunk myself by pure accident going to the landing to attend to some affairs a friend called me into a sutler's tent to take a glass of ale. Went on after getting through with my business and seeing all right to Capt. Gholson's tent to see if he would ride with me. He and some Kentuckians were about to drink. One of them had a wine glass in his hand and there were several other wine glasses but one of the company said he always hated to see a man drink out of a wine glass and puts in my hand a tumbler. Well the company turned off their glasses and I who had the most turned off mine. There being no water used helped the delusion. I had turned off instead of wine a considerable quantity of the strongest sort of raw whiskey. This added to the ale made me quite drunk. Came to my tent found a blacksmith and his friend fresh from Monterey seated perfectly happy at the door of my tent the blacksmith very drunk. Well sir what do you want here? "Why Captain I have brought my friend to tell you about the battle at Monterey". "Well did I not tell you to-day not to come here any more unless on business how dare you sir to take such liberties with me. Quit here this instant or I will send you to the guard house"—The friend used some dignity, I bowed him off assuring him I meant no offence to him that he had been misinformed by the blacksmith as to my desire to hear anything more about the battle at Monterey—But that nevertheless I would be glad if he would keep his seat. No sir said he if I have given offence I ask pardon and will go—"Not in the least sir no offence in the world, but sir I can not be annoyed by this man and unless he leaves I send him to the guardhouse instantly"—"Go away sir good evening sir"—Now had I not drank the whiskey I would have done as I did in all probability but I would not have spoken with such virulence the venom that I did. What now if the stalwart six foot friend who seemed really to be perfectly sober and a man of sense—What if he takes into his head that his laurels won at Monterey would be stained unless I made an apology or give him fight in some way—*Nous verrons*—Pack mules are to go in this train also. Padding of forage bags are lashed on the mules with ropes secured by a broad strap running behind the rump. Two sacks or bundles of provisions or whatever they are to carry are then lashed on with ropes a fold and knot on each side of the mules back. There is no bridle on the mule—There is one *arrero* or muleteer to every 8 mules—When they are all packed—they are started forward in a body. There is one mule selected to lead the drove and the other mules never go ahead of the leader. At night the drover stops near water the packs taken off and the mules fed or grazed. In travelling over the desert or badly watered parts of Mexico I learn from one of our interpreters—that the traveler does not arrange his stops so as to need water at night but at noon—The mule being able to do without water from evening to the next day at noon—But if he were marched without getting water from morning till night he could not stand it. The difference is between the heat of the day—the coolness of night and the dew of the herbage. Seeing my Mississippi friends to-day fresh from a field of glory at Monterey reminds me to put on record this history which is destined to survive me many years the orders of my superior which detained me here—they are as follow

Camp, Camargo, Mexico
Sept 5, 1846

Sir,
you will please to report to Captain Crosman, a. q. master,

U. S. A. to be assigned, for the present, to duty at this Depot.

> very respectfully
> I am, Sir
> your obt st
> Henry Whiting

Capt. Franklin Smith a. q. m. General
a. q. Master
M. S. Volunteers

Friday October 23d Capt. Arnold's train 136 wagons left this morning an hour by sun for Monterey. The steamer "Whiteville" carrying the mail which contains the letter inclosing the check of 80 dollars to my wife—left also to-day at 10 o'clock A.M. I wish it had left yesterday. Mr. Angel tells me that he went over to Capt. C.'s office last night and had a long talk with him—The Captain says he is perfectly satisfied and did not want to hear any more on the subject. That he now sees that malicious drunkard had endeavoured to mislead him—Mr. A. says he told him that he would glory in an investigation at all times that he challenged it and that hereafter he would ask it as a favour. That when there was the least suspicion as to the property on this side to come in person and if there should ever be found any thing wrong he was ready to suffer death and in fact would prefer it infinitely to dishonor. The Capt. was very clever as he always is—and I am glad now this charge was made—it will keep up vigilance and attention to the public good on the part of all the agents here. Going up the Ohio River last November on my way to Baltimore, Mr. Charles A. Raine now of Yazoo County Missi. and formerly of Virginia told me an anecdote of John Randolph[21] to this effect. Some gentleman being at his house on some occasion was surprised to see him get into a terrible passion with his overseer and servants as the gentleman thought most unreasonably—After the trembling hireling and slaves were dismissed Mr. R. noticed the gentleman's concern surprise and mortification remarked with his fascinating tone and deportment—"Dont be annoyed at this scene, Sir I pray you dont think of it it is all of design, all of design—I raise a row every now and then sir, it keeps things straight—if there is no cause sir, so much the better, it prevents there being any." I have a sort of idea that our good Captain has practiced in this instance this philosophy—if he did not it is nevertheless [a] very good philosophy and I am glad we have the benefit of it whether by design or not. Speaking of Mr. R. I could myself tell some anecdotes of him were it in good taste to introduce them here. Mr. R. was a member of Congress first of the lower house and then of the Senate when I was a school boy at Washington from 1823 to '26—one of the most exciting periods in our political history. I boarded at my uncle Nathan Smith's (or rather I was fed by his bounty he always refused any remuneration from my father) on 7th Street and went to school at the Washington Catholic Seminary on F Street Adam Mareschal Presdt. and subsequently the pious and good Wm. Matthews Rector of St. Patrick's. My uncle was then in good circumstances and took the Washington daily papers. I could generally tell when Mr. R. was expected to speak and during those times of [illegible] for his peculiar oratory he spoke a great deal. Every time I expected him to speak I would fain some excuse and steal off to go and hear him. Hastening from school at 12 I would run up into my room throw down my bag of books—descend to the kitchen in the basement story get the old cook (a negro woman raised by my father) to give me some dinner and get to the capitol and secure a seat before the order of the day was taken up which in the senate was *always* at one o'clock. Mr. R. interested me much more than any man I ever heard and I have heard frequently the most of our great men—I consider him by far the greatest, the most touching, the most fascinating orator that I have ever listened to. Mr. McDuffie[22] not as he is now but as he was then—next—(I mean next greatest—there was not much about him fascinating) and S. S. Prentiss next. It has often been a matter of wonder and speculation to me how it happens that (in this book-making age) no life of Mr. Randolph is published. Why have not some of Virginia's gifted sons—many of them Mr. Randolph's intimate friends and relatives why have not some of them given the world a biography of John Randolph? No son of Virginia ever loved him more and few that she ever gave birth to were brighter ornaments than he. Apropos of that strange brilliant weird man. Looking over the Baltimore Sun of Sept 15, 1846 this morning I saw here extracted the following article. [the article is missing from the journal] General Marshall was kind enough to ride to my tent this morning and bring me two papers—Baltimore Sun 15 Sept. Matamoros Flag[23] 17 Oct.—I find from articles in the Flag that public opinion is everywhere awakening to the impolicy of the present mode of warfare. As soon as the people learn that the gold and silver in our treasury have been expended to make glad the hearts of Mexicans without advancing one single step toward conquering a peace—there will be a universal demand for peace or war to the knife. Saw Capt. Scott[24] a. q. m. to the Illinois regt. a mild man of good deportment. The mules of the next train consisting of 50 wagons from Monterey (came down a few days ago) and ten from the depot—60 are being shod in a frame—The mule is walked into a machine with two uprights on each side from these uprights two broad leather straps are suspended which taking the mule under the belly lifts him from the ground the straps being shortened by pullies. His forefeet are spanseled his hind feet lashed to the hind uprights—each foot to either post—he is otherwise secured by ropes. His feet being turned upwards from the posts he is shod with ease. This machine was made because it took so much time to throw the mules which always had to be done before they would allow themselves to be shod—In the evening Capt. Sherman called to my tent—we rode out to-gether as we returned we were overtaken by a single horse man a Texian. He had left Monterey by himself travelling the whole distance alone and sleeping in the chaparral at night. He was well armed and said he had apprehended no danger at all now nor would apprehend any during the armistice. This is a strange confidence. He says the rumor that Santa Anna has arrived at San Luis Potosi is confirmed—He reached there a few days ago with 10 thousand regulars. Ampudia wished to fortify Saltillo and make a stand there but the inhabitants would not allow it telling him if he could not defend Monterey it would be idle to attempt to defend Saltillo—His army has formed a junction with that of Santa Anna. Ampudia is arrested and sent on to Mexico [Mexico City] for trial as a coward. Monterey was an awful affair. The Mexicans whipped yet their confidence in their prowess is restored. The defeated general and the victorious general both suffering in reputation— The victors in mourning and the vanquished elated. But woe betide the Mexicans now—Woe betide—Look out Don Santa Anna your career will soon be over—The days of glory beam upon you for the last time, if you will remain upon the next field until the close of the fight. This evening Dr. Patton calls on [me]. He was assigned for duty at the Matamoras hospitals the 15th Sept under a contract with

Dr. Craig[25]—head surgeon—at headquarters approved by General Taylor—he was to get $150 per month. At the time he was employed there was a great need of surgeons. Some of the regular surgeons being absent and none or but very few of the new appointees of the President having come on—He went to Matamoros and worked hard—A sufficiency of commissioned surgeons having reached there—He was relieved by the head surgeon at the post with orders to report to Major General Patterson. He reported to Genl. P. a few days ago Gen. P. ordered him to attend on the 4th Illinois regt now. The Illinois surgeon having arrived Gen. P. instead of sending him to Dr. Craig at Monterey dismisses him from the service on the grounds that there is no more need of surgeons—He then applied for his pay—The paymaster refused—It was then suggested that Capt. Crosman would pay if Genl. Patterson would give an order. Genl. P. will not take the responsibility. He is without a single dollar in his pocket having never drawn any pay either as a private or as a surgeon turned adrift in the midst of an enemys country without the means of getting home and without a single friend to apply to but myself—This is the history of his case—partly gathered from documents which he showed me partly from his own lips. I had reserved myself the smallest possible sum with which I could live on till next payday to wit $5—I placed that amount in his hands and gave him a note to Capt. Crosman requesting him to loan me $20 and hand the same to Dr. Patton and to take his receipt for $25 containing a promise to deliver the amount to my wife at Canton, Missi and also give Dr. P. a permit to go free of charge down the river and a right to a cabin passage.

Saturday October 24. The Rough and Ready comes up this morning bringing a small mail—Called at Capt. C.'s very busy said he had complied with my wishes in reference to Dr. Patton. Went to the post office mail not open waited some time. Saw Capt. Reynolds— Capt. Reynolds [and] some volunteers on our side killed a Mexican last night—That he was brought over and was then lying at Genl. Pillow's tent dead. Saw Major Carnes he has been very sick but is now recovering slowly. Capt. Baldwin called me aboard the Rough and Ready as I was coming over and gave me a Picayune of the 24th Oct in which is the first announcement of the battle—Called on board the "Corvette" steam boat to see Dr. Patton and found he had taken a fine state room—he was not aboard—but had stepped up town a few minutes in about an hour after I had reached my tent the other boat went down the river. He is aboard of course. The weather is excessively warm—it has been as hot for 3 days as it was in August—very dusty—Genl. P.'s troubles thicken upon him—guards report blacksmiths playing cards last night and refusing to put out lights and that when a try [was made] to seize them they all made their escape but one man whom they jugged. Sent for Stewart he reports one of the blacksmiths found the guard asleep—Took his gun and hat from him and hid them under the wagon in which he was asleep and in revenge he wishes to imprison the blacksmiths— Brewer one of the new interpreters a worthy man reports that the guard, this is a Ky soldier, has a habit of bringing all persons to a stand without the preliminary hail of "who goes there" that he had a musket cocked on him three times last night that he will have to quit here if this is to be the way things are to be conducted. I must give written orders and the objection to that course is that it is impolite to anticipate a case. Upon inquiry I learn from Mr. A. that the guard who was found asleep by the blacksmith is now in the guard house. That the blacksmith took the sleeping sentry's musket to Genl. Marshall and the Genl. had the guard arrested—Well that saves me the trouble on that score—Capt. Lincoln Judge Advocate to the General Court Marshall now being held across the river tells me that the 3 delinquent Ohio guards (previously spoken of) have been tried—Of course I could not learn the sentence as that is secret until approved. While the Capt. and myself were walking on the bank on the other side, the Captain going to his court and I going to Capt. Crosman's office, he said to me (pointing [to] a broken down sallow looking man with an old hat on his head and a tin cup in his hand) "There goes the former Judge Rice Garland[26] of Louisiana." "Sir said I nothing shows the mutability of all human things more than the contrast between his position now and and what it was when I saw him last. The only time I ever was in his company was in the winter of 1839 when I dined with him and Mr. S. S. Prentiss (on the invitation of the latter) at their boarding house. The table was covered with all the luxuries of Washington city high life—Mr. Rice Garland was then a member of Congress stood high and seemed to me a happy man—I now see him an outcast in a hostile land far from the scenes of past happiness and honor, wandering solitary unhonoured and unfriended on the banks of the San Juan "like a ghost on the banks of [some] Stygian lake". In the evening passed over the river and rode out with Capt. Crosman, Capt. Sherman and Capt. Taylor. While Capt. S. Captain Taylor and myself were standing at the door of the office waiting a moment while Capt. C. was despatching some business—I noticed a new dragoon uniform. I asked the Dragoon what Regt. he belonged to—he said the new Regt. of mounted riflemen, Capt. Mason's company. "What Mason"? "Capt. Stevens T. Mason[27]". "Capt. Stevens T. Mason formerly of Loudon County Va"? "The same" said he—where are you stationed? "Near Col. Riley's regt. east of the Town." "Well" I remarked to Capt. Crosman "I have found an acquaintance Capt. Mason—Let us ride by Col. Riley's camp where he is" we did so. I found Capt. Mason had not seen him since he waited on me when I was married a young man 19 or 20—delicate, spare, taciturn—now a manly looking officer of 26 or 27. He received me with great cordiality—must be sure and write to my wife that I had seen him etc. and give his respects. He takes great pride in his company—Said I must stay to see them form which I did. There were some four or five thousand applications for commissions when he received the appointment—camped by the side of Capt. Mason's company was Capt. Sam Walker's[28] company now commanded by the lieutenant the gallant Capt. being at Monterey. Capt. Mason introduced me to his lieutenants—Rhett[29] of South Carolina and Porter[30] son of Govr. Porter[31] of Michigan—These fellows may be killed but while they live they will be ever the first in the fray and the last to retreat—These dragoons have not got their horses yet they await Genl. Taylor's order to the quarter master to furnish them then they will go forward and see hard service. Sent Mr. Angel to Col. McKee to talk about the guard and to say to him that I will be down in the morning. Came home some Mexicans had camped near my tent—sent for the Interpreter and made them clear out. They stood out to go *Maniana*—but the interpreter convinced [them] that they must go *Las noches*—*Si si* said they very solemnly and went off. There is no guard around my tent which is remote from any one and I scorn to ask for one or to order one for my protection—It need not surprise my friends therefore between the discharged funosas[?]—and the yellow ones if I have my throat ingloriously cut. Allah is law—*Quod scriptum scriptum*—Capt. Mason is the son of the Mason killed in a duel by his cousin McCarty. He is the last of his family. Having no near relatives than an uncle Temple Mason.—

Sunday October 25th   Aroused from my bunk before sun rise by hearing some one cutting down the post where I fasten my horse— Looked out a Mexican was cutting it—another standing by—"No cut" said I *"bamos, bamos"*—(go off, go off) I thought surely they had desisted and gone—but to my surprise and indignation they commenced cutting again. My man having gone across the river and having no one to send for the interpreter I slipped on my panta- loons took down my rifle and went out at the sight. They stared— *"bamos"* said I—they still stood—cocking the rifle and taking aim— they understood that and left in a hurry. I felt confident there was no danger of me having to shoot—but sooner than my post should have been cut down after such repeated warnings—by an impudent rascal just from Monterey in all probability, I certainly would have shot him. Being up I thought it would be playing the sluggard too much to return to bed. The morning was delightful. I ordered out my horse and took a ride of three miles—read several chapters in the bible—and now it is Sunday morning 10 o'clock. What a scene of peace and content is every where presented now in the Towns and Cities in the United States. Now the parson is adjusting his tippet thinking to astonish his parishioners with a big sermon—Now the priest is listening to the honeyed tones of some fair penitent she thinking of divine relief through his ministry and he thinking of—her. Now the clerk is fitting himself out in his best bib and tucker to captivate the budding affections of some miss just from school—the said miss regarded by her parents as but a child but she better informed regarding herself as old enough for all the purposes of life. Now the lazy well paid sexton having taken a draft of strong ale at the next grocery or (to be more decent more to the point and to save appearances) some stronger draft in his own house—with pious and well tutored demeanour—rings the first bell most skillfully. Now the rich merchant deep in last weeks papers thrown aside till sunday—is reminded by his better half that it is high time he had dressed for church—most willingly would he give the church the go by—but a sense of duty to his family and a certain propriety make it a business transaction that he should go. He rises from his papers therefore promising himself rest and peace in the evening—And now (better to contemplate) thousands of pious Christians are indeed regarding this as a holy day pouring [*sic*] over their bibles or on bended knees in their retirement, they are now communing with their God—Praying for the afflicted and abasing themselves in the dust, they cry out as they think on God's blessings and their own unworthiness "Lord have mercy on me a sinner"! And where are we? In camp where but few think of God. The blacksmiths are hard at work shoing [*sic*] the horses that are to start in to-morrow's train—hundreds are playing cards in their tents or drinking smuggled liquor—What guns are firing—A platoon of one of the Kentucky companies over the grave of a fellow soldier. Born in a healthy district in Kentucky he never knew what fever was—With a heart struggling with suppressed emotions he tore himself away from the paternal hearth—his father mother and sisters all in tears and pressing around to take yet another farewell embrace. Even now they are talking of him and wishing poor Tom was there—After many weeks a letter will arrive. They will break the seal with anxiety but to learn that he whom they loved so well was long since dead—but on to-day at Camargo with the honors of war—poor consolation will that bring. Never will the sisters cease to bemoan the hard fate of their brother—Never will the broken hearted mother speak of her manly offspring but with tears—No more will the father take interest in the affairs of the world—the prop of his old age is cut away forever! Capt. Mason came over and dined with me. He was 29 days coming from Baltimore to Brazos—caught in the equinoctial storm—main mast lost—a dreadful time Capt. Stubbs was Captain of the Brig. In the evening Capt. Crosman comes over in the greatest possible hurry—Express in from Monterey—All the towns are to be occupied General Patterson had countermanded his order directing the two Alabama companies to go as the military escort to the train which is to start to-morrow—and orders three companies from Genl. Marshall's brigade to go—3 companies of Kentuckians. They must be ready to start at daylight in the morning (Monday and it is now four o'clock Sunday evening)—Now the Alabama companies are ready to march, their subsistence was in their wagons. This looks like a bungling piece of Genl. P.'s work—Why could not an additional Ala company been ordered if necessary to have three—After seeing the Ky Commander and commissary—I ordered the wagon master to have ready an additional wagon all complete and told Capt. Gholson when he was ready to load let me

know. This he soon did and to the credit of the Kentucky companies—
They got ready, cooked two days provisions, loaded their wagons,
and left camp about an hour by sun this morning.

Monday Oct 26 The train 60 wagons Col. Bell wagon master a
very efficient man left before sun rise—Having to put some men to
work grading the banks of a deep ravine a mile from town on the
Monterey road. I got my horse and rode out just as the Ky
companies were marching off. They marched off in order drums
beating and fifes blowing—They are much pleased to get from here.
I was soon joined by Genl. Marshall and Col. McKee—Col. McKee
goes with the troops—Having reached the place where the hands
were at work, I was about to stop there but General Marshall
requested that I would ride on with him until he saw the boys well
off and all right and then we would return to-gether. The hands
being at work at the proper place and superintended by the proper
officer, I rode on with Col. McK. and Genl. M. After riding on a
mile or two the General making suggestions to Col. McKee and the
different Captains about the care of the command etc. Genl. M. and
myself returned we were in advance of all the troops and of course
faced them as we returned. It was all the time "farewell Genl.
goodbye General, we hope you will come on". Genl. Marshall
"Farewell boys take care of yourselves—I hope to hear a good
report of you—never disgrace yourselves or your state in any way",
and expressions of that sort. There was no mistaking the relation
which the men bore to the commander and the commander to the
men. The affection between them was evident and can be compared
to nothing but the affection men bear for their fathers and the father
the sons. Another case of drunkenness—Here comes a blacksmith to
me, the foreman Presser is drunk and making a great riot in the
blacksmith's. Go to Angel and tell him I order Presser to the guard
house—Here comes Angel—guard wont execute his order "Did you
apply to the Sergeant of the guard"—"He is not there"—"Did you
go to the officer of the day?"—"There is none that I can find"—I
went down to the blacksmith's shop. There laid Presser drunk as a
dog lying flat on his back—Among other outrages he had attempted
to stab one of the men. Turning to the nearest guard I asked for the
sergeant. Some one had gone for him—he soon stepped up I
ordered the blacksmith taken to the guard house immediately—"I
order it sir, Capt. Smith the q. m. commanding here." "Certainly

sir." The man was immediately seized and carried off. Now this man Presser had worked most faithfully—one of the best smiths in the shop—Yet he must be discharged for this conduct. Drunkenness is not a vice only it is a great crime. There is no safety but in cold water. There is no temperate drinking with a grown up man. The tipler sleeps on a volcanic fire. The devil laughs at his composure. Soon will come occasional drunkenness—then habitual—And Oh! My God what is the condition of the drunkard. Liquor becomes his existence and every day the quantity *must be* increased. He finds himself sinking down to H——l amidst the scorn of the good, the curses of his family, the contempt of friends, the mockery of foes! Around his head hiss the snakes of the furies! His heart is a stone house where all the generous emotions all the ennobling principles of our nature are ossified, no petrified. Could I speak with the voice of a trumpet which could be heard from one end of the world to the other I would say to all youth as they value their souls—avoid strong drink and debt—A well raised youth who is at all industrious no matter what his calling may be *can not fail* if he will remain sober and keep out of debt. Yes he may fail even though he avoid these things but he is certain to fail irretrievably if he fasten upon himself a heavy debt and a habit of drinking. The first produces the latter the latter produces irretrievable ruin! Three Mississippians have just called. Two young Markhams[32] uncle and nephew and Mr. [W.?] Thompson[33] all of Vicksburg just from Monterey—They come with arms captured from the enemy and bearing on their persons wounds in front—enduring testimonials that they have fought like men and deserve the everlasting gratitude and affection of their country. The youngest Markham is fair as a lady—remarkably good looking and not quite 18 years old—yet he is now a hero. And as "None but the brave deserve the fair" so it must follow I would think that as he is unquestionably brave so if ever he addresses a lady and she rejects his overtures she will write herself down—unfair. When I was drawing the foregoing picture in reference to the young Kentuckian who was buried yesterday morning I suppose it an ordinary one applicable to hundreds who have gone before him. But no. The picture must receive a deeper shade and cast yet a more solemn gloom. The young man did not die of the fever as I supposed but was shot—shot by his own cousin. They went out hunting on friday—they came across some person on the banks of the river

some distance below the camp who had half a barrel of whiskey—
They both became drunk and returning to their camp and tent—a
pistol was carelessly discharged by the survivor which flourishing it
and boasting of its being the best in the word [world?] the deceased
received its contents in his breast and expired. The survivor I am
told swears that he never will drink again and is exhorting all to give
up the practice—He is represented to be utterly miserable. One
young man dead, the other wretched for life. There are the triumphs
of the demon of intoxications!—I have just learned from an authentic source a story which rivals anything in fiction. A Kentuckian
belonging to the Ky regiment of dragoons stationed four miles
below, took his poney, rifle, and two pistols and went out hunting.
He had shot a turkey and a deer and was returning to the camp with
his deer before him when he was attacked by a party of Camanges
[*sic*]—They showered their arrows and wounded him in many
places. He leaped from his horse as soon as he could with his rifle
and one pistol killed two Camanches. Before he could use the 2d
pistol he was seized—They carried him 15 or 20 miles into the
swamp stripped him and beat him with clubs—Before they completed their ceremonies of murder they became alarmed thinking a party
of white men were about to attack them. They threw themselves in
advance leaving one Indian to guard him. This Indian had his
pistol—he gave him first the unloaded pistol which he snapped
several times as if showing how it was used. The Indian drew close
he snatched the loaded pistol blew the Indian through jumped on
his horse made his escape and reached camp this morning naked and
covered with blood and wounds. Feverish headache, have had it for
three days—took medicine—

    Tuesday October 27th. Rose before sun-rise—wind from the East—
balmy delicious air—Wrote a letter to Fulton Anderson[34] Esq. on
business and one to my wife—expecting Lieut. Markham—While
drinking some coffee two Ky officers I dont remember which regt
they said they belonged to came and requested that I would give
them an order for a coffin that the man who had died though a
private was a man of distinction and character—that they would be
glad to get a coffin. I thought that when the granting of a coffin was
asked as a favour—a favour which my friends may have soon to ask
for me, I would comply—saying nothing, I wrote an order to the
carpenter to make the coffin. Gave Stewart an order to the officer of

the day to deliver into his custody—Presser—to be taken to Capt. C. to be paid off and discharged or employed on the other *side*. Writing a note to the Capt. that he was discharged from this side—the drunkenness might be pardoned but the attempt to wound his fellow labourers with a knife would render his further continuance unsafe and improper—as the feud would be certain to break out a new—Sent to a merchant across the river to buy a shawl blanket or something of that sort to send my wife—He had nothing on hand of the kind. A large train of pack mules leave to-day for Monterey loaded with subsistence—Various things are going on but as I could not leave my tent—they will have to go on for me. Fever is in my brain and quivers through my limbs—There goes the "Rough and Ready" carrying off my Vicksburg friends. Now I never could have supposed that these men would have left me thus without calling for the letters which they knew I was so anxious to send. But I feel confident that something must have occurred in their own affairs to detain them until the moment of departure and that they are now regretting their inability to call as much as I do. In the language of Jacob Faithful "Better luck next time". Capt. Lincoln called to see me in the evening and sat an hour or two. He tells me what all the officers tell me with whom I have conversed on the subject that all officers in the army look forward to the time when they may retire from the army and having some good snug retreat spend the evening of their day with their families and friends in quiet and peace—but that very few ever attain the desired object. It does appear to me that a sailor's or soldier's life is an awful calling. Torn from family and friends sometimes for three years at a time—the family kept in eternal suspense and anxiety. Children know not when they talk of their father whether they have one, wives find often they have been widows for months etc. But Horace's ode beginning *"Qui fit Macenas"* makes dissatisfaction universal to all trades and employments—And it all comes from the design of Heaven *that we should not be happy in this world* whatever may be our position but regard existence here as only a preparatory state and look only for peace and quiet in the world to come. There may be some things to amuse us for a while a woman's lip, a chew of tobacco, a glass of grog, the wedding and the merry meeting but whoever lives to thirty will agree with old Spencer and in agreeing with Spencer agree with the Bible

"That bliss may not abide in the estate of mortal man"

Brewer the interpreter a shrewd smart practical man—born in Massachusetts—but living for the last fifteen [years] in Mexico called yesterday evening. He got to talking of the Mexican character which he portrays in the most despicable light. He says from his intercourse with the Mexicans he is prepared to say that in his opinion there is not a Mexican man from the highest to the lowest who is not a thief and a rascal—there is not a Mexican married woman who will not when she has the chance and on sufficient consideration violate her marriage vow. That it is a nation of thieves and strumpets. The single girls among the decent classes are chaste. But as soon as they marry they then feel at liberty to do as they please. That among the low orders incest is a very common crime. Remembering just now what he said I have put in these things. There are doubtless many honourable exceptions. And the standards of morals and conduct in upper Mexico is not I expect the standard of the more wealthy and better informed portion of the country. But from all I can learn the picture is in the main correct. Every thing proves that the Mexicans as a people are capable of any treachery bribery corruption fraud and robbery. There is and must be in every country any ways civilized a class that has pride of character—the men honourable—the women virtuous but in Mexico this class must be smaller than in any other country called *civilized*.

Wednesday Oct 28 Health improving—the fever nearly gone—good nights sleep—etc. Two mails arrived last night sent over to the post office—no letter for me not at all surprised to learn that there is none—I have given out expecting letters. Rode out while I was gone a Mexican stole from the post the halter which I left. I called a Mexican and made him understand that my halter was stolen he expressed the greatest surprise. I started my man after the interpreter at which the Mexicans became alarmed sent the halter to me by a little boy and while I turned to call my man to put it on the horse the little boy ran away. I could not tell where. Sick again—rode out late in the evening with Capt. Gholson overtaken by a drunken man straining his horse by us and flying like the wind lying horizontal on his back throwing his head first one side and then the other. After a while he came galloping back and asked our pardon—swore he had some of the best whiskey in the world and if we would drink he would gallop back to his pack mule for it. Capt. G. said he would drink most certain—he soon came up in a half strain holding up a black bottle—He gave us the benefit of his company and entered into a long history about his home until we had gone as far as we intended—when we were about to return—He said "Boys you must not think hard of me". I looked at him rather sternly Gentlemen said he you are officers, I suppose Capt. Gholson explained. "Now said he were I to meet you any where" addressing Capt. Gholson "I would feel that I had the liberty to slap you on the back and say how are you, but if I met that gentleman" meaning me "I would not approach him in that way—there is something stern and dignified in his appearance no gentlemen I would not harm this is nature and there is a difference in men". We both exclaimed at once no offence in the world. Capt. G. was pleased at the compliment I thought and I felt equally so. We parted the best friends in the world.

Thursday Oct 29   The receiving clerk Mr. Cornel reports that from the steam boat (J. E. Roberts) he had received too many barrels of flour that finding an excess of one barrel over what was called for [in] the Bill of lading he mentioned the fact to the Capt. of the steam boat. That the captain told him to make a memorandum of the fact on the bill of lading which he did and returned the same to Capt. Crosman's office where it is now on file, that after the J. E. Roberts left for the Mouth of the Rio Grande one of the interpreters (Mr. Brewer) came to him and told him that the Captain had sold him a barrel of flour and claimed it—Sent Mr. B. to Capt. C. to report the facts—these are all worthy men—Mr. B. is certain that the Capt. of the boat must have had a barrel of his own and that it had been taken out by mistake and that is the way the excess occurred. From the smallness of the amount the open nature of the transaction and the irreproachable character of all concerned I am confident that this was the fact but I rather it had not happened. The barrel remained with the govt. property and here the matter dropped—Learned to-day that there had been a mutiny in one of the Ky Cos 2d Regt. A Company raised opposite Cincinnati. Lieut. Aiken in accounting for the mutiny said there were a parcel of notorious fellows called "the Fly Market Rangers" who being unable to get in from their own state crossed the river and joined the Ky Co. That one of these Cincinnati gentry named *Robertson* was elected 2d Lieut. that he commenced demagoguizing [*sic*] from the start against the first Lieut. [who] in the course of time got sick and resigned and went home. That having got the 1st Lieut out of the way—he then bent his energies against the Captain, that for the last two or three days he and his party have been treating the Capt. with every indignity. That they finally declared that they would sooner die than serve under him. That as soon as open disobedience to authority was made known to the Genl. they were offered pardon upon declaring their contrition and readiness to obey orders—Twenty nine of them professed their readiness to suffer any extremity rather than return to their allegiance. Today they were marched over to Camargo. Their punishment I further learned is to be doubly ironed and made to dig down the river bank for a wagon pass until they submit. I predict that they will submit before long. And if they do not I will say of them as the country man said of the dandy upon the latter saying to him "Some take me for an English man some for a French man what do you take me for"? "I take you for a damned fool"—So if the fly market or sky market rangers or whatever name they may rejoice in, prefer working irons to a compliance with their duty to their God and Country "I take them to be darned fools" that's all—So "good morrow to you good master Lieutenant Robertson" and may the Lord have mercy upon your soul! Twelve hundred pack mules are packing and 70 or 80 wagons loading for Monterey. Five Cos 2d Regt. Ohio, Col. Watson Commdg. escort the wagon train—2 Cos Ky the pack mules—Lieut. Aiken says he thinks Genl. Patterson has been much more courteous towards Genl. Marshall since his affair with Col. Peyton than he was before. A sword thrust into a charged bellows lets out the wind—and nothing is so effective to reduce a puffed up dignitary to decent dimensions as the dread of a bullet. There is a young man here named Gregory—sober sedate—clear skin—northern complexion— he is now keeper of the forage on this side (in the place of Mr. Levy gone to Monterey) he is a New Yorker by birth—He is about 28 years old. He has been living in New England and Canada until this last month or two—He has been working as a clerk from a boy getting $8, $10, $14 per month and once for a period of two months he got $50 per month as assistant to some engineer of a rail road—He was in Detroit and part of the time in Canada during the patriotic outburst in Canada. He was one of the party that burned Malden[35]. They numbered 150 they crossed from the American side

on the ice. The heat from the burning fort and the wind broke up
the ice in the river. Just as they were about to quit 2 British Regts
with 6 pieces of cannon arrived. They got on cakes of ice and
floated over, they floated 15 miles below before they reached the
American shore. He received two wounds. He says the people even
now are ready for revolt and fully able to whip the British part in
Canada. That they would have done so in the last struggle had not a
leader named Duncan proved a coward. He says that one of his
uncles who was somewhat deformed took a small bundle of clothes
when he was eight years old and walked off from his father's house
and was never heard of for 14 years—when he was found to be a
rich man in Buffalo worth $100,000—then he dipped into land
speculations in Illinois and came out minus $100,000—then he
went to Arkansas and he has learned from a Capt. of a steam boat
since he has been here that he died at Council Bluff in Arkansas in
1842 possessing a large property which for a wonder under such
circumstances is in the hands of faithful executors—He has written
on to Ark. and thinks he may do something in the line of inheritance—
his uncle having condescendingly remained a bachelor to the day of
his death. Heard a good anecdote to-day of Genl. Mirabeau Lamar[36].
I was introduced to this gentleman on the road near this place when
he left for Laredo a few days ago with a new company of Rangers
composed principally of Texians who had fought at Monterey and
were on their way home but agreed to serve under the Genl. for 12
months more. I looked at him with greater interest and curiosity
than any of the military characters that I have seen expecting Col.
Croghan[37] and Col. May—remembering all the while that I have
seen General Taylor and what is still more to the point the great
Genl. Patterson himself. The anecdote is the day before he left here
he walked into the pay office quietly unrolled his papers stating he
had never drawn any money but would now like to have a little. The
paymaster informed him that the papers were informal, he would
have to send them to Monterey on correction etc. The Genl. made
no reply but quietly folded up the papers and put them in his pocket
saying "It is the first time I ever asked for money and reckon it will
be the last I bid you goodbye Major" addressing himself to the
paymaster (Major Burns).

   Friday Oct 30th 1846   Preparation and hurry to get off the trains.
Wagons loading—pack mules packing. Wagon trains to start to-

morrow—Pack mules next day—Steamer Monroe [the] sutler's boat arrived to night *from the mouth*—nothing of any importance to-day—a blank day as it should be of any importance. A great number of Mexican blankets are being down to sell—they ask very high for them—The difference between the conduct of wagoners, volunteers, and others *now* to what it was before I made drunkenness a crime and cause of instant dismissal—the seizure of the liquor and the inspection of the train on its arrival by order of Genl. Patterson—is very striking. Formerly the arrival of a train from Monterey was the signal of universal drunkenness riot quarreling shouting and carousing—now order reigns and no man is seen drunk—the old topers regard the change as a great hardship but they dare not say a word—Besides the different heads of departments are drawing the reins so tight upon them Capt. Crosman requiring all my men to be ready at a moments warning and as soon as ready I report the same to him—he notifying the other departments of our readiness that the old drunken drones wake up in astonishment to find themselves in constant danger of losing their places—I believe there could not possibly be found a better officer for so important a depot as this than Capt. C. and I am sure from the assiduity with which he has laboured to take care of the public interests—to enforce order promptitude and system that his country is much more indebted to him than it is to hundreds whose name will go down in history while his will be forgotten.

Saturday October 31st I think the Mexicans look much more dejected than they did a few weeks since. Immediately after the battle of Monterey they were in the highest spirits and all along until within the past week smiling and happy—They have an inkling I believe that their days of delight are drawing to a close, that they are to get more iron and steel hereafter than gold and silver and that when the armistice is over they will find that they are at war and so will we, I think. Heard today from an authentic source that the gallant the noble the generous the brave the talented Randolph Ridgely[38] has met with an accident which in the opinion of his physicians admits of no hope of his recovery. Riding into Monterey a few days ago to dine with a friend he was thrown from his horse—A Mexican horse his head struck the rock pavement and his horse fell on him—up to the last account he was lying insensible. The blood flowing from his mouth and ears. Great God that so fearless a spirit so bright an ornament to his country after facing the enemy even to the cannon's mouth on so many a field should meet with such a fate. This is typical of all our dealings with the Mexicans—we trust them—give them money—they flee from us when in battle array—they stab us in our security—we trust their horses—they pace elegantly but true in their nature to their masters— as soon as the rider feels secure in the saddle he is dashed to the earth and killed. It was but ten days ago that I read in one of the newspapers the most beautiful and elegant response of this heroic young officer to the committee of Citizens of Baltimore who had presented him a sword. No letter was ever penned in better taste than that. It will now become history and that justice will be done to Randolph Ridgely now that he is dead which was refused him while living. Amaranthine be the laurel that shades his grave! Reported to-day that Santa Anna is at San Luis Potosi in great force that he has made the Mexicans about the capitol along his march uncommonly enthusiastic—that he designs putting his army into three divisions—one to oppose Genl. Wool in Chiahuahua the other to march to Tampico while he at the head of the reserve faces Genl. Taylor. Bravo! If these be your arrangements Don Santa Anna—the sun will soon set on you to rise no more. The first battle you get into with our men had you the lives of ten cats there are Texian bullets enough devoted to you to take them all—provided always you dont fly before they come in gun shot—Rode out with Capt. Taylor and Capt. Sherman on the other side. About four miles east of Camargo we saw a great many chaparral bushes covered with white shells—the shells are a species of snail resembling small oval sea shells—Capt. Taylor married in Annapolis and being acquainted with a great many people whom I knew we had a very pleasant ride talking about old acquaintances and by gone days—

Sunday Nov 1st   The Catholic church bells are ringing as if they were in for a day's work—a platoon of musketry is firing over the grave of a deceased volunteer. The birds are singing gayly—drums are beating—labourers and mechanicks laughing loud—the Mexican women and children on the banks of the Rio San Juan bathing hubbubbing. As for my individual self I am sick never shall I get well. If I could only hear from home and knew that all were well there I should feel content—but I am perfectly overwhelmed with anxiety—I must go home. Started over the river to see Capt. C. to know if it would be possible for me to go home—reached his office he was engaged—went to his lodging stating to him that I would wait until he can. I would not like to make the application but I know that my presence here now is not needed at all. There is but little boating doing here now few boats and they bring up little or no cargoes—went with Capt. Sherman to Dr. Wells' to get some medicine—blue mass and quinine—when we returned Capt. C. had reached his lodgings—Dinner—staid to it. After dinner I told Capt. C. my wishes he seconded them heartily and said if he were in my place he certainly would go if possible—I told him that I had understood that it was necessary to get Genl. Patterson's permission to go if so the matter must stop at once as I would ask no personal favour of Genl. Patterson. He said no. You will get permission from Col. Whiting with the approval of Genl. Taylor. I am to write a letter by Tuesday's express to Col. Whiting and the Capt. says I will get an answer on Friday—Heard in the course of the day many anecdotes of Genl. Taylor which indicate that he swears terribly worse if possible than Genl. Jackson ever did and that he is subject to gusts of passion and rage during which he is wholly unreasonable when he gives vent to his feelings by pummeling with his fist any one that comes in his way. Having two black men about him on one occasion he became incensed and being unable to get hold of the guilty one he fell to work on the innocent. At Monterey the other day after the capitulation had been signed a company of Mexican lancers had been ordered out to escort him back to his camp. The papers being all signed the Genl. and Col. May got on their horses and announced themselves to the officers as ready to leave. They were informed that they would have to wait a moment until the guide got ready—The General waited a moment or so saying I suppose we must have patience and then again asked if they were ready but received the same reply—again he said I suppose we must have patience but in two minutes he said "Come May I am going" and clapping spurs to his horse he darted off. As he was going someone hollowed to him "Stop General the guide has come". The General exclaiming "Go to Hell, you and your guide" dashed on at full speed. The officer and lancers thinking something dreadful would follow dashed on after the General with what speed they could. Col. May knowing that the picket guards were out and every body was on the *qui vive* at the American camp uncertain whether they would have peace or a fight with great difficulty got ahead of the General and warned the guards not to shoot thereby preventing what most likely would have been a dreadful Catastrophe. It was eight or nine o'clock at night. As the General rode up displeased with himself and every body else he hollowed to his men put out your lights you d——d fools and go to bed there is no enemy now—When things dont go right to please him most of the officers are afraid to come near him. Down at Matamoras when he was fretting about not being able to get on, officers were known to go without many things which they wanted rather than go near him. But it has not been always that his officers have shrunk before his violence of temper. On one occasion he became outraged at the delays of some men and rushed upon them thumping with his fist first one then the other. Lieut. Porter[39] (the old Commodore's son) was looking on and enjoying the sport mightily but presently the general took hold of a sick man and began pummeling him with his fist. The man crying out "General I am sick". "No you are not you d——d son of a b——ch" thump "You are drunk you rascal" thump. Lieut. Porter knowing the man to be sick stepped up to him and said "Genl. the man is sick and not drunk—I know him to be sick"—"I say it is a d——d drunk and not sick"—"I know him to be sick"—"I say it is a d——d lie" said Genl. Taylor shaking his fist in the Lieutenant's face "I say it is a d——d lie and G—d d—n you I will throw you into the river". The Lieut. shook his fist in the General's face exclaiming "You throw me in the river try it you d——d old rascal and I will throw you in the river"—The General put his hands behind him and walked into his tent. Soon afterwards Lieut. Porter made his men take up the sick man and brought him to the General's tent and laid him down saying "I wish to satisfy you General that the man is sick"—"very well" Mr. Porter said the General "I was too hasty sir I was too hasty all right sir I was too hasty". I am told he is very magnanimous in this respect always ready to do justice as soon as his passion is over but wholly unreasonable and outrageous while the passion is on him.

Monday Nov 2d 1846   Heard to-day that Major Graham[40] passed on Saturday to Monterey with despatches to General T. to break the armistice and fight the Mexicans with all fierceness! After the horse is stolen lock the stable! Capital error first in the Administration to expect so much from Santa Anna who had nothing to expect for himself but by gratifying his cowardly revengeful and perfidious countrymen. 2d To treat the Mexicans with a sublimated humanity—a refinement of feeling—Men incapable of regarding any act of magnanimity but as the offspring of cowardice—in fine men who are nothing more than barbarians and robbers. 3d *Ultimatum et maximum*—the last great error of all General Taylor's unaccountable leniency towards an insolent conquered foe—"Oh! What a fall was there my country men there you and I and all of us fell down" I will not say "while bloody treason flourished over us" but I will say "While stupidity Boeatian stupidity baptized in the heart's blood of brave men triumphed over reason judgement sense and patriotism". But it is easy to talk come it again old Rough and Ready. The next time there will be no lack of firmness I warrant you. The war is now to be prosecuted with the utmost vigor now that there is no cash in our treasury now that a goodly portion of our gold and silver has found its way through the hands of the govt. into the war chest of the Mexican army.

Monday Nov 2d 1846 [doubly dated entry] The "Whiteville" comes up with a mail but there is still no letter for me. Now were I twenty one my heart would break but a man of 39 is prepared or ought to be prepared for anything and be if he has not learned the motto *"Nil admirari"* he has lived to little purpose. The church bells ring nearly all day yesterday and all last night. I inquired of a Mexican who brought me water this morning what it meant he said it was *dias de todos santos*—all saint's day now whether yesterday or to day is all saint's day I had not a sufficient knowledge of the language to find out and I have forgotten what little I knew of the calendar of saints. Brewer the interpreter comes up says he wants his discharge there are too many Commanders at the landing. Mr. Cornel he says has been ordering him and his hands about in the most authoritative manner—Cant stand it either he or Mr. Cornel must go—I told him I would be sorry for him to go but he was his own man and would have to do as he pleased—Cornel comes and protests that he spoke to Mr. B. politely telling him that he wished a part of the Whiteville load placed at a particular place for convenience and This is the flour scrape—Smothered hatred and study of revenge seeking a vent. Raga the other interpreter gives notice that he will quit also—The Superintendent has griefs also Mr. C. rather haughty and presumptuous—Capt. C. has taken a liking to Mr. C.

and has been leagging [sic] him of me—Brewer went over to Capt.
C. who sent him back to me—I suggested to Capt. C. that it was
best perhaps all things considered to change Mr. Jones to this side
taking Mr. C. on his—that as to sacrificing a valuable worthy
honourable young man because he was disliked by his co-labourers
was not a thing to be thought of—but the arrangement I proposed
would obviate all difficulties—The Captain concurred with me in
every particular—and the arrangement was forth with made. The
Captain of sappers and miners, Capt. Swift[41], arrived yesterday—
they had a quick run 14 days from New York to Brazos—It will take
forty wagons to haul all the boxes and lumber they have along and
now we are quitting rivers and travelling among mountains—But a
great demand and outcry has been made by the army for this Corps
as if its whole destiny depended on it and now that the Administration
has furnished it why say the officers it is not wanted at all—The
truth is the want of their Corps and their bridge was made the
excuse for not pursuing Ampudia at Matamoras—when at the time
if Genl. Taylor had them he would not have used them nor had he
the least idea of pursuing Ampudia at the time so far as ever I could
learn.

Tuesday Nov 3d 1846 Brownsville came up this morning. I had
made a rough draft of a rough letter which I was copying in a fairer
hand asking leave of absence for six weeks when Mr. Cornel brought
me a letter from my wife brought by the Brownsville. Just at that
moment Lieut. Britton came in and knowing my wife's hand I laid
the letter aside afraid to open it—and wishing whether there was
good or bad news to read the letter by my self—When Lieut.
Britton left I read the letter and found all well—This took a
mountain off my heart. I did not send my letter to Col. Whiting as I
could not in honor make use of the main argument upon which I
founded my application perhaps it is as well—but had the letter
been deposited for the express which it would have been in half an
hour—I would probably been soon on my way home. It is slight
incidents of this sort which shape a man's destiny—had I gone
home I might have had so bad a voyage and hated a return so much
that I might have resigned. Well I am now in for it—Sappers and
miners camped near me—fine corps well disciplined—A Capt. Woods[42]
of Texas was arrested this evening for selling or failing to account
for public ordnance handed over to him for some of the Texas

troop. He was taken before Genl. Patterson but I do not know the deposition made of him—This evening one of Capt. Crossman's messengers took upon himself to order the Mexican horseman going express to Monterey to cross in the small ferry boat instead of the stream boat. In getting out on this side the horse fell in the river and despatches and letters got wet—Capt. Crosman was in a rage. Came over to see me about it had no one to blame he said but the stupid messenger—The packages were taken out saddle bags dried dry envelopes put on the packages—The letters were found uninjured—the express went on—

Wednesday Nov 4th Corvette came up a day or so since is being unloaded of ordnance, ordnance stores, and peculiarly constructed wagons[43] 4 in number for the sappers and miners—and ordinary wagons—Order from Capt. Crosman that a complete inventory be made of every thing now on this side of the river—Similar orders are being executed on the other side in all departments and bureaus—The information I understand is intended for Genl. Patterson who is now pretty certain is to march forthwith on Tampico. He went down the river this evening to review the troops. Soon after breakfast this morning I met Capt. Lincoln on my way to the landing—he begged to me help him with any information or suggestion as to his getting a servant. His servant left him two days ago and he had been living as he could—"I ate" said he "dry bread for breakfast"—"Why Captain" said I "why do you not come to my tent"?—well he did not know—go with me now and get breakfast I have just got up from the table and can have you in no time a mutton chop and tea or coffee as you like it—no he thanks me he had satisfied his appetite with the dry bread—Now I mention this to show *what camp life really is*. Here is the grandson of the bosom friend of the great Jefferson the son of the former gov of Massachusetts who was the only honest Whig (politically speaking) in the Congress of 1841—Himself a high toned gentleman and a Captain in the U. S. A. yet I have no doubt that most of his meals have been bread and water for the last two days—Saw Major Burns the paymaster from his conversation I have no doubt that Genl. P. is to march in a few days on Tampico—From conversations which I held yesterday and to-day I find that none of them will give specie for U.S. treasury notes but at 5 per cent discount. Beginning of the end! Tried to get a treasury note from the paymaster wishing to

send it to my wife inclosed in the letter about to send off in answer
to hers—Paymaster Major Burns said he had nothing less than $500
treasury note if I could change that he would pay! Yes certainly!
Well Mr. A. showed me a letter from Genl. Towson[44] Paymaster
genl. directing any paymaster to pay his account for acting q. m.
and commissary to a Texas Regt.—The acct is five hundred and
twenty odd dollars when that letter and account was presented—he
said he had no money—to call again in a week—From the manner
in which things go on when a man enters the pay office here he feels
as if he were going before a board of bank directors to ask a favor
instead of an officer of his government to demand his right. "Are
you there again old True Penny"—Genl. P. is at the bottom of this
business to hold fast so that *he* might not fail for the want of the
sinews of war and if he knew 10 million were coming it would be
all the same—he would never let slip an opportunity to indulge his
tyrannical feelings and *Petit Maitre* principles! A Mr. Clark[45] from
Texas (he came on for Woods) informs me he bore letters for Genl.
Taylor pledging him 2000 Texans to serve for 12 or 18 months as he
might prefer—That Hays[46] is fast completing his regt on Brazos—
and the whole country indignant at the armistice and thirsting for
revenge. Rode out with Capt. Swift Captain of the sappers and
miners He is a very sensible man was sent to Europe to attend at the
instructions and practice of similar corps—2000 he says are stationed
at Metz—5000 are in the French army—He traveled all over
Europe. He said that nothing he saw surpassed his expectations
except the inside of St. Peter's Church at Rome and Mount Vesuvius—

Thursday Nov 5 '46 Went over to see Capt. Crosman to know if
there was any thing certain about the movement on Tampico told
him I had heard it said that the matter was determined on and that
he was to go along. He said there was nothing fixed as yet and
to rest assured that as soon as he became acquainted with any
thing he would let me know immediately. Good man true friend!
—Captain Swift complained of a nuisance ordered it removed—
done accordingly—

Friday Nov 6th '46 Bought a Mexican blanket to send to my dear
wife at 18 dollars—bought it on the recommendation of Mr. Jones
the receiving clerk. Mr. Angel said it is a good bargain now nothing
would give me more pleasure in the world than to get from the pay
office my due send such money as I could after paying what I have

borrowed and answer my wife's letter and then send the present. Capt. Crosman came over early this morning Col. Taylor Capt. Linnard[47] Lieut. Roland[48] and other officers going on to Monterey he wished to see them properly provided for. Met with one of the officers of the new regt. of mounted Ky vols. They have just arrived came by land—they suffered a great deal from sickness. Lieutenant Brereton a noble young officer is over to-day attending in person to getting off the siege train and ordnance stores. Genl. Taylor will have every thing ready for the next fight. Lieut. Brereton dined with me. He said that before he was in one he felt a great curiosity to see a battle but after the battles of the 8th and 9th he became satisfied. He says the fighting is all well enough but none but a brute could contemplate unmoved and hear with a desire to hear again—The mangled corpses of friends and the piteous heart rending cries of the wounded and dying. I told him that I would like to see a battle well said he Capt. it is natural that you should so desire but if you see one you will never wish to see another—You might go into a second one from a sense of honor and duty as I would but you would never like it. "Rough and Ready" came up yesterday no mail—News in from Monterey this evening that Genl. Taylor moves on Tampico and not Saltillo—Troops will be drawn from Matamoras and this place for the former point also. The ablest officer with whom I have conversed says all points on this line ought to be abandoned except Matamoras and Monterey between which places there is a good road. The sensible officers depreciate the disposition to underrate Genl. Taylor by instituting comparisons between him and Genl. Worth. I have no doubt but that General Taylor is a magnanimous noble old man above every thing mean—Whatever faults he may otherwise possess—His giving Genl. Worth the post of honor at Monterey and allowing him to win honor and fame no friend of Genl. Worth should ever forget. Man drunk trying to steal ordered put in irons and sent down the river first boat—

Saturday 7 1846 Inquired the reason the mule train (1000 mules) had not got off. Waiting on the escort. What was the matter with the escort the 5 pack mules to be furnished them had not been furnished—because they had men off last night—sent to the contractors had the mules brought. The escort (1 copy Ky vols Capt. Fry[49]) and the train got off by about 9 o'clock. Capt. Crosman shewed me a letter from Col. Whiting dated Head Quarters Monterey—

stating that Genl. Taylors orders were such (those brought by Major Graham) that every energy must be used—the trains increased and the various stores transported to Monterey with all possible despatch. The express is just in from Monterey and along with the express and others from the same point came a thousand and one rumors. 1st that Santa Anna is at San Luis Potosi with 24 thousand men but his guns dismounted 2d That there is a fresh *pronunciamento* eminent or revolution in Mexico—a rush from different divisions of the Mexican army to the Capitol some declaring for Paredes some for Bravo[50] some for Bustamente[51] others for Santa Anna. 3d That Genl. Taylor has openly announced the plan of the Campaign a column from Monterey—a column from Matamoras and such troops as may be spared from this place to march on Tampico thence on the Capitol of Mexico as far as he can get 4th That Tampico is already taken by our navy. Wrote a letter to my wife inclosing a check for $55 drawn by Capt. Crosman on the Canal and Banking Co. New Orleans payable to her or order—Inclosed in a letter in the presence of Mr. Graham the p. m. and sealed by him—postage paid. Talked to an officer about abandoning all posts but Matamoras and Monterey—idea ridiculed—because water scarce between Monterey and Matamoras—a desert country and though there is a good road the scarcity of water caused Genl. Taylor to open the navigation to Camargo and establish a depot here. After writing a long letter to my wife my mind became so filled with the thoughts of her and the children that I could not sleep—My mind painted them desolate—then how they looked—what they would say when they heard from me—doubts whether I would ever see them again the horrible idea of being cut off without ever meeting them any more in this world—the thousand sources of annoyance to a poor woman left alone all this rushed on my mind and I remained awake until about an hour before day.

CHAPTER 3

November 8, 1846–January 7, 1847

When a man is at Camargo under the modern blue laws of
the narrow contracted Genl. Patterson and sick with diarrhea—
he is a great fool if he dont drink good liquor when he can
get it.

*On November 12, 1846, Maj. Robert W. McLane, a personal envoy
from President James K. Polk recently arrived from Washington, D. C.,
met with Gen. Zachary Taylor in Monterrey. President Polk, through
written and oral orders supplied to McLane, had countermanded previous plans for the capture of northern Mexico. Taylor was ordered to cease
any offensive actions in northern Mexico and not to advance beyond
Monterrey and positions necessary to secure that city. He was further
ordered to detach a force of 4,000 of his troops stationed in Camargo,
under the command of Gen. Robert Patterson, for an advance on Vera
Cruz. The War Department issued these orders directly to General
Patterson, a subordinate of General Taylor, violating both military
procedural policy and military command etiquette. General Taylor, a
Whig, was becoming increasingly disenchanted with the Democrat
administration of Polk. It appeared to Taylor that Polk, Marcy, and even
Gen. Winfield Scott were plotting to discredit him. But Taylor, as a result
of his military victories, continued to be popular in the eyes of the
American public, which viewed old "Rough and Ready" as the tallest of
"presidential timber."*

*General Taylor disobeyed his new orders and continued to follow the
recommendations that he had offered to President Polk on September 22,
1846. With a military garrison established in Saltillo under the command of Gen. William J. Worth, Taylor turned command of the garrison*

at Monterrey over to Gen. William O. Butler and busied himself with organizing an expedition which he would lead against Victoria, the capital city of the Mexican state of Tamaulipas. Taylor ordered General Patterson to proceed from Matamoros overland with a force of men for a rendezvous with him at Victoria. General Patterson would then continue with his forces from Victoria overland to Tampico. It was not known if the Mexicans would defend Victoria, but the city lay in the military district of Gen. Gabriel Valencia, who had a reputation for action. If military action were necessary against Victoria, Taylor, who had learned a valuable lesson at Monterrey, wanted an adequate force available to capture the city.

Santa Anna's spies were everywhere in northern Mexico and quickly detected the dilution of American forces. Small units of American soldiers were serving to garrison the principal cities and protect the supply routes, while the remainder was enroute to capture the distant city of Victoria. Santa Anna quickly saw a military opportunity and dispatched forces from his base at San Luis Potosi to overwhelm the small garrison remaining at Saltillo. General Worth received word of the Mexican advance on Saltillo on December 16, 1846, and hurriedly dispatched express riders to Taylor and the garrisons at Monterrey and Camargo with instructions to send aid at once. American relief forces were quickly dispatched to Saltillo. When Santa Anna received word of how quickly the Americans were moving to concentrate their forces at Saltillo, he sent orders to recall his forces. Santa Anna did not wish to provoke a major battle at that time. Taylor, who was on the road to Victoria, turned back with a portion of his forces to come to the aid of General Worth in Saltillo. However, before Taylor could reach Saltillo, Worth informed him that the Mexicans had turned back to San Luis Potosi. Taylor blamed Worth for a "false alarm" and turned his forces back in the direction of Victoria. The men in the ranks referred to this incident as a "stampede," and General Worth became known by many of the rank and file as "Granny Worth." Generals Taylor and Patterson both reached Victoria on January 4, 1847, and occupied the city without resistance.

Santa Anna was desperate for a Mexican military victory, no matter how small, which he believed would bolster the morale of his country. The Mexican army at San Luis Potosi, estimated by some observers to be as large as 20,000 men, had now become a force for Taylor and the American army in northern Mexico to reckon with. Total American forces in northern Mexico numbered only about 16,000 men, most of *whom were stationed on garrison duty in distant locations and would be difficult to concentrate. But this force was to be even further reduced as plans had now been completed in Washington, D. C., for the invasion of central Mexico through Vera Cruz. The majority of the forces needed for the Vera Cruz campaign was to be detached from Taylor's army in northern Mexico. The American army in northern Mexico was now weakened by this troop requisition to such an extent that it was extremely vulnerable to the Mexican forces at San Luis Potosi.*

Meanwhile, Gen. Winfield Scott, who was to command the planned invasion of central Mexico, was busy travelling up the Rio Grande on the steamboat Corvette. *Scott had written Taylor and requested a meeting on December 23, 1846, in Camargo, to discuss the upcoming offensive operations. Taylor received news of the meeting on December 17 while he was on the road to Victoria. He ignored the invitation to meet with Scott, as he had neither the time to reach Camargo by that date from his distant location nor the inclination to attend. Taylor was not certain whether Victoria would be defended by the Mexicans, and he could not abandon his army now in the field.*

Scott had proposed the meeting in Camargo to break the news to Taylor as diplomatically as possible about the troop reductions that had been ordered for Taylor's army in northern Mexico. About 9,000 of the most seasoned veterans in Taylor's command had been placed under the direct command of General Scott and relegated to the upcoming invasion of Vera Cruz. These troops included over 4,500 regulars in Worth's division, the backbone of the American army in northern Mexico. Taylor was to be left with fewer than 6,000 men. This count included all men on garrison duty from the mouth of the Rio Grande to Saltillo, so that Taylor was left with no more than 4,800 effective fighting troops. Among the 4,800 effectives, only about 600 were regular soldiers, the remainder being volunteers. Only about 700 of the volunteers had previously seen a battle. The important forces that remained with Taylor were three companies of regular artillery. With this small and inexperienced army, the planners in Washington expected Taylor to stand on the defensive and hold northern Mexico against the potential threat from a much larger Mexican army in San Luis Potosi.

General Scott arrived in Camargo on January 3, 1847, and after receiving word that Taylor was near Victoria, quickly sent dispatches to Taylor and to General Butler in Monterrey and proceeded on his return trip down the Rio Grande to Brazos Island. The set of dispatches sent to

Taylor was entrusted to young Lt. John Richey, fresh from West Point. Richey galloped toward Victoria from Monterrey with a small military escort, carrying in his saddle bags the plans for American military operations against Vera Cruz and the campaign in central Mexico. Lieutenant Richey, while carrying out his orders, was ambushed by rancheros in the little village of Villa Gran and brutally murdered. Scott's plans for central Mexico had now fallen into the hands of Santa Anna.

Meanwhile, back at Camargo, the inexperienced volunteer soldiers continued to die, not from armed conflict but from the illnesses brought on by communicable and water-borne diseases. Smith, who had contracted the fever and diarrhea by November 10, reported that the medicine he was taking produced a "happy effect," probably the result of an opiate. In this dreamy state of semi-consciousness he wrote one of his best entries (November 15) about the death of his fellow soldiers as the clouds of fine caliche dust that blew through Camargo settled about him in his sickbed. It is estimated that between 1,200 and 1,500 soldiers died from assorted maladies in Camargo while on garrison duty there during the war. One observer reported that the death march had been played so often at funeral services in Camargo by American burial details that the mockingbirds had memorized the tune and merrily whistled it from their perches in the trees.

Sunday Nov 8, 1846 This morning 63 wagons, Prime's train, came in from Monterey—General Marshall sent a request that the wagons be parked further than usual from his tents if the ground could not be wholly changed—There being no other place so suitable I directed that the wagons be parked at a greater distance on the same ground—Wagons drove to their ground. A great many oranges brought down in the wagons—several of the clerks made me presents of oranges—the finest I ever saw—their skin full of juice and sweet. The wagons being disposed of every thing became quiet and the rest of the day was observed as a Sabbath. Terrible wind from the S. East—driving the impalpable dust in clouds blinding the eyes and filling every place with dirt. It has not rained for a month. Capt. Mason came over and dined with me—I had bought a fish (which they called buffalo but which I think was of some other species) caught out of the San Juan. We dined on the fish and both of us pronounced it one of the sweetest and most delicious fish we ever ate. Grosbeck discharged clerk borrowed my old Mexican saddle to ride to Monterey and left with me three books declaring his intention most certainly to return—News that not only Tampico but Vera Cruz is taken by the navy I have no doubt of the truth of the first report but the latter is to good to be true—If it should be the gallant Navy would not only rival but once more shoot ahead of the army in the career of glory. Started to-night against my will— *invita religione*—to go to a Fandango Fortunately a part of our company reported themselves unable to go and the remainder after riding a mile concluded to return much to my secret gratification—

Monday Nov 9th "Col. Cross" comes up this morning and brings news that the capture of Tampico is believed by every body at Matamoras but still the report wants confirmation—50 wagons ordered to be loaded to-day with subsistence Prime the wagon master very indignant—no time to rest—no time to repair—no time to get provisions for the men. Could do nothing yesterday because he was told the offices were closed and to go to loading to-day throws him into confusion—*N'importe*—On on—Col. Whiting Aggs. Capt. L. and Capt. C. comes down on the wagon master with a sharp stick—The despatches have put the old Scratch into Genl. Taylor—he is at the bottom of all this haste. Woe to Santa Anna and his army if they are ever overtaken. As soon as Genl. Wool joins Genl. Taylor he will march forward and then the wool will fly and either Mexico be crushed at the blow or Taylor and his army destroyed. Four of the sappers and miners stationed near me (they are New Yorkers) assemble every morning before reveille around the cooks fire and curse every thing this side of the Hudson—They curse every thing up the Rio Grande then every thing down the Rio Grande—across the Gulf—around Cape Sable and so on to Sandy Hook—They complain most bitterly—Who dont when they first enter upon the miserable drudgery of camp life? Time, time the comforter will straighten them either in a grave poor fellows or to a dogged satisfaction—or rather indifference to all things. Went down to see Capt. Gholson—he is very sick but was setting up answering a letter from his wife—One sentence of which carried me back to days of child hood in the good old State of Maryland—"I have finished sowing wheat" writes Mrs. G. "And next week I will gather the apples"—After talking to him a while I started to ride on but was joined by a Kentucky youth with a gun. He was going out he said to try and shoot a rabbit or partridge for the Captain meaning Captain Gholson and if I had no objection he would ride on with [me]. To which I assented of course—he seemed to be about 15 years old—said I it is not possible that you come out here as a soldier? Oh yes he did. "How old are you"? "I was just 16 said he when I enlisted"—"A soldier at 16 well" said I "the officer that mustered you in ought to be broke, it is a shame". Said he my name is Towles, David Towles of Greene County Ky. I had two older brothers one was a constable involved in a great deal of business of his own and other mens—the other had just opened up [a] farm— they both wanted to come but *pap*—Knowing it would ruin them forever would not hear of it. Then in the last war there were ten Towles in it and the idea of there being a war without a Towles we all considered would be disgraceful to the name so I stepped forward and would come. I was just about to start to college—had my books packed up—but as my brothers could not come I determined to do so—I have had diarrhea and fever and the measles thrown in—The Dr. at one time told me that I had no business out here any how and whether I wished it or not I should be discharged. I told him said he "that it was no use for if I were discharged I would still remain, that I would rather die than go home before my time." He told me many amusing stories about shooting matches in Ky and I found the companion of my ride in every way agreeable. Can all the tyrants of the world combined put down a people boasting such sons? Never—when we fall if such ever be the decree of Heaven we will fall like the strong man by our own hands!

Tuesday Nov. 10   Sick all last night—night before had chill—last night and this morning a dreadful diarrhea cause fish on Sunday and ½ dozen large oranges yesterday. Every thing Mexican is perfidious deceptious and false! A thousand and one rumors about Tampico Vera Cruz San Luis Potosi negotiations and peace. Wagons go to-morrow—Escort Capt. Willis[1] 2 Regt Ky infantry—Pack mules go next day escort Capt. Strawham's[2] company of the mounted regt.—Sick. Sick—Mr. Thompson procures me some how about 2 spoonfuls of good brandy—Mr. Angel finds a red silk scarf for which he gave $2.50. Poor fellow I believe it cost six but fearing I would not take it at that price knowing how anxious I have been to get such things—I believe he has put down the price to get me to take it. I am assured from a source that I rely on that Louis

McLane's son as a bearer of despatches passed on to Monterey on Monday yesterday declaring that troops shall be sent on and to go ahead after his own notions and finish the war—That it cannot be managed at Washington.

Wednesday Nov 11   Rumors still floating in abundance—The bearer of dispatches certainly and I hear again that Vera Cruz and Tampico are taken—it is said by some that there be peace in a few days by others a worse war than was ever seen. Steamer Aid just came up—Robert McLane[3] was the bearer of the last despatches. The Ohio troops are getting to be outrageous—One of them went up to some bags of figs which a Mexican had in a cart and cut one of the bags open with his Bowie Knife and began taking the figs—The Mexican dexterously wrung the knife from the vols hand and as the vol endeavoured to get back his knife the Mexican drew it through his hand and cut him badly—The vol got back his knife *now* another vol knocked down the Mexican with a stone.

Thursday 12   Sick—sick—wrote to my wife and sent the letter by Richard Latham also the silk scarf wrapped in same envelope—Sent Mexican blanket that cost $18 by Marshall Smith[4] lent Richard Latham $5 which he is to pay over to my wife. When he arrives he is to deliver the scarf and letter in person so is Marshall Smith—to deliver the Blanket in person will they do it?—They went in the Exchange left here at 5 o'clock P.M. this evening Nov 12, 1846. Marshall Smith put the blanket in his knapsack—Latham put the scarf in his pocket. Mr. Angel became alarmed about me this morning and sent word to Capt. C. that I was ill. Capt. C. wrote to Dr. Wells that I was ill and demanded that he immediately go to me or send his assistant—He a cold selfish heartless witch who to get clear of the sick Mississippians reported 35 (out of 90 sick) to be well and fit for duty—men who could scarcely stand on their feet 2 minutes—he sent a Dr. Dunn of Georgia a wild salty fellow but a fine fellow. Dr. Dunn gave me some medicine which had a happy effect—

Friday Nov 13th   Dr. Dunn says General Taylor or Patterson or whoever made the order missed it awfully when they prohibited spirits Brandy Whiskey etc. that the ale cider poisonous beer and wine have given the troops diarrhea and killed hundreds—that no remedy can be found for the diarrhea after it becomes chronic—Said all I want is a little Brandy He undertook to try and get me some from Dr. Wells if he succeeded he was to leave it at Capt. C.'s office—sent over did not get the brandy—Dr. Dunn says he has known Dr. Wells to send Brandy to the regulars and refuse it to the Volunteers—When the vols apply he has none. When the regulars apply he has a plenty.

Saturday Nov 14 Sick—sick—The church bells are ringing most dolorously—one of the richest citizens of Camargo—a Mexican—was murdered on this side of the river about six miles from here on yesterday his horse came in covered with blood. He was found this morning dead in the chaparral. Our troops are not paid—then they have conceived an idea that they are to kill the Mexicans and rob—which is their late interpretation of the late despatches to carry on the war vigorously and to forage on the enemy. Capt. Mason and Lieut. Rhett severally called this morning they are on their way with their company to Monterey—they are ordered on and go as the escort to Duffield's train which leaves to-morrow—Col. Riley of the 2d infantry hearing somehow I suppose that I was sick and stood in need of the *critter* did me the honor to send by one of his soldiers a champagne bottle of good brandy—Presents thus bestowed unexpected unasked for are the most agreeable incidents in *life* and keep the chain of memory always bright. Bell's train just in from Monterey—Bell called to see me. His train is ordered to report to Col. Riley for orders—Orders are brought for Col. Riley to march to Tampico. Genl. Worth and Wool have marched for Saltillo—Genl. Taylor for Tampico—Tampico and Vera Cruz are to be attacked in succession. Genls. Wool and Worth will give battle to Santa Anna if he comes within striking distance—These seem to be the present plans—

Sunday Nov 15 Dies benedictus Dies Domini—Yet a miserable day—Heavy wind from the S. E.—no rain—no drop of water—dust dust dust—on the bed in the kneading trough—in the water bucket—on the towel—in the mouth down the throat. It is a wonder that the mere inconvenience of high wind and dust had not been one of the plagues of Egypt. I would gladly exchange them for frogs or any thing else in that line except lice—and I would gladly just now exchange this place for Okhotsk—Kamschatka [*sic*]—St. Helena—Madagascar—or the Punjaub [*sic*]—Damn it was a man *in viriditate* made only that he might not? To show how far a part of God creation called nerves and muscles may stand the warfare of a tropical sun cold nights dust and malaria? Platoon after platoon is firing around me every day from every point the soldiers are dying—But who thinks of a private a volunteer private? He dies and is buried uncoffined! The only announcement *not of his death* but that a man one of the genus *homo* is dead is the firing of a half dozen guns—the shooters trying to fire together and trying at nothing else and thinking of nothing else—The firing announces that *homo* is dead—Black Thompson Smith Jones Clay Polk Mason Brown Peterson whatever his name or lineage it boots not to say nor is it said or known except to *the man detailed to give him rice water and close his eyes—Barem* go the guns—*homo* is dead! That is all that is known to the surrounding thousands—Fallen poor fellow like a withered leaf of autumn in the stillness of the forest! Fallen like a drop of rain on the foamy surface of the deep in a night storm at sea! Unknown unpitied! Without an eye to pity or a heart to utter a prayer in his behalf—when the death shudder convulses the frame and the soul reeling and staggering beneath the heavy burthen of its last agonies gather with dreadful convulsion its last energies to meet its last final doom! Dreadful hour to him all important awful hour to him! Awful still more awful hours to her whose arms he left for this inhospitable shore! To those dear innocents sleeping in peace and quiet on the banks of the Illinois the Wabash the Ohio the Missi— the Cumberland or the Alabama and dreaming they will soon see their pa a dream never to be realized until father and offspring meet together in the land of spirits where if Holy men say true the joy and sympathies of the flesh are remembered but to be despised! And what has produced all this misery. Ah ye had better be after minding yourself Mr. James K. Polk may be you have done a bad thing—I must examine some questions when I get home and see who or what was the *detemina a causa belli*! Mason's company left this morning—Capt. Taylor's ditto with the big guns—Duffield's train of wagons ditto Major McCall and Col. Belknap[5] with an escort of dragoons all for Monterey. Went over to see Capt. Crosman to tell him I must move from this place and to ascertain what prospects he had of ever getting away—He says he has applied for leave of absence and will get an answer next saturday when he goes to the army. I shall go if he does not succeed I will apply separately—I must quit this hole if possible—A few days ago a pupsy looking fellow with a yellow face and a squeaky voice took the liberty to call on me and introduce him self as the cook for the sappers and miners and said "may be captain as you seem sick and weakly you would like a quail or partridge or something of that sort and if you will allow me and not be offended I will cook you some things nice and bring it over"—I told him it was very kind and I certainly could not say I would be offended—Thereupon taking a seat he proceeded to say that "his father was well to do in the world that he was under no necessity to come out here but wished to travel and see the world that he had cooked for President Harrison (?) Mr. Van Buren (?) and you know said he when Governor Bouck and his party visited Long Island they gave him a big dinner?"—Oh certainly said I—well rising in all the gravity his person and features would admit of, "I" and he "I am the man who cooked that dinner." It is possible said I "yes sir I am the very man that did it." Sir said I you astonish me you have been really a distinguished man—The thought seemed suddenly to strike him that there might be some irony in all this—I looked at the sky and he looked at me and after sitting a minute or so which was evidently an unpleasant period of silence to both parties—He withdrew with a "Well good morning Captain I hope you will soon recover." I thanked him with much sincerity—He has not called again and I fear I shall never be blessed with the superb dishes of an *artist de cuisine* who had cooked for two presidents of the United States one Gov. of New York and is now diurnally dispensing the benefits of good living to the rank and file of the sappers and miners! Got a paper this evening "Daily Picayune" of the 31st Oct. Elections in Ohio and Pennsylvania [have] gone against the Administrations signal guns of distress. This war must end quick or there is an end to the Powers that be—Mr. Polk sees and feels this now—But now no alternative is left him—There was a time for reflection caution statesmanlike doubts before the army was ordered across the Nueces and above all before it was made to quit Corpus Christi and set down against Matamoras. But now *cita mors aut victoria lata* is all that is left Mr. Polk—I reserve these questions however for a hereafter for a *post bellum* examination—*Flagrante bello* all the patriot can do is uphold his country right or wrong— Capt. Crosman came over this evening and *proh pudor*! Taking the agent from this side we rode 8 miles to a *fandango*! Spirits of Fore and Wesley—founders of the faith of my fathers. Spirits of my fathers ye who when ye were in the flesh worked 6 days in the week and kept the 7th Holy mourning praying and singing hymns how must ye have grieved as you beheld this degenerate descendant sallying forth half dead with disease amidst clouds of dust going *per fas et nefas* on a sabbath evening to a Mexican *Fandango*! When we arrived there were but few assembled—The fandango was to be at the house or rather in the yard of one of the express riders—Silvester—to this man and many of his acquaintances and friends for various services in the Qr Master's departments many a good dollar had been paid out at Crosman's office. The arrival of Capt. Crosman then it may be well imagined was regarded as a distinguished honor *El Capitano El Capitano* could be heard on every side! Three or four were at his horse immediately and as the number increased their attentions at last extended to the horse of *Autro Capitano*—at last Mr. Angel's and mine were admitted to full fellowship and Silvester ordering and directing began to cry out—*tres—los tres caballos*. So our horses and *appahos* [?] were secured a great point gained for at Fandangos the American's horse is often stolen. The yard was swept clean—three antique looking vessels—earthen ware about the size of an ordinary spittoon—filled with some kind of grease or oil blazed along the east side of the yard—these gave the light—wide benches were placed along on the sides of the yard. The yard was inclosed by a fence made of upright logs placed in the ground endwise. One half of the yard was dedicated to the horses who were eating fodder and corn. Our great coats being taken we were carried into the house by Silvester and his wife and wife's sister saluting us with a hug after the Spanish fashion—we were set down on a bench cushions being first placed on it one for the Captain and one for myself—We were then handed very good coffee and sweet light bread or rusks. Many apologies made the while to the *Capitano* for not having a better supper—that if they had only known we were coming—They would have got a good supper etc. The belles of the big city may know and remember that their fashionable hours are observed by these barbarians—The senioras and segniorettas [*sic*] did not congregate until about 10 o'clock. An old Mexican was the fiddler—his the only instrument—I was surprised to hear so many tunes familiar to me among others was Fisher's hornpipe. The waltz is their great dance—they are fondest of it—and I think they danced other figures mostly at the suggestion of the young vol. officers a great many of whom were present. They waltz to the greatest perfection—with great ease and grace and are capable of continuing

on the floor longer than an American would think it possible—
when they waltzed the Mexican youth generally got a show—but
few of the *voluntarios* could go the waltz—the women were dressed
principally in silk, with gold beads around their neck. On the N. E.
corner of the yard near one of the lights heavy gambling was going
on at Monte—at the S. E. corner an old woman had a large table
loaded with oranges pecans and dried figs. I noticed the girls giving
back to the old woman the presents of fruit which the vols. gave
them—I remarked this and was told that it was a regular perquisite
of the old crone. From what I saw heard and witnessed at this
fandango I am sure Brewer's account of the Mexican woman is
correct. The young girls are generally inaccessible—the married
women only want the opportunity to cuckold their husbands—One
fact speaks volumes a proposal to a married woman if there be any
cause to prevent her acceding to it *is never regarded as an insult but
always as a compliment to her charms*. If she takes a fancy to you or
thinks you will pay her well your suit is greater if she takes a
different view she is at least complimented and her respect for you
heightened—now if any one thinks from what I have said that I
took personal advantage of this accommodating spirit—he or she
will form an erroneous opinion—for after setting up until 12
o'clock the symptoms of my diarrhea returned on me and too weak
longer to stand or set up Sylvester took me into his hacal [*sic*] and
laid me on his bed where I lay until day break catching such
snatches of sleep as the noise would permit—but I found out every
thing that was going on from a young man attached to the quarter
master's department who spoke both Mexican and English. The
waltz and the gambling continued until day break—at which time
the party broke up and we being treated to hot cakes and coffee
returned to Camargo. We were about to leave at 3 o'clock—when
the Alcalde of the village (which is called Wardaw[6] [*sic*]) hearing of
it came in person and urged Silvester to insist that the Captain and
myself should not leave until day—that from what he could learn
and pick up we would be carried off by a party of robbers at a
certain ravine—We thought it prudent to remain I understood that
the object was not to kill us but to abduct the Captain and myself
on a ransom speculation—

Monday Nov 16th 1846 Reached the depot by an hour by
sun—everything straight—about sunrise a very large snake was

crossing our road. Silvester dashed up on his fiery little pony and fired at it with a revolver—the horse jumped ten feet—the snake retreated to a bush. Silvester immediately had his poney at the spot reined down stock still by the powerful Mexican bridle and firing twice sent the 2d ball through the snake's head—got some newspapers—read and slept—all day—

Tuesday Nov 17 Dust Dust Dust—clouds of dust—Mr. Winfield the Commissary's clerk told me this morning a most thrilling incident in reference to two Kentuckians of the mounted Regt. now stationed on the other side of the River below Camargo—Two young men brothers named Hayden applied for their discharge because of sickness Genl. Patterson opposed it—Finding they could not get their discharge the one that was least sick endeavoured to carry the other to the river so that they might drown together—being unable to do so he (the one least sick) went down to the river and drowned himself—His body was found sunday morning and about the same time the body was found the other died! Now often and often in the service as well as in every other service I have learned that a sick leave has been granted to young officers in perfect health and here when men are really sick and dying it is refused—Had they been discharged the hope of reaching home and the excitement of travel might have saved them! There are *hardcases* in this world of ours! One of the interpreters at this depot named Raga (talking of thrilling incidents brings to mind this story) was one of the Mier Prisoners—It will be remembered that while being conveyed to Mexico they rose on their guard and beat them off but getting lost afterwards were recaptured and decimated—One of his friends [was] a Texian with a large family having drawn a black bean—Raga went to the Mexican officer and enquired whether he might not be shot in his stead which was agreed to his friend was plunged into the greatest distress. Raga came to him and told him to cheer up that he would be shot in his place—that he should yet see his wife and children—and as for himself he had none and did not care about dying at all. The man embraced him and said not for the world would he allow such a thing—and marching out with the rest died with the utmost firmness—This instance of Roman fortitude and magnanimity which I get from a reliable source I have thought worthy of being remembered—Passed over this evening to Capt. Crosman's office in company with Capt. Scott a. q. m. of

Illinois. Capt. Scott is ordered to Tampico in charge of 50 wagons (Bell's train) to carry the provisions tents etc. of Col. Riley's Regt.—They are to set out on thursday the 19th inst.—They will get off in all probability on friday the 20th Capt. Scott told me that Col. Whiting said he expected to fall in with him at some point between this and Tampico and being anxious to quit this pestilential hole on any terms. I went over to consult with Capt. C. whether we had not better address a letter to Col. W. by Capt. Scott. Capt. C. bade me be easy that Capt. S. might fall in with Col. W. but it would be later in the campaign before he did—The "J. E. Roberts" came up just as we crossed with a small mail. After I left Capt. C.'s office I went to the Post office with the dim glimmering hope that there was another letter from me from my wife no letter—on my return I fell in with Capt. Scott and we adjourned to a sutler's where we had the good fortune to stumble on a bottle of gin which I bought at $2.00 and we drank half of it before we parted—I am so well satisfied since I had this last attack of diarrhea that about 500 men have died here from drinking cider and eating Pelonceau [*sic*] and that I myself would have but for the brandy furnished me by Col. Riley and Mr. Angel—that I drink now from spite and will never regard here after *a bold abstinence pledge* but with contempt. I am satisfied that such a pledge is folly—Drunkenness is a crime a homble damning evil—but alcohol brandy—gin is as good as a medicine as calomel or quinine. So long live the memory of Horace—he was right—though he wrote 1800 years ago—*dulce est decipere in loco*, which means when a man is at Camargo under the modern blue laws of the narrow contracted Genl. Patterson and sick with the diarrhea—he is a great fool if he dont drink good liquor when he can get it. Though I say this I do not retract one iota of what I have written above against the unabating bestializing habit of intoxication—Ovid is right—*in medio tutissimus ibis*—a man of sense (not brutes or those in danger of becoming such) should observe a just medium occasionally—i.e. half brandy and half water—Oh. I am heartily tired of this place and would resign instantly had I seen a battle. I asked the sutler to give me some papers, he gave me half a dozen and when I opened them I found a tract with the following title "The Conversion of the World or the Claims of Six Hundred Millions and the Ability and Duty of the Churches *Respecting* Them" Published by the American Tract Society and sold at their depository re etc. New York. The writer says there in the world 800 millions people—200 millions are *nominally* Christians—600 millions never heard the gospel and that it is time Christians had sent out (after 1800 years delay) missionaries to preach the gospel—I think so too—but alas! he proposes to do this wonder work not on the Falstaff principle of "avoiding their potations and addicting ourselves to sack" alias brandy but by appropriating all the money expended for strong drink in fitting out Missionaries—I would have sympathized with the writer four weeks ago—but now I have an idea that he is a "tarnation fool" yet God grant that his truth may triumph and I doubt not but it will.

Wednesday Nov 18th, 1846 Waked this morning with a stifling sensation—could hardly breathe it was so hot and sultry went out and raised the sides of the tent—returned and had just got to sleep when down came a Norther—with the roar of a hundred steam boats. I hardly had time to fasten down the tent and after I did so I expected every minute that I would be blown away—very cold—I have on two thick blanket coats and yarn socks. Genl. Marshall came to my tent this morning and sat two or three hours chatting. Having a good opportunity I enquired of him in reference to Winfield's story about the two Haydens—I find the story was true as related to the letter and what is worse Genl. Marshall said the surgeon gave them a certificate of their being sick and unfit for further service and that their Col. and himself (Genl. M.) made personal efforts to get Genl. Patterson to agree that they might be discharged—but in vain—and the young men died as above stated—q. master guard to the depot taken from the Ohio Regt. in a state of insubordination. Angel ordered one of them to the guard house for misconduct—Major Wall comdg the Ohio Regt sent for him and told him he had no authority to order one of his men arrested—demanded to know what commission he held etc.—when the guard was ordered off by Angel all the rest of the guard hissed and shouted in derision they had doubtless got their cue from their commander. Capt. Turpin[7] witnessed the manner Angel was treated and was exceedingly indignant at the conduct of the Ohioans. Passed over the river with Capt. Turpin where after spending an hour or two returned to my tent. Capt. Dunn of the "Whiteville" which came up this morning had kindly brought me a bundle of late papers—I read after supper until from the cold and small print I could no longer see—had no company and knowing what a long cold night there was before me I dreaded going to bed and the way I passed the time was to sit still until tattoo wrapped in my two coats—

Thursday Nov. 19 Though I had three blankets and an India rubber coat—(one blanket coat for a pillow one across my feet) I slept quite cold. The wolves howled nearer the camp and fiercer than I had heard them before—Crossed the river and saw 5 companies of Col. Riley's regt march off for Tampico—They marched off with bright arms fixed bayonets band of musick and moved like machinery and with a proud look and step which seemed to say we are the boys to rely on—We are the men to face danger and follow whereever our commander leads. Immediately behind the troops followed the train of 50 wagons—Bell the wagon master—Scott a. q. m.—called on Genl. Marshall and got from him a written order that when the Ohio guard misbehave hereafter to bring them before him and he will see them punished declaring that it was useless to expect the Ohio officers to punish them past experience showed that whatever their conduct was their officers would screen their men. I hope I shall now have some chance to protect public property and enforce discipline hereafter. Col. McKee who is stationed at Seralvo came down day before yesterday and left to-day—wrote a long letter to my wife—health improved with the cold weather—

Friday Nov 20th Sick wretched miserable. Rode out in the evening with Genl. Marshall and Col. Marshall[8] on their invitation—Took along Raga one of the our interpreters. I believe their object was to find some Mexican at New Camargo and make a purchase of him.

Saturday Nov. 21. Still sick—worse—wretched diarrhea dreadful. Wallace comes over with a written complaint in his hand signed by Major Wall—The latter without saying anything to me had gone to Capt. Crosman and made out a written complaint that the quarter guard furnished from his regt was quartered in a stable where there were horses and a heap of manure. I did not think this possible so I went down to look—I found the statement true to my great mortification. A new tarpaulin having been up near the old guard tent—I ordered the latter removed. Mr. Angel selected the stable intended to have it cleaned out. There was some neglect—and the guard went into it before it was ready and then Major Wall glad of a chance to cover over the many bad acts and violations of orders by his men without saying anything to me goes over to Capt. Crosman—I ordered immediately guard tents to be put up selecting the location myself which was accordingly done this evening—

Sunday Nov 22d Took medicine last night—little or no relief getting very weak—go over to see Capt. Crosman—told him I must go some where—question leave of absence to go home or leave of absence to go to Monterey. I believe I could get either—but my fate cries out. I must see something if possible—will go to Monterey. Called on Dr. Wells and considered with him he said he would cure me in a week and if he did not "write him down an ass". That the ride to Monterey with the use of medicine ought certainly to restore me. Wrote a request to Capt. Crosman for the leave of absence. He is to get the comdg Genl. Patterson to grant it in the morning. If granted I go about wednesday—I retract all I have said against Dr. Wells—He said if he had known it was my request personally that he should come over he certainly [would] have done so. He is too gentlemanly and a man of too much science to speak disrespectfully of—He gave me a box of pills—"Col. Cross" came up this morning bringing a large mail not yet opened—when I came over this evening I found that Genl. Marshall had sent me an invitation to dinner. Mr. Gregory poor fellow had taken the trouble to go out on purpose to kill me some birds he brought me a couple of partridges—

Monday Nov. 23rd Leave of absence granted—I am to start to-morrow for Monterey in company with some 8 or 10 officers. Sent to my wife (God bless her and the children) a check for $50—drawn by Capt. G. H. Crosman. It is all I could send her—Would to God I could send $5000. Inclosed the check in a letter and handed the same and 10 cents for postage to Mr. Graham the P. M. at Camargo—handed the letter and money in the presence of Mr. Wagaman the Post Master General's agent—About sun down this evening returned to my quarters and employed Wilson Van Dike[9] one of the Mier prisoners a tolerable speaker of Mexican to go with me to Monterey and ordered all things ready for a start by 10 o'clock.

Tuesday Nov. 24th Left Camargo at 12 o'clock in the company of Col. Whistler[10] of the 4th infantry. Capt. Bradley[11] 1st Ohio Regt and Capt. Walton[12] 1st Tennessee. The two last were returning from their respective states where they had been on leave of absence on account of bad health—They are now entirely recovered and anxious to join their companies. I look on them both as gallant men and fine soldiers—These three gentlemen and myself travelled together and pitched our tents by each other at night. We got along very well and never had the least jar—We frequently rode ahead of the wagons and stopped under the shade until they came up. The train consisted of 7 wagons of provisions to Pontagooda[13] [*sic*]—2 of specie to Monterey—2 small ones of officer's baggage—and 2 wagons belonging to the military escort—A company of the 1st Regt. of dragoons commanded by Capt. Kearney[14]. Major Weston[15] a paymaster was along to see after the specie. There was also Lieut. Hunt[16] of Duncan's artillery—He and Lieut. Ewell[17] and Kearney travelled together—Major Weston the paymaster progged along on his own hook sometimes far before sometimes far behind every body—we travelled 11 miles to-day amidst clouds of dust and camped on the banks of the Rio Grande. The wind blowing stiffly all day from the N. W. terminated in a Norther at night—I slept in under a shed in front of a Mexican house. I put my mattress down where the dog staid and was much annoyed by fleas—during the night I noticed some four or five men dressed like volunteers passed by me into the house—I was awakened just before day by their going off. The first sounds that I heard in the morning were *blanketo blanketo*—The *seniora* was complaining bitterly—the scoundrels who had thrust themselves into the house uninvited and had slept on the floor where there was a sick child had gone off in the morning with one of her blankets—I thought this one of the meanest things I ever heard—to partake of the shelter of a man's roof unbidden and then steal the blanket furnished to keep them warm. Van Dike had taken care to tell the woman that I was a *Captaino*—as soon as I got up she complained to me—I told Van Dike they were none of our men but robbers and devils and that her husband had better go with us to Mier and see if he could find them out. Before we got to Mier we found that the same rascals had stolen two horses and 80 dollars—when we got to Mier we found that they had committed some depredations in that vicinity and that an armed party was in pursuit of them, whether they were caught or not I can not say.

Wednesday Nov 25th We camped at Mier having traveled 12 miles. After we had pitched our tents Col. Mitchell[18] of the 1st

Ohio Regt. wounded in the leg and his adjutant Lieut. Armstrong[19] one leg shot off—came along in a wagon and were about to pass us to camp at Mier. They were hailed by Capt. Bradley[20] and they concluded to stay where they were. I contemplate these men with great interest Lieut. Armstrong is a young man about 22 years old—The only son of a widow in Cincinnati—with what feelings will that widowed mother meet that son—there is one consolation— he gets a good pension for life. Col. Mitchell is a remarkably handsome man about 35 he is a lawyer in Cincinnati—I would think that if his career hereafter be not brilliant—it will be his own fault. There is a fine bold broad creek on which Mier is built and on whose margin we encamped called Alcantro—it empties into the Rio Grande some two or three miles below. This creek winds its way along from Seralvo and is called higher up Alamo—

Thursday Nov 26th We traveled 15 miles and camped on the Alamo—whose banks are covered with ash trees which caused Captain Walton to dub it Ash Creek—the lands on both sides of the creek are as fertile as any in the world—fine water power—splendid sites for towns and plantations. I who had been so long removed from the sights of large trees and running streams could scarcely satisfy myself with contemplating those beautiful features of nature—

Friday Nov 27th We travelled 15 miles and camped at Pontagooda (a small Mexican village) again on the banks of the Alamo. I walked a half a mile down the banks of the stream here and found it one of the most delightful spots I ever saw—At one point there was a stone dam causing a beautiful cascade—from the dam there was a large stone aqueduct leading the water off to irrigate the plantations. Some of the Ohio troops stationed there told me they had been three miles down the creek—that as far as the eye could reach there was a succession of as fine fields of corn as they had ever seen in Ohio—That the land was not half cultivated but the crops full and abundant. Lieut. Ewell of the dragoons went to one of the planters to buy corn and found him among his Peons (some 50 in number) grinding the sugar cane—This planter was very polite to the Lieut. sold him corn at a dollar a bushel but complained bitterly of having been robbed of 1000 dollars and his wife of her jewelry—even her ear rings were taken off her ears—on Friday Van Dike was thrown from the pony I had bought being nearly killed—he did not hate his injury half so much as the idea that a Mexican horse had thrown him having caused injury to him self perfectly and fast at riding Mexican horses—I had to put Van in the wagon and procure the services *pro tempore* of [an] other servant

Saturday Nov 29th   Travelled to-day 20 miles and camped still on the banks of the Alamo where stood two live oak trees bearing moss—the first I had seen—Capt. Walton dubbed this Live Oak Creek—land still rich along this stream. Here we were met by Genl. Shields on his way to Tampico—passed through Seralvo to-day once a beautiful village mountain torrents aqueducts dashing through in every direction but every thing bears the aspect now of dilapidation— the place Seralvo is very sickly. The Mexicans have no doctors but old women and depend much more on amulets and holy water than they do on medicine.

Sunday Nov 29   Travelled 24 miles this day and camped east of a village called Ramos among the mountains and on a mountain stream. The mountain scenery along this day's travel was quite grand—and increasing in grandeur the further we went—

Monday Nov 30   Travelled this day 27 miles and camped on a beautiful stream at the foot of grand mountains within 3 miles of Genl. Taylor's camp and 8 miles of Monterey—Passed through a town called Marin—a beautiful place—nothing can exceed the fertility of the soil and the grandeur of the scenery from Marin to Monterey. After you pass Marin look back and you behold the mountains piled up as it were from the plain to the Heavens—look forward "Hills peep o'er Hills and Alps on Alps arise". Grander and grander becomes the scenery deeper and deeper becomes your interest as you approach the closer to Monterey—Mountain torrents travel around you rich fields and pastures challenge your attention and mountain after mountain higher and still higher is thrown into view at every turn in your path—

Tuesday December 1st   Set forward about half hour by sun later than we had started before—when we got opposite the camp I turned to the left to find the Mississippians—they were camped next to a point beyond their brave associates in peril and in glory—The Tennesseans. Enquiring for some officer's tents whom I knew of one of our soldiers—I was pointed to Genl. Quitman's[21] tent hard by. I rode to it, he received me with evident marks of pleasure and with great urbanity. I need not attempt to describe the joy with which I took by the hand the brave men whom I knew—Genl. Q. took his hat and walked round with me and expressing a wish to see the positions of the different Corps on the field he said to me that I had but to name my time and that he would ride with me with the greatest pleasure. That he was anxious that I should see as he wished all our people could see the true positions of the army and the ground—I told him I would certainly avail myself of his kind invitation. Finding the train was about to pass on to Town I returned for my horse to Genl. Quitman's tent and there I found Col. Crogan—I had mentioned that I wished to call on Col. Whiting and Genl. Q. as I was about to mount my horse telling me where I would find his tent Col. Crogan said he was going there and then to Town and would be happy of my company—He looks now much better than he did when I saw him last August. Rode by Col. Whiting's tent who very politely extended my leave of absence (Genl. Patterson had only given it for 7 days) till such time as it would suit my health—he said Capt. I am ready to employ you here but having heard the army was to stop here and not go to San Luis Potosi—I determined not to commit myself for it if I am to get down and see no foughten field I had as leave be at Camargo as here. I replied Col. I am only on leave and expected to return to Camargo—he said very well and extended my leave indefinitely— He then enquired about wagons and mules and teamsters etc. at Camargo how many wagons complete could be furnished etc. I soon took my leave and joined Col. Crogan who was talking with an officer and waiting for me and we rode on—Gen. Taylors camp is in a valley gently sloping hills and bubbling fountains bursting out of the ground and dashing through the middle of it. It is shaded by splendid oaks the finest in this region—the troops are making sad heavock [*sic*] upon the timber lopping off the branches and leaving the trunks—If there ever was a valley deserving the name of Happy Valley this is it—Just as Col. Crogan and myself remounted our horses the clouds which had all morning concealed the sun from view cleared away. The air was balmy and delicious—the golden sun bringing all the panorama of mountains suddenly to view—the giant trees half concealing—half disclosing the glories around—the laughing streams and gushing fountains the rich soil and last not least to make my heart bound with joy and delight—there encamped— there they stood the brave and glorious troops of the Great republic who had fought and won but a few weeks ago a victory almost unparalleled in the history of the world. Col. Crogan pointed to the nearest mountain on the right said that mountain gives the name to the place[22]—"Observe said he those crested peaks rising up some-what in the form of a tiara or crown—thence the name Monterey—Mont-el Rey—The King's Mountain—We had a King's Mountain in the revolution and we have a King's Mountain here" "Yes" said I "and at each there was as hard fighting as ever witnessed on earth"—"When you come to see the strength of the town, its fortifications and its defenses natural and artificial you will see that it was utterly disgraceful to the Mexicans to give it up—to surrender such a place to such a force was utterly disgraceful—unheard of and astonishing—our men have gained great honor they did all men could do—the Mexicans are eternally disgraced. He spoke of the Mississippians with praise—They had done all they were required to do and when he said that he said he felt he was saying all he could for any soldier. I had not gone a mile with Col. Crogan until I fell in with the wagon master who having got his wagons divided while delivering officer's baggage begged that I would ride with the specie wagons while he hunted up the others—I hated to separate from the Col. It was a great draw back to me and I felt like refusing but a moment's reflection convinced me I ought to comply with the request. Major Weston had gone ahead and there was no other guard than 2 privates the teamster and some man traveling on his own hook. I rode in front with the traveller who said he was a Texian and in the fight—the guards rode behind—the traveller had been spoken to by Major Weston to see the wagons safe to the quarter master's office. The approach to Monterey is most singular—When I inquired of my Texian [where] is the Town—between this, said he and that mountain in front—Now from where we were to the mountain in front appeared to me to be about a mile I could have sworn that I could see every thing like a house between where I was riding and the mountain. I strained my eyes I could see only some bushes—As we proceeded further my Texian said he saw the dome of the church. I told him I thought I could see it too but when I came to explain myself I was looking at a conical peak half way up the mountains—finally—however I saw the dome then the black fort then the bishop's castle then the white houses stuck in among the orange groves. Reached the quarter master's office announced to the q. m. and the paymaster the arrival of the specie asked a. q. m. Sibley[23] for some place to pitch my tent at or where I could stay etc. He cut me very short—There was he believed a boarding house in Town some thing to that effect—Major Van Buren volunteered to speak to him which I greatly regret having allowed him to do—I was greatly pestered. Now here is human nature—officers could give no satisfaction—I determined to hunt round on my own hook. I met with a man discharged from the quarter master's employment at Camargo for cheating some of the clerks at cards—he took the pains to walk with me half way up one of these narrow streets to introduce me to a man who had rooms to rent. In a case of distress or requiring sympathy those worst treated by the world or most humble or even the most depraved are the most likely to render assistance. I put this down as an axiom—It is on the principle that Dido proffered hospitality [to] Aeneas—*haud ignara mali misens succumire disco*—got quarters. In the evening rode with a young friend to the Bishop's castle to the height where Gillespie fell and is buried—where Worth pulled up the cannon. Took a view of Arista's palace[24] and garden and returned in the night—as I intended to give a description of these things after I see them again I will not say anything more of them now—

Wednesday December 2nd 1846   Rose early and went to the large church—one of the most beautiful buildings I ever saw—built of white stone—front covered all over with architectural ornamental work carved in uses and surmounted by little turrets—inside beautiful— the back of the church behind the altar glittering with gold gilding and paintings. The large pulpit or altar is like a Grecian temple in miniature—there are several pulpits and confessionals—the priest was saying mass at a side altar. I never saw more beautiful architecture in my life—The roof is supported by three or four arches which look as if they ought to fall in every moment from their long span or scope—The church bears the marks outside of one or two balls thrown by Worth and Webster[25]. It is said that this church situated on the N W corner of the main plaza was filled with arms and ammunition during the fight and it was the dread of an explosion from the church which caused Ampudia to cave in as quick as he did—other accounts represent that it was to save the *church itself* without reference to the ordnance stores which caused the white flag to be sent in—All agree that as soon as it was ascertained that our guns were about to play on the church and demolish it that the white flag was sent in. Met with Capt. Rogers and Major Bradford of the Mississippi Regt. in the street—They were very glad to see me. Rogers says his company when they made the charge was directly before the cannon—Downing's and McManus' to the left of him—All agree that McClung was the first man in the fort and that he led the way that he pursued the Mexicans out of the fort and entered a house in pursuit of Mexicans where his comrades though following him regarded that it was certain and inevitable death to enter—that the Mexicans shut the door in his face that he rushed against the door like a tiger. Drove a Mexican officer to the far side of the room and was about to receive his sword when he was shot—promised to ride out to the camp with Rogers but being late getting my horse he left me—called on Col. McClung a soldier pointed out his quarters—as I rode up to the door he could see me from his room and the first thing I heard was his voice crying out before I had got from my horse "Why Smith is that you when the Hell did you get here tie your horse and come in". I went into his room a fine airy one he seemed very glad to see me—Dr. Halsey was with him—He was in fine spirits said he was never in better health all to his d——d wounds that were so slow in healing he feared he would never get any better that the d——d bones were eternally coming out and that he believed he was doomed to lie just as he was—no danger of dying he showed me his wounds—left hand shot all to pieces and a large hole in his right side. The ball ranging and coming out near the back bone shattering the pelvis bone—McClung said it was he who gave the order to charge—Lieut. Townsend[26] of [the] Tombigbee Company says the same—All say had not McClung been shot down he would have continued to pursue the Mexicans into the next fort and that the Mississippians would have continued to follow—That no order to halt would have been listened to had he continued on his feet. Called on Captain Mason and his gentlemanly officers—found them snugly quartered in a house that had evidently been the dwelling place of some of the aristocracy—flower pots wells stone enclosured ornamental trees papered chambers and all the appurtenances bespeaking wealth and good taste. Lieut. Porter gave me a glass of gin and Capt. Mason toast and chocolate— returned to my quarters—beautiful moonlight night—wandered with a friend to the lower part of the Town where we heard there was a fandango—but we could not find the place—to look at the white house the sparkling streams the palm and orange trees and the mountains by moon light was all our reward—

Thursday Dec 3rd Went early out to camp to get Genl. Quitman to ride with me agreeable to promise over the battlefield—When I got there he informed me that Genl. Hamer had died last night about 11 o'clock that he would have to forego the pleasure of riding with me until to-morrow—said that the funeral ceremonies would be interesting that the General would be buried to-morrow at 10 o'clock—invited me to come out in the morning and attend the funeral and after an early dinner we would return together and visit the field—As I returned I fell in with an officer who took me to the fort the Mississippians captured showed me where Watson fell and where he was buried where were the Ohioans the Kentuckians the Tennesseans—as we rode over the ground we saw several soldiers half out of the graves some entirely out—my companion thought this done by Mexicans—I believe it was done by wild beasts[27]. As I hope to have the benefit of fuller information I will say no more now. Learned from high officers that Quitman's brigade and Twigg's[28] division have orders to march on Thursday next to Victoria—Now as I believe there is to be a mere occupation of posts and no fighting and as my health is precarious I would as leave be at Camargo as a post further south. This evening at sunset received information from the wagon master that he would leave for Camargo early to-morrow morning and he wished to know if I desired to go and whether he should call for my baggage—Capt. Sibley the q.m. at Monterey on inquiring said that he did not think there would be another train for some weeks—determined to go—

Friday Dec 4th Wagon called at sunrise and took my baggage— Last night I rode around the battle ground by moon light—Yesterday on my return from visiting Genl. Quitman I rode around and over the ground with an Ohio officer—but I was still not satisfied—so I went to Lieut. Townsend of the Mississippi Regt. Tombigbee Co., he had no horse I got down and told him to take mine and I would walk in this way we went over the battle ground where the vols and the 3rd and 4th infantry fought. After we had occupied two hours or more in this way we parted near the bridge where stands a statue of the Virgin Mary[29] surmounting a pillar. Just as I turned my horses head for the camp I saw Col. Percifor L. Smith[30] Capt. S. T. Mason and another officer of the mounted riflemen as we rode on

Col. Smith pointed out the positions of the troops the forts etc.
Soon we started for the camp and the Col. finding from his watch
he was rather late we went at a gallop—When I reached Col.
Whiting's tent I found that he and Genl. Taylor and all the officers
had gone to attend Genl. Hamer's funeral. I had supposed that the
wagons would be delayed at the camp but to my surprise I learned
the party had left some half hour or more. Fearful of being cut off
from them I galloped on without seeing anyone. Having the sailor's
superstition about getting out on Friday I apprehended some
misfortune—I overtook the wagons after going two or 3 miles—My
horse while at Monterey having been fed entirely on new corn, in
the evening I found him badly foundered and it was with difficulty
that I reached Marine 27 miles from Monterey where we staid all
night. The party being in advance of me had applied to the Alcalde
and obtained a house for us to stay in—After we had tied our horses
established our quarters and set the servants to cooking we began to
think of the helpless condition we were in. There were six or seven
sick men Georgians under the charge of Dr. Hoxie[31], there was a
sick man of the Louisville Legion, myself, the wagon master,
teamsters and cooks constituted our force. Among us were the
following arms—2 holster pistols belonging to Dr. Hoxie, 2 rifles,
and I had 2 pistols. The wagon master was told that he would [be]
overtaken by Lt. Col. Henry Clay[32] with an escort of dragoons—Dr.
Hoxie and myself having directed the arms to be loaded made all the
preparations for defence we could went and took some coffee with a
old fat Mexican who invited the officiales to take Cafe—he stuck to
his invitation he furnished coffee and nothing else but some sweet
bread which he produced from a dirty towel—Thinking that it
would offend him to call for other dishes we sat about an hour
jabbering with the old Rascal. Hoxie more for form than for any
thing else asked him what we should pay he said what we pleased—
Hoxie put down 4 bits—American half dollar—the old rascal was
evidently surprised that he did not get more and set to examining
the money with all his two eyes turning it over and over jingling it
on the table etc. He barely took time to say *buenos tardes seniores*—
leaving him to his scrutiny and his suspicions we returned to our
quarters very hungry and thoroughly disgusted at our mistaking a
mere huckster for a grand Don as the President in one of his
principal appointments made the same mistake. I suppose we may

escape the charge of folly and stupidity. Soon after we had later a hardy supper at our quarters about 8 o'clock Col. Clay and 4 dragoons arrived—we were greatly pleased at this timely succor—Col. Clay had a bottle of good brandy—He got it out and when we were settling down to conviviality our old Mexican came in. Col. Clay must go with him he should have every thing he wanted. Having explained the nature of the invitation to the Col. He took his bottle of brandy and invited us to accompany him—We went with him, Hoxie who could speak Mexican very well inquired of the Col. what he should tell the Mexican to have for him—this was done—The Mexican was delighted when he found so many things called for—Hoxie told the old Mexican that Col. Clay would be at Marine in a few days with troops and would be governor of Marine. It was amusing to see how the old Mexican's heart warmed toward him—He made his daughter, a very pretty girl of about 16, put on a flaming new red dress—the table groaned with new dishes—and as the Col.'s brandy took more and more effect of which on the Col.'s invitation he partook truly the fame was kittered [?] and the compliments doubled. Col. commandante should board with him when he came etc. made him cigars with his own hands out of corn shucks and leaf tobacco—Col. Clay not understanding a word that was said to him would let much happen but when he found the old man particularly pressing and earnest he would get Hoxie to explain and his acknowledgments to the Mexican was somewhat after this order "*si si* old horse that is right old governor we'll get along first rate—take some more brandy" pointing to the bottle "that; you old cock I'll be d——d if you dont love it"—eating and bowing the Mexican would drink and return to the charge drawing his chair closer and closer—the scene was a rich one—comic in the extreme—Col. Clay gave him a dollar his supper was better worth five dollars than ours was worth a pic. A young man one of the Georgia discharged vols learned some two or 3 hours after his friends left camp that they were gone—he mounted his poney and rode on by himself and was almost dead when he got to Marine about 10 o'clock at night. He rode up to a house and tried to make enquiries about us but could not make himself understood—The Mexican lit a candle and came out and scrutinized his face and felt of his pulse and finding the young man sick he took him into his house had him prepared a good supper and bed and fed his poney etc. in the morning would receive no pay—The women are universally kind and generous—I have known several instances of the men treating sick and destitute persons with great kindness when it was entirely in their power to rob and murder—

Saturday Dec 5 We set out before sunrise after we had travelled some ten or 12 miles from Marine and 4 miles and a half from Ramos we over took a company of Kentuckians returning from Monterey (whither they had been as an escort) to Seralvo. They had found a murdered man—murdered they day before a hale hearty looking young man about 27 years old—Nobody knew—I have learned since that his name was Downing—clerk to Mann a sutler. The bush from which he was shot was directly on the road and so full of branches and leaves that a man could be completely concealed in it. Opposite to this bush and on for thirty or forty yards could be seen his blood—then could be seen a puddle of blood and signs of something dragged over the ground—The Kentuckians had no difficulty in finding the body by the trail on the ground and the blood. The body was in a thicket about 200 yards from the road—a ball had passed through the body entering one side and coming out the other—There was also five stabs with a knife or sword either of which would have proved mortal. The Kentuckians having no spade or hoe placed the body in a small gully and covered it with branches and stones—The wolves doubtless got him—It is as well as any other way—*quod scriptum scriptum*—I have learned that he had fallen back only some fifteen minutes behind the party he was travelling with. When we got to the deserted Rancho some 12 miles from Marine we camped for the day here. Col. Clay sent back the dragoons and taking with him such of the Kentuckians as had horses he pushed on to Seralvo—

Sunday Dec 6 Camped at Seralvo—Col. McKee invited me to sleep in his quarters a large stone house which I did throwing down on his floor my mattress and blankets. Col. Clay was with him. I was attacked with a burning heat my flesh covered with whelks—I could not sleep—I got up and stripped up my sleeve and asked Col. McKee what it meant "Oh nothing Captain take a little more muscal" D——n it sir said I I believe muscal constitutes your *materia medica*—Remarking on the great mortality among the Mexican children Col. McKee said the Mexicans contended that they were afflicted with a new fever[33] which the Mississippians brought among them (Capt. Sharpe's[34] Co. and Capt. Delay's[35] had been stationed at this place) I replied that owing to the Kentuckians keeping their mothers and sisters so much engaged that they had no time to attend on them—A young man Lt. Bennett and two other wayfarers arrived in the night—Bennett had gone to Louisville for his health and had just returned. He reported Polk below par and Owsley[36] the gov of Ky—Money scarce in Ky and Henry Clay still spoken of as a candidate for the presidency—

Monday Dec 7   Camped at Ash Creek—

Tuesday Dec 8   Camped at Mier—There we found a plenty of very good American whiskey. The Kentuckians stationed at Mier under command of Capt. Willis were very hospitable and kind—I slept in my tent however not liking the damp Mexican houses. In the evening I visited the church where the priest said mass it was some festival day—There was an organ in the quoir [*sic*] which while the organist played was supplied with wind by two bellows behind upon the handles of which a boy was alternately working— all in sight—The church is a fine spanish building elegantly decorated and adorned with many paintings statues and gold leaf or gilding of some sort. The prettiest women I ever saw in Mexico I saw in this church piously kneeling on the stone floor. The pronunciation of Latin by a spaniard is so different from that of an Englishman that I did not distinguish a single word—He rolled it off as if his tongue was running a race. In the evening I went to the Fandango— There I saw some two or three dozen Mexican women well dressed after the American fashion—Their hair clubbed and adorned with artificial flowers—They danced well and were a sort of Aristocracy to any thing I had yet seen—They waltzed splendidly and have a beautiful dance they call the *Lanceros* in which the object seems to be to emulate the motions of Cavalry as near as possible. I retired at 10 o'clock. Before night a Kentuckian whipped a Mexican with a strap for some insolence. A woman came out and demanded who did it. A very large good natured young fellow was pointed out to her. She went up to him she scolded and berated him as a woman only can. The Kentuckian took it all and said after she had gone on for three or four minutes—"*no entiende*"—This enraged her beyond measure—violently gesticulating and repeating the words *entiende entiende* she retired amidst the shouts of the volunteers—Those who understood her said that the substance of her speech was that the whipped Mexican was her Peon that she and her husband were responsible for his good conduct that if her husband had been applied to he would have punished him if he deserved it but that it was very wrong and base to be whipping a poor slave etc.—I have no doubt but that the peon deserved what he got—he had picked up a stone to throw at the volunteer the day before and when ordered away by the officers he would not go this latter conduct I witnessed—He remained until his mistress came and at her order he departed immediately. I visited the house from which the 200 Texians did the most of their fighting when they fought Ampudia with 3000 men the house and the whole street bear the marks of the battle—The battle lasted from day light until noon. Between 700 and 800 mexicans were killed—The water spouts of one of the largest houses where the Mexicans were stationed ran blood. The Texians could have escaped had it not been for the folly of the officers—These were the celebrated Mier prisoners—one of them I had in my employ as a servant on my trip to Monterey—he explained to me every thing about them

Wednesday Dec 9th   reached Camargo about 4 o'clock P.M. found parts of the 7th and 8th infantry under command of Major Wright[37] and Major Hawkins[38] camped around my tent—Mr. Elisha Peyton and his son[39] (the latter had fought in the battles at Monterey) staid with me awaiting the departure of a boat—

Thursday Dec 10th   Knocked about town visiting friends I found Genl. Patterson and Genl. Pillow and most of the troops stationed here when I left, gone to Tampico—and Genl. Marshall had moved across the River as the commanding General of the Post.

Friday Dec 11th   Major Hawkins and Major Wright with their troops left for Monterey. Old Mr. Peyton and his son left for Missi on the Enterprise. I sent by Mr. Peyton a letter to my wife another Mexican blanket pair of Mexican slippers which I bought in Monterey—some lancero buttons—a Mexican whip—and a small Mexican reticule for my daughter—

Saturday Dec 12th   Reported in the evening that Canales with a large force would make an attack on this place to-night—great anxiety and preparation for the attack—This report grows out of the fact that 2 Ky Lieuts were chased last night from Wardaw nine miles off—and from the fact that thursday night the Ohio troops stationed at Pontagooda sent down for ammunition and from the tales of the

Mexicans who are always ready to make out any thing so long as they can find listeners—

Sunday Dec 13   I loaded my rifle and pistols and slept in my clothes until late in the night when thinking there could not be the least danger as our troops were on their guard—I got up and undressed and slept soundly the rest of the night. I find this morning that there was no harm done last night with the exception of one of our men being murdered by one of his comrades for his money—read the bible and rode out—threatening to rain but alas the sun comes out hot and dispels the clouds—if it would only rain there would be something like life here as it is one is ever in the ways of *"dusty death"*. Happy Genl. Patterson to escape such awful dust as there is here now—No rain for more than 2 months. The whole hill cut up by pack mules and wagons—and all the thorough-fares covered with inhalable powder more than ankle deep. Just learned that the murdered man was a private in one of the compa-nies of regulars—artillerists—He was murdered for his money by 3 or 4 of his comrades. The guard came upon them before they could get more than 15 dollars—The man had some hundred or more in a belt around his waist—such was the hurry of the murderers they left their hats and the knife with which he was murdered. Others of the same company identified the murderers by the articles left on the ground—they are arrested and under guard and will doubtless be tried and shot—So must it be—base villains—every rascality hereto-fore has been attributed to the volunteers. I begin to believe that many crimes have been committed in their name and they are as much sinned against as sinning—1st Regt. of Indiana troops came up on the corvette on their way to join Genl. Taylor. On my way down from Monterey I met Major Coffee[40] and Capt. Cassius M. Clay[41]. I was introduced to the latter by the former—he is a well made fierce looking man—something dark and repulsive—this may be prejudice however—he is certainly a well made bold looking man—but he has not in my estimation a countenance sufficiently open and candid to wit confidence or friendship. He and the great orator Thomas F. Marshall[42] now a captain in the same regt and here at Camargo had I understand a quarrel a few days before I came back. Marshall has been in a big spree—I am told that he says when he signed the temperance pledge he did so under the belief that it would be always in his power to get good cold water—that he did so without having read or heard of such a place as Lavacca in fine he takes a lawyer's distinction that the pledge was made with a view to the surrounding circumstances—*secundum subjectam materiam*—Now here is genius. He is now under arrest—confined to his tent—for improper conduct during a drunken frolick—The man that chained the attention of all the wise men at Washington—struck with wonder and admiration listening thousands in all the large cities and had he not been so much a man of genius might have been in Congress for life. For had he been less high toned he would not have defied Henry Clay in the Lexington district and here he is entirely out of his sphere and calling—when oratory can do no good and temperance lectures excite no sympathy or praise in durance vile in an insignificant Mexican Town—so go the great! Found that I had an acquaintance in the Ky Cavalry—Dr. Price formerly of Canton now Capt. Price[43]. He went on a visit to Ky and while there was elected a Captain so here he is—

Monday Dec 14　　Last night there was an alarm—some hundred of the Ky cavalry ordered out—they are to go on a secret expedition to-day to capture some of Canales' men. They will not find them of course—Canales' friends among the Mexicans here will give a warning of their approach. By order of Genl. Marshall the streets in Camargo are being barricaded again—but the dirt is being thrown on the right side this time—Heard that 9 new regts are coming on from the States—This evening the J. E. Roberts came up bringing I hear Col. Davis and Capt. Willis on their way to join their regt.

Tuesday Dec 15　　Met on the landing by a young man who said that Col. Davis was at Capt. Crosman's office and that I must come over. Went over he knew nothing of my family—crops bad—cotton high in price but the planters did not make much while every thing our people buy is higher in proportion than the cotton—gloomy times—I told him we had been battling with federal measures 15 years but this war would resuscitate tariff paper money banks and every other political quackery—he said he feared I was right that many thought Starke now running for his place would beat Ellet[44] that he could not believe it—I told him I did. He was inquiring about horses—I offered to sell him mine—he came over to look at him—I told him he should have him for a hundred dollars and praised the horse very much. What was my mortification and regret when we went to look at the horse to find him foundered. There had been employed a new ostler at the wagon yard [a] stupid Dutch Man—Who probably before his arrival here had never come within 20 yards of a horse of any kind. He had starved my horse two days though I had full forage on my requisition and finding at last it was the Captain's horse that he had starved—He stuffed him with food until he nearly burst—This stuffing operation had been going on for 24 hours and more when the Col. and myself went to look at the horse. I told the Col. that I would not let him have him—the horse walked off as though he had at least 3 wooden legs—bad luck—foundered—stiff—paid Col. Davis $50 money lent at the Mouth (camp at the mouth of the Rio Grande) last august—paid in the presence of Philips brother to the Missi sutler and Capt. Reed of the J. E. Roberts. 2nd Regt. from Indiana up on the way to Monterey—They are fine looking men—

Wednesday Dec 16   Col. Davis informed me that poor Kemp. S. Holland A. C. S. to Missi Regt. is dead[45]—poor fellow destined to be cut off and buried at the same old camp which we left with so much pleasure—the Mouth of the Rio Grande—he was very kind to me and I deplore his fate most sincerely. How often have we stood together and talked over the delightful times when we should be blessed by a return to our friends and family—Poor fellow buried in the sands at our old camp on his way home. Col. Davis and Capt. Crosman dined with me to-day—The Capt. and myself rode a mile or two with the Col. Capt. Willis and some five or 6 others [who] go with him—Rather dangerous but the Col. said he would not wait for more Cos. Capt. Gholson came down from Mier and staid with me all night.

Thursday 17th   When I came down from Monterey, there came with the train a man named John Puett of Fannin County Texas—he and two others were made prisoners at the Presidio on the Rio Grande some time in August last. They were taken on to Saltillo where they remained until the battle of Monterey when he and his companions were hurried on to San Luis Potosi. San Luis Potosi is 265 miles from Saltillo—called by the Mexicans 100 leagues—Saltillo is about 70 miles from Monterey—From San Luis Potosi to Carretro [*sic*] is a hundred Mexican leagues and from Carretro to the city of Mexico is 100 Mexican leagues. The road from Saltillo to San Luis Potosi is a very fine one and well watered all except about 90 miles or 4 days march—Along these 90 miles there is no fresh water—All the water being salt and collected in deep holes dug in the ground from ten to 20 acres large called tanks—There having been no rain for a long time when Puett came on he said the water was very bad indeed—Goats asses mules and other cattle in heads from one to ten thousand are eternally about the tanks muddying the water and otherwise rendering it offensive. Puett says the Mexicans fully calculated on whipping the Americans at Monterey—That there were a thousand troops stopped at Saltillo who were on their way to the fight—stopped as he was told because there were already enough at Monterey to defend the place against double Taylor's force. He says they were informed at first that Taylor's army was destroyed—but one of the prisoners who knew their habits well boldly told the Mexicans that he knew better—for if they told truth there would be ringing of bells and fandangos instead of the funeral silence every where observed—when they got to Saltillo they were pretty roughly treated and were informed that when Santa Anna came (he was then daily expected) they would be shot—Santa Anna came soon afterwards and instead of being shot they had much better fare and treatment and were allowed the large yard within the barracks to walk in at pleasure. He says the house Santa Anna occupied was in full view of his prison—that he saw Ampudia when he returned after the battle—that pulling off his hat he made a very low bow to Santa Anna as to a master—that Santa Anna conversed with him a while then bowed him away—that Ampudia was then taken to quarters and put under strict guard as a prisoner. He said he saw about 40 deserters from our army—that they were all irish or Dutch—that he conversed with the most of them and that they all deeply regretted the step they had taken and that they all alleged the same excuse for their conduct bad treatment by their officers. He says that these men are in a most deplorable condition treated with utter scorn by English Americans and Mexicans—that they were promised money land and commissions—they get their food only from the govt—and dare not stir beyond the precincts of the city if they did the Rancheros would murder them. He says Santa Anna has thirty thousand men—the regulars are principally those that fought at Monterey—that men are daily driven into town lavetted like mules—half naked and half savage—these men are forced to join the army—that the recruits are most such men—and they swear they will only pretend to fight and will run as soon as they can do so without being suspected of running willingly. He says Santa Anna has some 500 men his enemies among the Mexicans working on the fortifications and entrenchments many of them the first men of Mexico. He thinks Santa Anna will do all he can to get the Mexican Congress to make peace—that the clergy either cannot or will not furnish any more money—He says soon after the battle of Monterey the Mexican officers resorted to the most disreputable means to stir up hatred against the Americans—that they read forged letters stating that the Americans had made *stables* of the churches at Monterey and ravished the women etc. that for three or four days the stratagem produced a great excitement but traders and others from Monterey Mexicans and English gave the whole story the lie and the result was great injury to the Mexican cause—the citizens rejecting afterwards even accounts which were true—Puett came on here and finding some men were to leave in a few days for San Antonio went to work as a labourer in the quarter master's department to await the departure of his party. By some accident mistake or neglect the party went off and left him. He told me of his situation on sunday—that he could not sleep and did not know what course to adopt—that he believed he would go to Laredo and take chances to get home that way. I mentioned his case to Mr. W. E. Winfield clerk in the Commissary's department a Texian. He said to me with great generosity and promptness—"I wish you to tell Puett to come to me, I have heard of him—he must go by water and if he has not money enough I will lend him what he wants"—seeing Puett next morning I carried him to Winfield—Puett came to me in the evening in good spirits said Winfield had raised him among the Texians $30—that he had sold the poney he had bought to ride to Laredo and had made two dollars on his trade—that the $32 together with $20 which he already had would take him like a book. Winfield had issued him also 15 days provisions and Capt. Crosman had given him free transportation to New Orleans—I was delighted to find that he had done so well—The poor fellow left here yesterday evening on the steam boat "Rough and Ready." His family and friends have long since given [him] up as dead—what a happy hearth there will be when he gets home to his wife and 8 children— fair be the winds propitious be the seas, safe the machinery which carries him on. The joy of such a return I envy—it will be worth all the toils and privations which he has endured! When we were going to Monterey we saw a great many flocks of wild turkeys and innumerable tracks of them in the road especially between our first camping ground beyond Mier and Marine—Talking of animals one of our company said there were a plenty of tigers panthers and leopards in this country—This was confided by an old man named Larkins across whose breast a wagon past a few weeks ago giving him a hacking cough in words a consumptive look outwards and a streak of black and blue entirely across his once robust frame—The said Larkins said it was his purpose if he lived to collect specimens of all the strange beasts and birds in Mexico to show in the States. We all thought the scheme a good one to raise the wind bag[?]—As I returned from Monterey I saw with my own eyes two large flocks of parrots[46]—not paraquetes [sic] but bona fide full grown green parrots fly by us in quick succession a few miles this side of Seralvo—I looked at them with childish wonder remembering that when I was a boy there was a tradition in our family that a sea captain had made the present of a parrot to one of our aunts when a handsome young lady—My aunt and the parrot were both dead at the time I speak of—the former misfortune I did not appreciate having had no recollection of her but the death of the latter I most sincerely deplored regretting I had come into the world so late as to miss seeing one of the wonders of the world—and now how things are changed—I have got some how away south into the land of parrots and see them fly by me in flocks! If I ever get to Maryland again I shall of course speak of it and then in a few years there will be a new tradition for the modern youngsters that one of their old uncles (long since dead) had seen in his time in Mexico parrots flying about as thick as blackbirds—They are ditching barricading throwing the govt stores on the plaza and playing the devil generally in Camargo—were we about to be invaded by the Duke of Brunswick and the allied armies there would not be more clatter bustle preparation and dismay—I am sick of all this. I have heard so long of danger until I almost desire to see it (N. B.—Puett is named Elisha and not John) There are all manners of Rumors—Rancheros arising—no wood to be purchased by the boats on the Rio Grande— all the Mexicans gone—Camargo to be attacked—Matamoras to be attacked—Monterey to be attacked on Christmas day—a hard fight ahead and in case of a repulse to Genl. Taylor—The knife to cross every American throat—

Friday Dec 18th   Detachment of Ky Cavalry sent out 2 days ago returned last night having captured a Mexican officer and some 20 or 30 armed Mexicans the latter they disarmed and sent on the former they brought in—very cold this morning washed my feet and stood on the floor while Van Dike was blacking my boots— caught a dreadful cold sick all day—borrowed a weekly Picayune of Beeth Commsy's clerk of date 17th Nov—no mention here from New Orleans for about one month. The few stray new papers which have reached us in that time have been brought by captains of steam boats—The steam ship Alabama I am told left New Orleans in the night and the captain sent to the post office but there was no one in it—Now the P. M. and all his subordinates unquestionably deserve hanging—for such vile abuses to suffer about 10 days getting ready to leave without the mail—cut my finger fixing a string in my shoe and other like accidents mark this as an inauspicious day.

Saturday Dec 19   An express arrived last night 24 hours from Monterey—He killed 3 horses—He brings news that Santa Anna is marching on Saltillo with 30000 men that Genl. Butler is taking all the force at Monterey to the aid of Genl. Worth who is at Saltillo with only 1200 men—that troops must be hurried on hence with all proposed despatch. I am also informed that an express goes to Matamoras to Genl. Patterson to bring on troops from there— Whether Genl. Wool has been cut off or whether he will be able to form a junction with Genl. Worth appears to be uncertain—An express left Monterey it is said for Genl. Taylor to hasten back to Monterey—Santa Anna it is further said has played his game with consummate skill having cut off all spies and effectually prevented his movements from being known to Genl. Worth—what a dreadful calamity would befall us should Worth and Wool be severally conquered but it is not so written—they will unite and make the pass near Saltillo another Thermopylae—should Worth be overpowered another big fight will come on at somewhere in the neighborhood of Monterey—as soon as the express arrived last night Genl. Marshall ordered the Indianians to move—their drums beat two or 3 hours before day and the 1st Regt. and all of the 2nd that were ready were on the march by day light—The rest of the 2nd are now going 10 o'clock A.M.—They are able bodied healthy fine looking men. They (all the Inda troops) have been more disposed to work take hold and facilitate than any troops I have seen—finding there was a difficulty in their way on account of wild mules—they went to work and broke the mules—they found the mules could not be shod by the quarter master's blacksmiths for the wont of time—they furnished their own blacksmiths and shod the mules in the night time. Poor Indianians going off as they did so rejoiced and happy leaving as they thought all the hated camping places and stopping places behind them! Poor fellows after spending the summer at the Mouth of the Rio Grande and thinking themselves safe at last bound for fields of glory leaving the fields of disease and degradation behind them—going on all together two Regts from the same state officered from their state from genl. down to corporal—an express has left here to bring back six companies of the 1st Regt to relieve the 5 Cos. 2d Regt Ohio now here the latter being ordered forward as a part of Genl. Marshall's brigade who goes forward to-day. I met Capt. Crosman this evening near the Genl.'s quarters. He held in his hand what he had just received from the ordnance dept. a requisition for the transportation of 47000 lbs of ammunition—Said he Capt. this has been the darkest day that I have ever seen in Mexico! From what I can learn Santa Anna and His forces were within 3 days marching of Genl. Worth—It is uncertain whether Genl. Wool can join Worth also uncertain whether Genl. Butler with 2 Regt. from Monterey can arrive in time—"here I have a requisition on me for immediate transportation of ordnance stores requiring 24 wagons to transport and have no teams". All the horses and mules have been drawn for the transportation of the troops! Nothing daunted he went on to his office had his agents running and galloping in every direction and when I left him ½ hour afterwards—he had made up teams for 14 wagons—This thing will be an example to show the awful waste attending a state of war—when the war broke out and up to within the last 6 weeks mules were bought in the United States original cost transportation here and losses by the way made the cost of the mules which reached here average $200 *a piece*. For the last six weeks the mules of this country have been supplied to the quarter master at an average of 15 dollars a piece and I am told the contractor got them at an average of $10 a piece—Making by his contract $5 a mule—I suppose at least 1000 have been furnished at this depot at the above rates—now see a 1000 mules purchased in U. S. $200000 a 1000 mules purchased in Mexico $15000 a snug little loss on one item. Now some clerk or drunken member of Congress will be keen sighted in looking over small accounts and big speeches will be made while probably not a word will be said in reference to these mule contracts steam boat contracts etc. spite holes will be stopped while the head of the barrel will be kicked out without ceremony or observation! Capt. Smith[47] of 3rd infantry returned yesterday evening—His and Col. Davis' three horse wagon broke down the other side of Mier—returned for an other wagon which he got. He tells me the Rancheros with their families are with drawing to the hills—that their camp fires can be seen in every direction now I think we are in a bad fix. Santa Anna be a great genl. He will whip Wool and Worth *seriatim* Crush Butler on his march descend on Monterey like an avalanche—and then sweep with the bosom of destruction all our little garrisons—cut off our steam boats and hem in Taylor and starve him and whip him before before he could get succor—what a chance for a Napoleon and for such troops as Napoleon had! But Santa Anna is not a Napoleon nor the Mexican soldiers the *viele garde!*—

Sunday Dec 20 '46 Went out this morning for the second time since I have been here with Mr. Gregory gunning. We had fine sport and I was just entering into it with boyish excitement when Mr. Angel came whooping and galloping to us with a sealed letter in his hand from Capt. C. I broke it open. It was an order that all the wagons should be immersed in water to make them swell to the bands from which (being made of green wood) they had shrunk. I handed the note back to him and told him hereafter to break open all notes directed to me in my absence and if on business of the capt. attend to it. but remembering a great deal was to be done I saw that my sport must stop and returned—We killed while out some dozen birds a wolf and a skunk. Black smiths and wheel wrights wagon masters and teamsters hard at work all day shoing horses and preparing wagons—the wagons for the ordnance were ready by this time the ordnance was and loaded before night ready for an early start—

Monday Dec 21–'46 Ky Cavalry Gen. Marshall and Capt. Kim's Company of dragoons with the 6 wagons [of] ammunition left to-day—In consequence of a distressing letter received from my wife to-day dated 21st Nov I must apply for leave of absence or resign so soon as the danger of an attack becomes less imminent—I am [certain] that the Indiana genl. has refused to his troops return—So the Indianians are beyond the reach of condolence and are on their way to Monterey rejoicing. As I crossed the river to-day I crossed on the boat with Thomas F. Marshall. Having addressed himself to me I introduced myself to him and we had some chat etc. The letter from my wife received to-day using terms of bitterness and despair on account of her desolate condition the sickness of the children and the derangement of my affairs gave me great pain. Spent the day and most of the night in great anguish of mind. Resolved to write to Col. Whiting and Col. Davis. There being no more horse and mule teams here and transportation for additional ordnance stores being required by the ordnance department ten Mexican ox carts (two oxen to a cart) carrying 800 lbs each were furnished by our department as a *pis aller* and dispatched for Monterey—Col. Cummings thinks that the news about Santa Anna's marching on Saltillo is false—that Santa Anna has managed by throwing out a large scouting party or something of that sort to impress our folks with the idea that he is marching on Saltillo with a view to divert Genl. Taylor's attention or confuse his plans—If this be so he must be very adroit to put to Genl. Worth and Butler so much at fault as their late expresses and orders must make them should it turn out that they were mistaken.

Tuesday Dec 22d 1846   Agonized at the character of my wife's letter—after a most painful and almost desperate council between my heart and head as to what was proper and right to do, I adopted the course of writing the following letters—The one addressed to Col. Whiting was indorsed by Capt. Crosman recommending the leave to be granted—it was then with the one addressed to Col. Davis inclosed in an envelope directed to Col. Davis[48] at Monterey and sent on by this evening's express-copy of the letters—

opposite Camargo
Dec 22d, 1846

Dear Sir:

I received letters from home yesterday of such a character that I am bound by every tie to visit home if possible. My wife's health is delicate one of my children sick the negroes disobedient my business neglected and ruinous. There is a report here that there will soon be a big fight somewhere in the neighbourhood of Monterey. Conversing with Col. A. Cummings (recently from Monterey) he informs me that it is his opinion that the many

rumors in reference to Santa Anna's movements and the prospect of a fight soon will prove false. Anxious as I am to go home as speedily as possible yet I would be loath to do so on the eve of a battle provided I could have any chance to be in it. I should like therefore if there be the well founded prospect of a battle within two or three weeks after this reaches you that you will get me ordered up to report to you or Genl. Quitman with the view of enabling me to be by your side or his in the fight and if I could be of no service in such a position then to take a rifle and stand in the ranks. I would not wish to open new accounts or be compelled to assume the quarter master's duties there for the present, that would defeat my object but to have a chance to mingle in the fight and that if I escaped unhurt to get a leave of absence immediately for home. If there be no prospect of active service soon or I can not get to it as it be over then please lose no time in obtaining for me if you can a leave of absence for sixty days and send it to me as soon as possible. I hope you will have embraced in the order that I report at the expiration of my leave to Col. Hunt N Orleans so that I might avail myself of the contingency of peace should it occur in the interim, if not I would get Col. Hunt to order me to report to Capt. Crosman and if he be not here where he might be or to you or Genl. Quitman. By complying with the requests of this letter you will place me under lasting obligations. I am sure Genl. Quitman would with the greatest pleasure unite with you if desired or his aid would be necessary. I saw young Howel[49] yesterday he is well and pleased I think with his position.   very respectfully
your frd and obt st

Franklin Smith
a. q. m.

Col. Jefferson Davis
1st Regt. Missi Riflemen
    P.S. Inclosed you will receive a letter to Col. Whiting as it is necessary I suppose that some document should be filed as an official application   F. S.

copy

opposite Camargo
Dec 22d, 1846

Sir

I am compelled by the state of my health and that of my family from which I have just heard to ask a leave of absence for sixty days. Col. Davis of the Missi Regt. will more fully explain my situation.

very respectfully
your obt st.

Col. Henry Whiting
a. q. m. Genl.

Franklin Smith
a. q. m.

Wrote to my wife that I had applied for leave and encouraging her all I could.

Wednesday Dec 23d   Nothing new or strange from any quarter. Sold my horse to adjutant Joline for $80—$20 less than he is worth—but if I got leave of absence I might have to sell him for less. Paid Mr. Angel $50 which he had lent me. Now square with every body—Corvette came up passed over the river to get letters and papers got no letters—while waiting for the P. M. who had gone to supper—Major Burns invited me to take tea with him saying he had a letter from Wm. C. Richards which he allowed me to read. All New Orleans was out and in procession it appears in honor of Ringold's remains[50]. Most true and sensible was the remark of Dr. Johnson that if Alcibiades and Socrates were out before the same crowd and Alcibiades said "go with me to Battle"—and Socrates "go with me to hear a lecture"—there would not be a man in the crowd but would be ashamed to follow Socrates—You may cultivate the intellect and exult the "standard of morality" as high as you may yet I fear among all charges and after all improvements it must ever remain the characteristic and opprobrium of our race— that 9 tenths of the men women and children in the world will pay more honor to military men than to any class of public benefactors—

Thursday Dec 24   Christmas eve—the 2d Christmas that I have passed like an outcast and a wretch—last Christmas beat about by Northern winds in the Atlantic on a voyage from Baltimore to N. Orleans. This Christmas in a hostile land a thousand miles from home. There are about 300 men here now one company of artillery in the town and 250 Ohio Regt. on this side. Easily taken now— The Ohio men on this side are fortifying the place—Rumors this evening from Monterey that firing of cannon was heard far from that Worth had retreated to the mountain passes and that Wool was in one days march of him—we must soon know the truth as the regular express will be in in a day or two—Capt. C. and myself took a ride around Camargo to see what we could see—They have got the town completely fortified barricaded cannon pointing out—

Friday 25 Dec 1846　Christmas day—Got up early—foggy morning—the first thing I could see was the Ohio troops with spades on their shoulders going to work on the fortifications on this side—This is fine employment for Christmas on the day on which the *Prince of Peace* was born—Two nations of Christians who profess the religion of Him who taught that we should love one another, celebrate His nativity by preparations to cut each other's throats. Yet these things must be—Even Saints have been known to prove their doctrines orthodox by apostolic blows and knocks and however fighting may be deplored by the wise and humane human frailty it is feared will continue to the end of the world to prove too strong for human reason. Read two chapters in the bible and wrote a long letter to my mother—passed over the river mailed it and paid the postage. Dined with Angel good dinner—went to sleep—[the remainder of this page has been torn out, possibly by Smith. The remainder of December 25 as well as December 26 has been lost; the narrative continued on an undated page and the next page is headed December 27 continued, so a part of December 27 is likewise lost.] . . . he had returned to secure his march towards Victoria. Genl. Worth has been joined by Genl. Wool. Every thing straight and placed in status quo—The fortifications are still being completed here however—a wise measure of precaution. Some of the Agents Messengers and whipsters from the other side having behaved in a very presumptuous manner on this giving orders without communicating them to me or the superintendent and one or two of the master workmen having stated to me that they were getting into confusion by reason of contradictory orders and multiplicity of commands. I stated the facts to and enquired of the Captain whether these things were by his orders or connivance as I expected I find that these underlings were directed in all instances to report to me or the superintendent what was required of this side. But this general direction having not been repeated of late the understrappers had swelled into the importance of full authority giving orders which had not been issued and ordering the hands as if there was no other head here—I have directed my men to obey no orders but those coming from me Capt. Crosman or the superintendent on this side—These agents and underlings are eternally endeavouring to supplant each other! *Peste!* [the remainder of this page has also been torn out]

Sunday Dec 27 contd   The gun was fired by a soldier from the bank on the other side of the river—have heard of several deaths in this way in the camps below and I have no doubt more have happened in the same way but never reported—perhaps not even known. Passed over the river saw Capt. DeHart[51] very intelligent gentleman recently from the States—Genl. Scott is certainly to take the command and is on his way whether to make his headquarters at Brazos or Tampico uncertain. Rode with Gregory into the woods— he took his gun with him and in a short ride killed four partridges a wild pigeon a rabbit and a wolf. Talking of wolves there is no place that I have been camped at that I have not heard them howling at night except at the Mouth of the Rio Grande and at Monterey. When I was at Monterey I met in the street a pale tall young man hobbling along on a cane with a handkerchief tied across the right half of his face. He came up to me and saluted me very familiarly saying "Why how are you captain. I am really glad to see you". I told him that I knew I had seen him at Camargo but that he was so changed that I could not call his name. "Scudder" said he "dont you know how bothered I was about the quarter master's duties" I remembered him at once he begged me to call to see him at the hospital. I promised to do so but had not the time. He was in the battle (in the Tennessee Regt.) and had received a ball when within a short distance of the fort and while running forward. The ball struck him in the corner of the right eye tearing away the bone and flesh. His recovery was for a long time very doubtful—He said that he just had sense enough left to crawl in a little gulley which prevented him from being shot or run over. He was pronounced out of danger when I saw him. He said he had suffered a thousand deaths. He lost his right eye of course. Noble youth may he recover. A more sprightly brave active intelligent young man I never saw than he was when passing through Camargo on his way to Monterey— If my memory does not betray me I think I have already spoken of him and the impressions he made on me while here.

Monday Dec 28th 1846.   The alcalde delivered up this morning a mexican who he says murdered two volunteers of the 2d Ohio Regt at Puntiagooda—He is in prison and in irons to await his doom. Col. Morgan is bringing in the mexicans from the surrounding villages and forcing them to work on the fortifications. I am told they are to be paid the prices paid the quarter master's labourers 6 bits a day—If this be not so, if I mean they are forced to put up cannon and intrenchments for the slaughter of their own countrymen without pay—not being prisoners of war nor soldiers but quiet citizens—then the proceeding would be at once damnable and unpolitick—even if paid it would be outrageous with any other people but Mexicans. As to them so they are paid I expect they are glad of being forced thereby getting money and saving their throats when the American army is withdrawn. My favorites the Hoosiers have not escaped calumny The hard things said of them I will not repeat but the following account given by the pilot of the "Rough and ready" is rather amusing. The steamer Rough and Ready brought the Hoosiers from the Mouth. On their way up they arrived at Matamoras a little before day break. Those whose business it was to cook were allowed to go ashore as usual with their camp kettles and cooking apparatus. A guard was stationed about the boat to keep all others aboard unless they had a permit from the captains to go ashore. About daylight the Col. or some superior officer came out and found the men going ashore *en masse*. "Gentlemen" said he, "it is against the orders for you to go to town you know this. Now let me request you as men of sense and soldiers not to go ashore unless you get your captain's permit." The men all stopped at this and those who had stepped off the boat returned. The officer seemed highly pleased and returned to the cabin and made a sort of speech to the other officers to the following effect "Now Gentlemen I only spoke to our men kindly and they obliged me cheerfully. Freemen must not be insulted. The thing must be handled according to the character of the men. Some men you have to drive it is true, but the most of them will listen to reason if you approach them properly etc. to that effect. Well all seemed well pleased but unfortunately while this was going on the men were departing and when the officer came out again almost every body had departed. Cooks left their camp kettles and had gone privates went in a body all but the guards. Most of the captains and lieutenants had left under pretense of bringing back the men. The Col. then sent off a detachment of those left to bring in the others.

The first grocery they got at all the detachment got drunk. One party after another was sent and one officer after another was sent fast as they reached the Town they lost sight of their errand and went it on the liquor at a rush. This business progressed until by ten o'clock there was no one left of all the troops Col.s Majors Capts. Lieuts. or privates except the Genl. and his staff. About 12 or one o'clock the tide began to flow back. The steam was puffing and bells ringing and the idea began to occur to those least drunk that their frolick must end—Then such a scene was never witnessed. Some were lead down some driven before a file of men with bayonets— Some after they got nearly to the boat turned back to hunt their guns. The most drunken were brought down on mules and horses laid across like dead hogs—others on litters made of muskets. Whooping yelling running falling staggering reeling—they got in the boat the most of them and at 3 o'clock the boat pushed off. About forty were left behind but they ran along the banks and got in. A great many guns were lost or thrown away or stolen by the Mexicans while they were drinking. Though far removed from what would be called refined society and its allurements we are not altogether destitute of the material for amusement: and any one of a humored turn might pick up a rich fund of anecdote by mingling for a short time with the volunteer portion of our army—A few days since a fair specimen of the genus *Homo*; as far as body, limbs, flesh and bones go to make one, entered the Post Office at this place, and coolly surveying the Post Master enquired if there were any letters in the office. To which he received in a tone as serious as his own a reply that there were. Who are they for enquired he? For various persons was the reply. Where are they from continued the interrogator? Different places answered the Post Master. Any from Old Keintuck? I presume there are was the reply. Wall look and see if ther is ones for me. It was now the Post Master's turn to ask questions so he commenced: Who is me? A. Douglass. What Regiment? (for the letters here are assorted by regiments) Why the Keintuck regiment. What Kentucky regiment? Capt. S——'s Company. Yes, but what regiment returned the Post Master with an accent on the word. Oh, Col. Marshall's ridgeament of Mounted Cavalry. Being informed that there was no letter for him, he left the office with as much self complaisancy as if he had acquitted himself on some important mission with great ability. Wonder if the Post

Masters sides shook any after that chap sloped! An instance similar to Pab's "Sure the name is on the letter" occurred here. A soldier about fifty years of age came to the Post Office and in broken English enquired for a letter for some name the sound of which seemed impossible to be produced by any combination of the English Alphabet—The Post Master asked him: *what name*—The same unintelligible combination of sounds was given in reply. Here was a dilemma from which the Post Master endeavored to extricate himself by asking how this name was spelled: thinking he would be able to understand the letters even if pronounced in dutch—But No. 1 did not feel inclined to satisfy him and answered "Vy the name ish sphelt on the letter". By the way it would amuse any one not conversant with queer things to take a peep into the Post office here—Such directions—superscriptions—their like could not be found in a literary museum. Letters directed to some "John Smith" "Capt. Jones Co. Point Isabel To be forwarded if the regiment has left" And mind you minus the name of the Regt. and perhaps without a post mark. No wonder the poor volunteers have so many of their letters missing . . . I have heard of this direction on one of the letters at Point Isabel "Mr. John Williams Care of Genl. Taylor Army of Invitation, Mexico John volunteered to fight for his country so dont forget him"—This evening Lieut. Mills of Baltimore arrived from Monterey bringing with him the mortal remains of Col. Watson, Capt. Randolph Ridgely, Thomas, Pierson, Graham, Capt. Gillespie and some one else I forget who—there are seven corpses—

Tuesday Dec 29th 1846 Went down this morning to one of our tarpaulins where the bodies of the illustrious dead are deposited awaiting the arrival and departure of some of the steamers (there happens to be none here now). There lie the poor fellows whose names just now are more in the hearts and the thoughts of men than any other names known to history—there they lie in rough square boxes of coarse pine plank—heaped up among other boxes of quarter master's stores awaiting transportation! Muskets, old escopetas, swords, and broken lances (which some of those who survived the battle are carrying home for relicks) are scattered loosely upon and around the boxes—a single sentinel of the quarter guard is stationed at the entrance of the tarpaulin frame! I walked in and surveyed these boxes and accompaniments! It was impossible to feel scarcely a single heroic emotion so much does the sight affect the imagination. Hearing the corpses had arrived I went to see them foolishly expecting I dont know how or why to find elegant coffins! When I saw the rough pine boxes laying about as the convenience of our hands required—(like the ordinary gun boxes of the ordnance departments) among barrels corn sacks and undistinguished that precious and heroic dust from the trash around I felt how vain and futile the attempt to impart the honors of the living to the dead! To prolong our interest in dull inanimate matter after "the heavenly flame" which gave it life and lustre—this soul—has fled! Better poor fellows that they had been left in the gory bed where they fell under the blue vault of the cloudless skies above them was the sublime mountains the witnesses of their heroism around them and in the precincts of that beautiful city of groves waterfalls and Palaces now destined to be a city of pilgrimages throughout all time—immortal through their illustrious deeds and those of their associates! I have stood on the height above the Bishop's Palace where Gillespie fell! and paused long enough to contemplate the humble grave of rude stone which his fellow soldiers had carved out of the mountain rock at the spot where it was crimsoned by his lifes' blood. There he fought, there he bled, there he died and there he ought to have rested forever! God and nature had made his monuments his life and character had made him worthy of it, his death consecrated it. How many an American, how many a traveller would ascend that sacred height and holding in his hand the eulogy of Governor Henderson muse long on the virtues of Gillespie while he stood beside his tomb! Now half of the charm half of the interest of the spot is broken and dissipated forever! I know not by whose direction Gillespie was removed—but if by the order of anyone but his family—however noble and generous the feeling which prompted it—it was in my humble opinion a mistaken act of friendship and in exceedingly bad taste. In that connexion I will relate the following anecdote which I got from Dr. Hoxsie's own lips while I was at Monterey. He said he acted as a surgeon to Hays' Regt. That as he ascended the height of the bishop's palace during the fight (among the Texians when a fight comes on there is no such a thing as a field or staff officer proper Genls. quarter masters commissarys and surgeons all take to the rifle) he was told to go to Gillespie that he was wounded. He did so. Gillespie fixed his gaze steadily upon him as he examined the wound and when he was through asked him if the wound was mortal—He hesitated to give a reply "Oh" said he "feel no reluctance in telling me the truth I want you to speak candidly and tell me what you think". "Gillespie" said Asa "you are in the hands of God" "I understand you" said Gillespie as he laid his head down—about this time the Mexicans were expecting to be about making a sortie and Hays was stationing his men among the rocks and giving them their orders—as he was stationing them he was crying out "now boys dont one of you fire until they get within 15 feet—short fifteen—let them come jam up—" etc. This scene and these words aroused Gillespie—Raising himself on his arm he called out "Boys place me behind that ledge and rock" pointing to a particular spot "and give me my revolver, I will do some execution on them yet before I die". Passed over the river to see if I could buy some thing of Mexican manufacture to send to my friends in Baltimore by Lieut. Mills—but failed—I could find nothing suitable in the stores. During my ride I fell in with a Hoosier just from Monterey—he says that Genl. Taylor said he expected no more fighting at least for three months. He says that the 3rd Indiana regt is on its way down here to relieve the remnants of the 2d Ohio now at this place—They did not get any farther than Seralvo—Among other stores which I visited is one kept by my old host and amigo—Don Gaspar—there I found him and his fat wife looking very happy. Don Gaspar (whose information can generally be relied on) told me that Santa Anna is now in the city of Mexico. He said something about the Mexican Congress but I could not understand him—Lieut. Tilden[52] and his party came down yesterday evening from their expedition up the Rio Grande. The number of deaths that has taken place here and in the surrounding country has been wonderful a few weeks ago there were 29 dead bodies carried to the church in one day. They are all taken to the church for the priest to chant the funeral service over them and thence to the consecrated burying ground. The bodies are dressed as fine as the purses of their friends will admit of. Decked with fine clothes artificial flowers crowns and furbelows—while going to the burying ground a man preceeds the corpses shooting off fire crackers to frighten away the devil and give the soul a lift upwards towards Heaven. The burying grounds surrounded by quadrangular stone walls have become too small to hold the dead and give each a place. The Mexicans are too lazy to enlarge the enclosures to accommodate the newcomers so they dig up skeletons with sang froid and pile the bones in a corner of the burying ground[53]. In all the burying grounds that I have seen, I have observed in one of the angles a stack of human bones. The day I arrived at Mier on my way to Monterey, a funeral was just over and one of the Kentucky officers told me that he saw three skeletons dug up to make room for the woman that was buried. They fill the grave with the earth thats dug out and beat it down level with the surrounding earth. This presents a horrible reflection when it is remembered that the bodies are buried without coffins. When the Mexicans marry they marry in the church at midnight. The couple kneel a long time and a part of the ceremony is to tie them together with a silken cord. But I have broken the thread of my discourse. I was talking of the dead and here I will insert a few lines of *poetry* which I wrote about the middle of November when all the world was dying and I thought that I was about to be in the fashion.

> Tis even-one bright beaming star
> Twinkles in the East afar
> The Norther's breath's expended
> Summer's with the winter blended
> The sweet South lifts her balmy voice
> All nature doth rejoice!
> Not so the poor volunteer!
> For him disease death the bier.
> What means that drum with tones so low?
> To the volunteers grave they go!
> The firing of that distant platoon?
> The soldier's buried that died at noon.
> Why strikes so sad the spanish church bell?
> 'Tis a Mexican's funeral knell
> Death on his pale horse careens around
> Death on his pale horse tramps the ground
> The victors and the vanquished all
> Before his fatal darts here fall!

Invited Lieut. Mills to ride with me—he promised to come to my tent—I happened to be out when he came—sent for him—he had gone to Capt. C.'s to get the necessary orders in reference to the transportation of the corpses and him self—Rode to the chaparral after supper. Lane came after me and invited me to an Egg Knog drinking at his tent. Found there Col. Morgan (now commdg officer at this place) Lieut. Mills Mr. Watson and Adjutant Joline. The latter gave me the agreeable information that he had brought with him $100—to pay me for my horse when he came to buy him—that he mentioned $80 with no hope that I would take him up and was greatly surprised at my doing so—$20 low because no horse jockey but an honest man to wit a d——d fool!

Wednesday Dec 30th 1846 Fourteen wagon loads yesterday evening with subsistence for Seralvo—8 wagons loaded this morning with medicines ordnance and other stores for Monterey to start to-morrow morning under one escort commanded by Capt. Thornton[54]. Went down to the landing this morning after breakfast and found that Brewer the interpreter was about to take the Mexican hands down to the tarpaulin to load the wagons with the dead bodies. Went down with him and saw the Mexicans take out the boxes containing the bodies of the dead heroes one by one— The wagon having taken them down to the river bank, I passed on to the other side of the river to make an other effort to buy some thing Mexican to send to my wife's mother Mrs. Spencer by Lieut. Mills—After enquiring at many places I found the only purchase which I could make was a coarse red bag at the store of a man named Wolf—a name which he well deserved—I paid him his price—as I returned to the river to recross I saw that the "Troy", the steamer which was to carry the corpses had steam up and was about to start—I was all anxiety to get over in time to bid Mills and Watson (Col. Watson's uncle of Orleans) farewell and deliver to the former my humble offering—While my eye was anxiously fixed on the ferry boat I was accosted by a messenger from Captain Crosman requiring my presence at the office immediately. Considering all hope of reaching the steam boat before her departure as gone I repaired to the office. Capt. Crosman told me that it was necessary that I should go to Seralvo in charge of funds for the quarter master at that point. I was greatly distressed at this because on Saturday I expected a leave of absence by the express—I made no demur only to state to the Captain that I would go cheerfully but if the leave came I should regard myself as a truly unfortunate man. He said I would have to go as there was no proper officer going to whom he could entrust the money—It was arranged therefore that I should come over about 5 o'clock sign the receipts and take the money. I again hurried to the river, the Troy was still puffing at the landing the last trunks and packages seemed being put aboard—I hurried on crossed the river and as I got on the opposite bank the hands were untying the ropes to cast off—I had barely time to get aboard place the bag in Mills' hands bid Lieut. Watson farewell and get ashore— as I did so I fell in with Winfield he informed me that Capt. Caldwell of the Ohio Regt. was going to Seralvo we went to see him he promised to take the money got him to go with me to see Capt. C. when we got to the office—The first words Capt. C. said to me was to inform me that May or Dix the paymaster was going to Seralvo that he would take charge of the funds to hear this was indeed a relief. I thanked Capt. Caldwell for his good intentions and crossed the river returning to my tent happy for the time being— what a misfortune it is that the pleasure of escaping from a dilemma does not last more than 20 minutes—wave succeeds to wave alps on alps and I now look to the express with the same solicitude that I did this morning—"Man never *is* but always to be blessed". This day has been as hot here as ever I felt the weather in June. Yesterday at 3 o'clock while waiting on the East bank of the river for the ferry boat I was struck with a very bad pain in the head and had I not taken to the shade I believe I would have been struck down with a regular *coup de soleil* as it was my forehead burned and ached the whole evening. There has been no frost here. Frost was never here and the Mexicans say *their winter is now over*!!! The sun sets here are beautiful—All that poets have written about oriental sunsets—as the sun goes down half the Heavens are rose coloured. The moon is much more perceptible here in the day time than it is in Missi—

Thursday Dec 31st Captain Thornton's company of dragoons (fine horses—men dressed in red flannel shirts—presenting a very warlike appearance) escorting Major Dix[55] two wagon loads of specie and about fifty other wagons loaded with various stores—left about 11 A.M. Major Van Buren paymaster on his way to New Orleans after money call[ed] at my tent and borrowed my cap while he could ride after Capt. DeHart to give him a broad brimmed straw hat. The said Major advising the said Captain that he would suffer on the road with the narrow visored black hat which he had—Major Van Buren having come down from Monterey two or 3 days [ago]—This incident will give some idea of the heat here—Col.

Morgan (the commdg. officer here) received information yesterday that the Alcalde had sent an express to some *Ladrones* (robbers) informing them that a large quantity of specie was going with the train today. The Col. sent for the Alcalde of this place and the Alcaldes of the surrounding villages (I understand) and told them that if the train was attacked he would hang them all. They said it was a hard case; that they were innocent and nevertheless the train might be attacked (this looks somewhat reasonable) the Col. however told them that he believed what he had heard that he relied on the information given him—and to prevent the train being attacked was their look out—that as sure as God reigned if it was attacked he would have the whole of them. Col. Morgan when I saw him the other night told the following anecdote on Thomas F. Marshall when the news arrived that Ridgley had lost his life from a fall from his horse. Marshall speaking of it over his cups remarked "As well might one expect to hear of an eagle dying from the fall of his own wings as to hear of Randolph Ridgely's dying from the fall of his horse"—The beauty of this remark will be appreciated when it is remembered that Capt. Ridgely had the character of being one of the best horsemen in the army. Another anecdote of Marshall. Lane (Baker the sutler's clerk) tells me that one night he got drunk at their store and talked and talked and drank until about two o'clock when striking out God knows where he stumbled on the camp of the sappers and miners in the opposite direction from his quarters. "Who goes there" thundered the sentinel "oh G—d d——n it old horse none of your d——n regular doings with me give me a light, give me a light". "Stand" shouted the sentinel bringing down his piece. "Why you are not in earnest, why you are a d——der fool than I thought would you shoot a volunteer officer?" The sergeant of the guard happened to be near—Marshall told him he wanted to light his cigar whereupon the sergeant took him to the guard fire and there Marshall stood talking with the guard until day break. Soon after day light he came back to Baker's store—And the Sappers and Miners having found out who their guest was—A man of whom they had all heard so much—they came down to the store almost *en masse* to see him. As I am telling anecdotes I will tell two more. As General Twiggs was riding up to the head of his division when balls were falling in showers and death dealt on all sides he saw an officer of the Baltimore Battallion lying behind a rock—

"Wounded?" said Twiggs—"No" said the fellow gently raising his head and peeping over the rock "No damn you and you dont intend to be" said Twiggs as he rode away—One day a man apparently in great haste dashed into Capt. Crosman's office nearly out of breath. "Is Col. Cross in?" "No" said Capt. C. throwing himself back in his chair "Where is he?" said the fellow "He is dead" said Capt. C. "Dead why they told me he lived here"—a pause—"No I believe I made a mistake, it is Capt. Crosman I am looking for" "dont know him" said Capt. C.—"Then sir . . .". Capt. Crosman said the fellow [was becoming] indignant, his American blood getting up—"Yes sir I am the man what do you want?" Bought a pony this evening for 8 dollars from a discharged regular just from Monterey discharged from expiration of his term of service—

Friday Janry 1st 1847   Last night at 9 o'clock a Norther came on threatening demolition to tents. The old year departed and the new year came in in a hurricane—To-day every thing still. 1st Indiana regt. arrived from above on their way to Matamoras—Mexicans came down from Wardaw and charged them with stealing their blankets and saddles—appeal made to me in their behalf by our interpreter Brewer—sent him to Col. Morgan—saw a Mexican woman in the streets of Camargo weeping bitterly complaining of having her box containing clothes trinkets money etc. rifled by one of the guards in town—a regular. This evening complaint that some 8 or 10 trunks left in a tarpaulin by the Ky mounted men were broken open and robbed. Supposed to have been done by the teamsters who camped near them last night—Night before last some villain went into my kitchen tent and stole a ham of bacon for which I gave 15 cts per and a dozen eggs for which I gave 3 bits. The Dd rascals are going it strong—Robbery like drunkenness a short time ago is becoming an epidemic—"Col. Cross" went down this evening taking off most of the Inda regt.—the rest of them go to-morrow— Capt. Crosman Lieut. Brereton and myself went by the trunks as we were riding—they had been left a hundred yards from any where— under no guard or care—so thoughtless are the Kentuckians and in such hurry did they leave. Every thing in each trunk had been stolen except a parchment Diploma from the Transylvania University constituting some very learned youth a Doctor of Medicine. The only thing thought of no value! Applicable to human life! The honors of literature the triumph of science the evidence of intellect are of no value towards clothing the naked feeding the hungry or putting money in the purse. If your child is hungry can you satisfy him by talking to him Latin. If your wife wants a bonnet or a new carpet can you appease her with Mathematicks Roman Antiquity or Cicero's orations? In such cases a few pounds of flour and a few Doublons would be worth more than all the learning of Oxford Cambridge Pisa and the Sorbonne. Let not the youth who is pressing forward for collegiate honors despise the nider occupations by which men are clothed and fed! He will be very fortunate if he does not find at some period of his life or on some occasion that a check shirt is of more value than a diploma! Fresh news this evening from Saltillo the Mexicans are said now to be advancing on Saltillo in earnest! I dont believe a word of it. I believe these rumors are put afloat to divert our attention from other designs and other points of attack! Read the President's message this morning—good paper puts Mexico in the wrong. Shuts her mouth as to any cause of complaint. But still the question occurs not for the Mexicans or their friends (they can not say a word) but for Americans to decide. Did the administration bona fide apprehend that a Mexican army would cross the Rio Grande *at the time* it ordered the army to quit Corpus Christi and camp at Matamoras? Had not Genl. Taylor in a recent despatch notified the govt. that that *no* Mexican army was collecting at Matamoras? Could it not have been left to Genl. Taylor's discretion to move when the Mexicans moved? Had not the army been ordered to Matamoras *would the war have taken place*? Now this war may end soon and in a blaze of glory new territories be acquired the command given us if the trade of Asia the East Indies and the Pacific and we become the factors and carriers of the world, but if it continue long and entail on the country a large national debt and restore the reign of federalism banks high tariffs etc. Mr. Polk will have proved the worst enemy that Democracy ever had. And if he ordered the army to Matamoras not under a bona fide apprehension that our territories were about to be invaded but *with the design—the animus*—to bring on a fight *under the belief that unless he did so, the fight would not come on* then he acted improperly and he and his cabinet are responsible for whatever evils this war may produce. God grant that the war may end speedily and honorably and the government be saved from the federal vortex towards which it is now drifting.

Saturday January 2d 1847. Lieut. *Botts*[56] (*Expende Hannibalem; quantas libras invenies*) son of the Honble. John M. Botts of Virginia, died at his quarters in Camargo yesterday and was buried to-day at one o'clock. Tis said by all the officers (I conversed with a half dozen) that he died from homesickness the doctor being unable to locate or designate his disease by any other name than melancholy. Poor young man just from West Point but appalled unto death by the wont of humanity which every where presented itself to him in this region of death and under the bloody code of military rule—Doubtless his heart was the seat of generous emotions his soul alive to all that is honourable but he was not prepared for the misery of Camargo—so he died! Peace to his remains—He was buried with the honors of war—a fine coffin covered with velvet and enveloped with the flag of stars and stripes followed to the grave by two companies and all the regular officers at this post— Some officers (Dr. Gregory[57] Tombigbee Co. was one of them) came down from Monterey this evening and reported that Santa Anna is obliged to fight or disband—that he is now believed to be marching on Victoria scouting parties having been thrown on the San Luis and Saltillo roads and the late rumors put afloat on purpose to conceal his purpose of attacking our troops at or near Victoria. This is the last *stampede* as the officers humorously term the flurry which a new report creates. I believe this news. Others say again that Vera Cruz will be taken and then there will be no more fighting that Santa Anna is in Mexico—Capt. C. told me to-day that he would have to send me to Seralvo to be stationed there. I would as leave go to the devil—I reminded the Captain that I expected a leave of absence next express that if it did not come i.e. if it was refused me I should certainly either perform my duty at whatever point I should be ordered or resign—that I thought I should take the latter course that I could not be insensible to the miserable condition in which my family was placed nor resist the appeal made to me by my wife to return: that I would be more or less than ruin not to go home. He accordingly let me off until I could hear from the request letter. There is in fact no real necessity for my going to Seralvo—there is a quarter mr. there already but by guess some things have gone wrong and the Captain knowing that I would do all in my power to promote the public service he has got a notion that I must go—he will soon write a letter to the Qr. Mr. waking him up—He will be attentive and avoid unjust complaints and I shall hear no more of Seralvo. It would clearly be great folly for me to go to Seralvo to be stationed there and by the time I received the property get a leave of absence which would be of no avail to me as I could not trust another in my absence with the property in my name—

Sunday Janry 3rd 1847   The great mogul of the army Major General Winfield Scott commander in chief etc. arrived this morning in the "Corvette" at half past 10 A.M. and departs this evening I understand at 6 P.M. This looks like business—H—ll to pay—and that the taste for "a *hasty* plate of soup" is changed to a taste for a *hasty* view of Towns and fortifications. To speak a la President Tyler this is an improvement *per se*—Caesar wrote to the Senate *veni vidi vici*—The General can write to the Secretary of war in relation to Camargo "*veni vidi avisi*"—(this is not original but the inventive language which the bitter old cynic Tristram Burges[58] applied to Mr. Randolph's mission to Russia)—All other business was suspended in the quarter master's department so that all hands might go to unloading the Corvette to get her ready to return as soon as possible—Officers in uniform swarmed thicker than I have ever seen them since I have been here except on yesterday when they attended Lieut. Botts funeral. They went through a ceremony then they have gone through a ceremony to-day. Genl. Scott was in fact treated with much respect. Officers and men women and children thronged the streets while cannon roared a salute. I had a delightful ride this morning—As I got beyond the camp I fell in with two privates of the 2d Ohio Regt. Each had his rifle. I continued to ride with them until we reached the Rio Grande about 2 ½ miles from Camargo at a beautiful spot. A large meadow clothed with green encircled by the arrowy [?] River. They had come out to shoot geese. I looked upon the green landscape, the fat cattle roaming among groves of the golden willow the noble game filling the air the rushing Rio Grande the glorious sun the bright skies—I thought of childhood—I was happy—I returned to Camargo, I witnessed pageantry show the arrival and the steam boats the fitting out of wagons etc. and I feel wretched. This is no way for a man to pass his life. I have had enough of it—I want retirement where I can see the sun rise and set in peace—When the Sabbath morn is halted as a day of rest—home—where amidst the prattling of children, the chirping of birds, the lowing of herds a man may feel that there is a God above him and that he had made his sabbath holy. Express goes this evening to Genl. Taylor at Victoria, from Genl. Scott. Lieut. Anderson carries the despatches accompanied by 15 dragoons—sent by him a letter to Col. Whiting fearful that my other has miscarried—Lieut. Malone[59], Lafayette Co. Missi Regt. just returned from Missi—goes with them to join his regt.—53 wagons go to-morrow to Monterey loaded with clothing ordnance stores and subsistence—

Monday January 4th 1847 The results of yesterdays operations, rumors, etc. is this—Capt. Montgomery (I dont know what Regt.) a regular put under arrest or sent under arrest or directed *to consider* himself arrested and to go to his regt. (I dont know which is the proper phrase fame gives it either)—Genl. Scott had heard below of Genl. Worth's alarm express the first great stampede and was on his way to take command when he heard not far from here that the expected attack on Saltillo was all in my eye and Elizabeth Martin's so he came to Camargo like the soul of a dead infant just to look out upon the world and return to the source from which he came—The object of his despatch to Taylor is to hurry troops to Vera Cruz—Vera Cruz is about to be attacked by land and sea— bomb shooters, artillerists, hot shotists, sappers and miners, soldiers and sailors, marines and infantry all are to have a show—*Delenda est Carthago*—Vera Cruz must fall. But if Santa Anna were indeed a Napoleon a Tell a Washington Marion or a Morgan instead of being as he is a tyrant and a villain—or even being as *he is* with so large an army use that army bravely he would descend down upon the unorganized and sheltered troops in the neighborhood of Victoria and sweep them from the face of the earth—then wheel along that comparatively unprotected line destroy the detachments and garrisons *seriatim* and be ready for a Bannockburn at Vera Cruz. He holds a central position he could do these things were he a brave man and a patriot fighting in a just cause and his army composed of freemen!!! Mr. Aynsworth the wagon master reported ready to start at 10 o'clock—went to see the superintendent to direct him to report the same to Capt. C. and to know if there were any further orders—found the superintendent had already gone to the office— took no further concern and went to the post office for letters and papers—Late in the evening found out that the escort had not started with the wagons and the reason given by the commander of the detachment of the Ky mounted men (the escort) was that his horse was tired—that he was a fine horse had been offered on the way out $150 for him and he be G—d d——d if he would ruin his horse. The train had to be stopped—the Kentuckian at last being convinced that it was necessary in great operations to disregard a tired horse and that there was a such a thing as a court martial and that he was incurring a greater responsibility by refusing to go than by further tiring an already tired horse—agreed to go on and overtake the wagons—Among the papers loaned me by the P. M. to read was a number of Graham's Magazine on the margin of a page which was "Dear Charley

Please keep my letter private—even from your most *intimate friend* for reasons that I will explain hereafter—Dont let any one know *that I wrote*". This memorandum or note was in a neat female hand. Here was food for reflection. Who was dear Charley? Perhaps dead—perhaps a living hero—who was the lady some beautiful young woman engaged to him who had told him all she felt and how much she loved and then would appear to shrink at the bold disclosure—and then again perhaps it was some Mrs. Myers—I intend returning the magazine prompt the P. M. to the note and if there be any possibility of dear Charley getting it it shall be done.

Tuesday January 5th 1847 —*Dies non*—being bitten to death by the fleas last night—driven almost to madness (I never knew anything like the fleas here they lived in the dirt and sand like ants—lice bred in the same way) I got out of bed went to see a friend at 11 o'clock sat up drinking wine all night—and as a just punishment was sick all day—

Wednesday January 6th 1847 Took over Graham's magazine— find that it had been directed to a dear Charley at Santa Fe—Done all that honour could require. Reported last night that Col. May and 200 dragoons and 40 wagons have been cut off between Monterey and Victoria—perhaps a Mexican lie—may be so true—Towards evening it clouded up and looked as if it was about to rain. About sun down a Norther came on more fierce and terrible than any wind I ever knew—Compared to which the Northers we have had were but mere zephyrs. Great God what will become of the shipping provided this wind swept the gulf as it did here—Never did I witness such an awful and terrible night! I sat up until it became so cold that I feared pleurisy momentarily expecting that at some blast my tent and the tarpaulin over it (put up by Capt. Sherman) would be swept away. I had great difficulty to keep a light even in the lamp. I never felt more desolate—darkness without—fright and consternation within. The dust was thrown over every thing within the tent a quarter of an inch deep. Outside it resembled a snow storm. At last I became so sleepy and cold that I was forced to lie down. There came soon after a blast which tore away the kitchen tent hurling benches boxes tin pans crockery etc. into everlasting smash. I thought it was all over with me I jumped up and ran to the windward side of the tent so that I might escape timbers as much as possible—I looked and saw the extent of the injury—I returned and drawing my great coat around me sat down on my chest cold frightened shivering the impersonation of despair. Still the storm raged with unabated fierceness each puff appearing stronger and stronger while the cold grew more and more intense. While sitting on my chest awaiting the event I thought of the nothingness of my life, how often I had formed good resolutions on similar occasions how unworthy I would be to meet God and thus pondering I made a vow which I propose by the assistance of Almighty God to keep if possible—"Ah! the fool hath said in his heart there is no God!" But even a fool would have acknowledged one last night. Seriously and candidly I think considering that we are certain to die in a few years—may die to-morrow to-night next hour next minute—that it is the greatest folly for a man not to live strictly up to the religion he believes and to the practice of all those virtues and all that course of conduct which in his heart and under the dictates of enlightened reason he believes best calculated to prepare him to meet his God. A greater delusion surely can not possess the human heart than to allow *any thing* to soothe the mind into security, when the question of everlasting and eternal happiness is undecided and unattended to. Thinking on life death and immortality and promising amendment I at last determined to sally forth for the double purpose of seeing if the sentinels were at their posts and if there was any chance to find company. Taking my pistols in my great coat pocket I went along slowly to the landing and the magazine. I saw no human being going or returning—I passed unchallenged and so returned. Every light was extinguished save one where slept the laundress. Never did I feel so desolate. It was 12 or 1 o'clock at night—I returned so cold that I was glad to lie down with great coat and all on and draw the cover over me as thick as possible. I got into a doze *whew whew crash* several times I was started up horror struck—thinking the tarpaulin was down on me—Some time before day I recollect observing that the blasts were much less fierce. I fell into a profound sleep and when I awoke the sun was shining and the wind lulled to a light breeze. The winter is not over. *Ice* was found in the ordinary water tubs this morning *a quarter of an inch thick*, in wash pans and similar vessels *the ice was half an inch thick*. The Mexicans refuse to work to-day pronouncing it *Mucho fresco no bueno* etc.

Thursday Janry 7th 1847 When I went down through the depot—I found tents thrown down tarpaulins ripped from the frames as if cut with a knife—barrels blown, the ferry flats driven from their moorings etc. Every body had some thing to say about the dreadful night. Met with an old acquaintance—Coffee—who used to keep bar for McMackin at Jackson. He is now in Phelps' store on the other side. This evening the "J. E. Roberts" came up bringing it is said a considerable mail—News brought this evening by express from Saltillo that ten men of Col. May's Dragoons and 25 wagons had been cut off by a party of Mexicans. This is the origin of the report that Col. May himself had been taken—The Lieut. and Sergeant accompanying the troops were lame struck and fled—They have been put under arrest to be tried for cowardice—

CHAPTER 4

January 8–February 3, 1847

... 'The Corvette' carrying Genl. Worth and staff and the gallant but unfortunate 4th descended the river all decks crowded and the band of the 4th playing splendidly—got a look at Genl. Worth—I expected to see a young looking man—and he is as to carriage and deportment but his hair is gray ... 'The Corvette' having on board Genl. Worth etc. is fast on a bar about 15 miles below the mouth of the San Juan—That the Genl. is tearing out his hair and in the language of my rough informant 'he has cursed the bow off the boat d——ning quartermasters steam boat captains and all creation.'

American troops fresh from Monterrey and Saltillo were now arriving in Camargo to embark for central Mexico and the planned capture of Vera Cruz. With the capture of Vera Cruz completed, Gen. Winfield Scott planned to push inland over the National Highway to capture Mexico City. Steamboats lined the docks at Camargo to transport the troops of Gen. William J. Worth's division down the Rio Grande to Brazos Island for a rendezvous with the fleet carrying Scott's army. Taylor's small army, now manning the garrisons at Saltillo and Monterrey, was in grave danger of destruction by the forces of General Santa Anna.

Santa Anna, basing his information on an extensive network of spies and the detailed dispatches carried by Lieutenant Richey, realized that a Mexican victory was now possible against Taylor's weakened forces. The Mexican army at San Luis Potosi moved quickly to respond to this military opportunity and took the road to attack the American garrison at Saltillo by January 28, 1847. The army leaving San Luis Potosi on this date was estimated at 15,000 men, although no more than about

12,000 would remain with the army after the harrowing 250-mile march northward through the high deserts to Saltillo. Facing this army, General Taylor had concentrated 4,691 officers and men. American defensive efforts were centered in a valley through which the main road south from Saltillo passed, at a location known locally as Angostura (The Narrows). The battle fought on this location would be named by historians for the small hacienda located at the northern end of the pass: Buena Vista.

It is no exaggeration to say that the battle of Buena Vista was the most strategically important battle of the Mexican War. The war would have taken a decidedly different tack had Taylor and his small force been decisively defeated at Buena Vista—and they very nearly were. To his critics after the battle, General Santa Anna remarked that he had "won the victory, only General Taylor did not know when he was whipped."

Many sobering lessons were learned from the defensive victory at Buena Vista, if victory was even the correct word to apply to the struggle. The most important lesson followed from the simple maxim that poorly led soldiers make poor fighting men. During the crucial times of this battle entire regiments of American volunteers had turned their backs on the enemy and fled the field in a state of panic. At other times, groups of volunteer officers could be seen arguing among themselves as to who would command combined units of volunteers. In one case, this bickering over command was quieted only by an attack from Mexican lancers. On the other hand, well-disciplined volunteer regiments under good leadership fought with heroic resolve. The Mississippi, Kentucky, and Illinois Volunteer Regiments refused to retreat against the unequal odds and stood their ground despite high casualty rates. The key to a regiment's success as a fighting unit at Buena Vista was almost without exception the caliber of its officers' leadership. But more than valor would be required to save the outnumbered American forces from defeat at Buena Vista. The American military edge was due to the superior firepower and deployment tactics of three companies of regular artillery armed with the highly mobile horse-drawn field artillery. These field artillery pieces could be quickly moved to any location on the battlefield and unlimbered by their skilled teams in a matter of a few minutes to deliver a lethal array of grapeshot, shell, or solid shot.

The battle of Buena Vista was fought on February 22–23, 1847, and marked the end of formal warfare in northern Mexico between the belligerent armies. But guerilla warfare was to continue in northern Mexico until the end of the war. With the approach of Santa Anna's army from San Luis Potosi in February, guerilla activity in northern Mexico, under the leadership of Gen. Antonio Canales, began to increase markedly. Canales's forces claimed to have killed 161 Americans during that month alone. Franklin Smith's diary recounts several of these ambushes and minor encounters that resulted in such a casualty figure.

In early February, Gen. Jose Urrea, under orders from Santa Anna, led a Mexican cavalry force through the mountains at Tula Pass near Victoria and followed a route into northern Mexico that bypassed Saltillo. Urrea's mission was to link up with Canales's guerilla forces and cut off the flow of supplies and reinforcements to Taylor's army that regularly travelled the route between Camargo and Monterrey. General Urrea's forces captured an American supply train on February 24, destroying more than 150 wagons and slaughtering all of the captured teamsters by most horrible means. The loss of the wagon train was assessed at a value of $96,000, and the citizens of Nuevo Leon and Tamaulipas were blamed for the attack. General Taylor placed a levy upon the citizens of the states of Nuevo Leon and Tamaulipas to repay these losses. To collect this levy and track down guerillas, a force of "Texan Rangers" was employed against the Mexican populace of these states. Samuel Chamberlain, an American dragoon with Taylor's army, recorded the infamy of these Rangers' deeds:

> Between the Rangers and the Guerillars [sic] the unfortunate inhabitants of the states of Nuevo Leon and Tamaulipas had a hard time of it during the summer of 1847, plundered by both sides, their lives often taken, and their wives and daughters outraged and carried off. The names of "Old Reid," Captain Bayley [sic], Harry Love, Ben McCullough and more terrible than all, "Mustang" Gray will always remain fresh in the memory of the Mexicans, as the atrocities committed by them now form a part of the Nursery Legends of the country.

From Franklin Smith's diary entries of this period, we learn that the steamboat J. E. Roberts made a round trip to Camargo (about 800 river miles) in thirteen days, which was probably pretty good time considering how low the water in the Rio Grande was at that time of the year. Smith left Camargo on January 26 to accompany an American army expedition sent to relieve a supply train trapped by Mexican guerillas. Smith ominously noted in his diary that the villages along the Rio San Juan were populated only by women, old men, and children. The young men were away, no doubt, with the forces of Canales and Urrea. Smith and his party were probably very fortunate not to be ambushed themselves by the large parties of Mexican guerillas then roaming the region south of Camargo. The force of 400 men sighted by Franklin Smith and his party on February 5, 1846, was quite likely a part of Canales's rancheros.

Franklin Smith's resignation from the army was approved in February 1847, and he left northern Mexico just prior to the battle of Buena Vista. His greatest wish, to participate in "a desperate battle," was not fulfilled, but he returned to his home in Mississippi a man who had witnessed the terrible evils of war. with the parting salutation "Vale—Vale—Vale" Franklin Smith departed from Camargo, and the pen that had recorded the life and times of northern Mexico during the Mexican War fell silent.

Friday January 8th 1847. Never can this glorious day return but that the name of the immortal Andrew Jackson shall be associated with it. 8th of January[1] hail! No salute is fired no drum beat no cannon roars in honor of the glorious anniversary, yet as in history its great heroes will live—his name flourish in amaranthine vitality when the names of Scott and Taylor will be forgotten—their bodies rot and their memories perish along with the ten thousand small potato heroes who have preceded them—Passed over the river found that the Express of last night had brought no new answer from Col. Whiting although there were dispatches from Head quarters Addressed a letter to Genl. Jessup to go by the "J. E. Roberts" asking of him the leave of absence—wrote the letter at the suggestion of Capt. Crosman—stated in the letter that if leave were refused I must frankly acknowledge that such was the necessity of my presence home that I would have to resign! which I did not desire to do. Wilbur the commissary's clerk who has been living a long time in Mexico and has a Mexican wife says that Perez one of Canales' men was in Camargo last night. that he has a commission to take all he can and hold all he gets of the Americans. I thought the news about May's rear guard being cut off[2] official but—I find it is not—It wonts confirmation—

Saturday January 9th 1847 The Mexican Congress has been in session since the 6th day of December—now a month and three days—They have had a month to deliberate. They will have found by this time that Vera Cruz the heart of Mexico—must fall unless they make their great battle. If they send their force there they *know* that it will be demolished—if they let the castle of San Juan de Ulloa fall with out a struggle ruin must be the consequence—now as they are cowards and slaves ruled by military chiefs is it not likely that Santa Anna and his congress will call a halt and make peace? —Unless the Mexicans are made of better material than I think *there will be in my opinion peace in 30 days from this present greeting*. If they are made of the right material and patriotism really exerts in the interior they must defend Vera Cruz and then will be fought there a terrible battle. In such a case those in the fort would whip our men our men whipping those outside the final issue therefore would be with us but after a long siege—A courier can go from the city of Mexico to Vera Cruz in four days—Santa Anna may risque a battle and if disastrous then make peace before the castle falls—the Chiefs and Educated men seem to care much less about their country and the results of battles and negotiations than they do about their character for bravery—As soon as they think they have satisfied the world that they are brave *men and can fight well* I believe they will be ready for any kind of peace.

> When lovely woman stoops to folly
> And finds too late that men betray
> What charm can soothe her melancholy
> What tears can wash her guilt away
> The only charm her guilt to cover
> To hide her shame from every eye
> To win compassion from her lover
> And wring his heart—is to die

Parody

> When a man of forty stoops to folly
> And sells his soul to Moloch's shrine
> What charm can soothe his melancholy
> And with fresh hopes his heart entwine
> The only charm to soothe his sorrow
> To free him from remorse and pain
> Is to rush to the battle on the morrow

And die, or live in glory's train
But if the right to him's denied
Either to fight or run away
To quarter master's duties tied
From such a scrape where lies the way?

Resign!

Caetera desunt—
Resign—no—no—no—that will not do—It is ever wrong to act hastily and without reflection. From the time that Capt. Crosman suggested to me yesterday that I had better write to Genl. Jesup (now at Brazos) up to the moment when I had the letter in the post office, was not ten minutes. If the leave of absence be refused me I must send whatever money is coming to me to my wife and go to whatever post I am ordered and make the best of it, trusting in God that he will guard and protect my poor wife and little ones. It will never do to resign in face of the foe—What if there should be a battle along the line after I left? No private reasons would save me from reproach. In vain would I refer to the many perils I had undergone—my despair of life twice—my six months residence among the dying and the dead—those living being in a worse condition than those dead—this would all go for nothing. This is a dreadful situation—If I go to Seralvo I shall have to open new accounts and owing to the irregular calls constantly made there by persons travelling—I shall probably be ruined. In the mean time my wife is in a miserable condition reproaching me for abandoning her. Yet now I think on it deliberately I dont see how I can resign. *Nulla vistigia retrorsum jacta est alea.* I pray God the leave may come but if it does not I must save my honor though I lose my life. This Honor view of the subject never occurred to me before. *Stabitur decisioni—* 1st If the leave come—well—2d If peace come—well—3d No leave no peace then hold on and abide the trial by God and the country—A mexican was killed this morning at a Ranche on the Rio Grande by the Camanches they crossed the river in the night—Killed the Mexicans and plundered the Ranche recrossed the river before day—The murderers were known by the signs they left poisoned arrows etc. The dead body and the arrows etc. were carried over to-day by the Mexicans to Col. Morgan—Heard from a man from

Monterey that McClung is dead! Our heroic lights are extinguished here with as little noise or observation as one by one go out the lights of a large city in the stillness of a winter night. But though like drops of rain on the surface of the deep they fall noiselessly and unheededly, the papers show that there are myriads of hearts elsewhere which beat high at their praises, while tears fall fast and heavy at the memory of their fate. and yet we know not but that the glorious end of these brave men is not rather to be envied than deplored. To die is the lot of humanity. And in a few short years we shall all alike—"Dust thou art and to dust thou shalt return". Was it not better than to have died at Monterey like McClung and give a fresh name to history, for heraldry and song to tongue throughout all time than to *live here, here at Camargo* where God's curse on the serpent—to eat of the dust of the earth—is transferred to man? Poor McClung pronounced out of danger chronicled throughout the Union as fast recovering! with what a shock will the news of his death be now received by his friends! Much harder will it go with them now than if he had died at the head of his troops. Then it would have appeared natural. He was known to be the bravest of the brave, and not to fall in the desperate charge which he led would have appeared less wonderful than to escape unhurt! But now, now he was regarded as alive and convalescent his sudden death strikes me with awe and anguish! God did not design us to be happy in this world! The brave man rushed on danger and dies at thirty, the coward screens himself and lives till eighty "Loathing his life but fearing still to die". Each lives as much and in enjoyment as long. I was just going to bed when I had written thus far, when the tramp of horses and the clash of arms warned me that something was astir. I went down to the depot and found a 100 infantry (2d Ohio) and 20 dragoons from the other side leaving for the ranches on the Rio Grande 15 miles off where a Mexican express to Col. Morgan states that there are collected 300 Camanches—the said Camanches having murdered this evening he reports some ½ dozen families—The Camanches are by this time 50 miles off—But it is proper to send out. ½ past 11 o'clock *nocte Dormiturio* God bless the United States and the army of occupation.

Sunday January 10—1847 Oh God what weather a terrible Norther sprung up in the night, this morning it was bitter cold. I got out of bed but was glad to get back—a hail and rain was falling and of course I could not enjoy the fire—Very very cold! I ate breakfast in bed. Soon after Bee sent me word that he had a good fire—went over—Lieut. Scudder[3] from Monterey now on his way to Tennessee hunted me up—I took him to my tent and gave him a first rate dinner. Talking of his home he said that before he left home his mother had done all she could to persuade him not to come but when she found she could not she resigned herself to it and the last word she said to him were to stand firm and fight like a man! Spartan mother may you soon hold in your arms your noble son. Scudder says McClung is not dead but thought to be in a critical condition. I thought it was strange. He will come out. Yet if so a brilliant career will reward his sacrifices—I must quit these diggings I fear after all. It is out of the question for a man voluntarily to endure this miserable condition in one of the worst offices in the world without the hope of honor profit or reward when the yearnings of nature cry out to him to return. Ohio men saw nothing of the Camanches of course—One might as well expect to find the eagle at the spot where he had pounced on his prey as to find a Camanche at the ranche of a mexican which he had plundered— After dinner I put Scudder in my bed and went and sallied out on adventures. I found a fire by which I sat until near dark designing not to return until Scudder might have had a good sleep—I came home just at night Scudder was still asleep—I sat down by my fire in the rain until Scudder awoke—Soon after he left me for his tent—After supper having put my feet over a frying pan of coals which I had brought into my tent. Feeling somewhat composed forgetting all ills and reading a chapter in the book of Jeremiah, a head was thrust in under the folds of my tent inviting me to Capt. Walker's[4] tent (pitched hard by) with his compliments—The head belonged to Capt. Walker's servant. Capt. Walker was another officer from Worth's command had come down with Scudder and other officers—They were all together—Though the night was inclement raining and hailing (I dont know exactly as to the hailing but one thing was certain the tops of the tents were stiff with ice) and I was engaged in a good cause and for the first time in 3 days felt comfortable "taking mine own ease in mine own inn" yet the temptation of good company and the very polite invitation was not to be resisted I drew on my great coat and passed over—I was much pleased heard much news had the battle of Monterey fought Wool's march through Chiahuahua detailed discussed many subjects and among other agreeable topics four rounds of Egg Knog dealt out in large tumblers—*Hinc iloe lachryme*—which means hence the staggering paragraphs—who is [torn MS] would not have drank egg knog on *such* [torn MS] *ye prudes in temperance say what would* [torn MS] done? The Capt. Walker spoken of here is the brother of J. Knox Walker—Polk's secretary—May God have mercy on my soul for I am very wretched after all and shall stand out in misery to-morrow like a mountain enveloped in clouds upon whose peak a glimpse of sun shine had been fleeing but for a moment.

Monday Jany 11. 1847 I have said that frost was never in this country. There was a plenty of it this morning and the tents were white with ice. The Mexicans say they never knew such weather— they never had such a flood as last spring—never so much sickness— never so cold weather—"Troy and Whitesville" came up to-day. Two camp women down from Monterey on the way to join their husbands at Tampico Vera Cruz or somewhere else have pitched their tents not far from mine—Their tent Capt. Walker's and mine forming a triangle—To night 11 o'clock just as I was going to undress I heard an infant cry so piteously and coughing so badly as if it would lose its breath and addressed so rudely by a boy who seemed to be minding it that it was impossible for me to resist going to see after it thinking it surely was some orphan as I heard no female voice—I went over a fire was burning in front of the tents a woman was standing out by the fire entirely unconcerned. As I came up I asked if the child had no mother. "Oh yes." "Is that your child?" said I "No sir it is the lady's" pointing to a woman coming out of a tent. "Well" said I walking off "as the child has its mother along surely it will be attended to"—"Take him into the tent" said the mother addressing the boy that was holding it—The other one remarked "it is a very obstinate child" the mother asked her companion sneeringly "Who is that? one would think it was the child's father." Such a life do they lead that the idea that my motive for interference was humanity never entered the woman's head. This is a cold night yet an infant crying itself to death and nearly choked with a cough is allowed by its mother to be rudely handled by its brother in the open air paying its piteous cries no more attention than if it were a bleating sheep or a barking dog and yet this child perhaps will live and die at a good old age after enjoying uninterrupted good health while the well cared for children of the rich and great die by thousands. While I have been writing the mother has taken the child and immediately the child stopped crying and is doubtless now sound asleep happy in its mothers [torn MS] which I can never be anywhere. I can now appreciate [torn MS] drawn by Smollet of the birth and education of [torn MS] Lathom (which I thought many years ago ridiculously extravagant) as founded in nature and supported by experience. I have not seen children fed on whiskey out of the touch hole of a gun barrel but I have seen them subjected to every other bad treatment likely to kill them and yet I have seen the little fellows like the hardy growth of a mountain's brow flourish despite the unnatural position which they occupy. I learn from my neighbours that Wool's command passed through a country well watered and abounding in rich valleys wheat corn and cattle. The corn they learned from the Mexicans before the Americans came along used to sell for ten to 30 cents per bushel. The Americans paid $3—a *finagre* (about 2 bushels and 3 pecks) being about 9 bits per bushel—That Genl. Wool was very honeying toward the Alcaldes—Genl. Patterson and all the rest of the generals have pursued the same course under the instructions of the government of course. What if this war was undertaken with the *quo animo* not as a last necessity to vindicate the rights of the nation but to obtain California and all upper Mexico—because all the action of our armies as yet has had just as little to do with conquering Mexico into a peace, or reducing her to extremity as if they had invaded Nova Scotia or New Brunswick. Had the government after the battles of the 8th and 9th landed an army of 20000 men at Tampico and marched on the city of Mexico the war might have been ended in 3 months. What if the object of the Administration was not so much to obtain redress for our insulted honor and just rights as to obtain territory—not to vindicate and fix firmly on an indisputable basis the power and majesty of the republic but to make out of a weak nation remuneration for mutilated Oregon yielded to a stronger power? What if in carrying out this plan of the young democracy and the small potato statesman that sprung into notice on the annexation question, the administration deliberately risqued the exhaustion of the treasury the waste of life and the energies of the troops in occupying chaparral and sparsely populated regions and in the subjugation of barbarians thereby compelling them *to commence the war* (for as yet we have done nothing towards the conquest of *the people* of Mexico though we have covered much Mexican territory) with an exhausted treasury to end in entailing on the government a heavy national debt the incubus of banks tariffs and federal power? Our government was founded in justice and in right, virtue, truth, integrity, and the love of liberty are its pillars. Whenever we lose sight of these we shall drift away amidst the rubbish of ruined empires—Like the rubble of Rome and the canaile of France we shall first conquer the world then fall by our own hands. Brewer the interpreter who has been electioneering for a discharge for a week got drunk and was discharged yesterday—In honor of their boss or probably instigated by him all the Mexicans stopped work this morning—The Mexicans were brought back and willingly went to work. Brewer was ordered to the guard house until the steam boat starts down the river then to be sent away on it—These Ohio men have greatly redeemed themselves in my estimation. Col. Morgan marched with the detachment when they went out as was said against the Camanch but this was to prevent suspicion. The real object of the movement was to take Canales, Col. Morgan having received information that he was at a Ranche about forty miles off—The men he tells me marched with the utmost alacrity and the real object was not disclosed to them until they had got 19 miles—They were delighted when they knew it—They made the march of 40 miles in 16 hours—Being in first rate spirits the whole way. The remnant of the regt (about 250 men) have worked hard under the superintendence of Major Wall and have thrown up in a few weeks a fortification which will stand as a monument to their industry and the skill of Major Wall. Major Wall has proved a vigilant thorough going officer and though the Ohio men have been a long time standing guard at the depot there has been no complaint made of their conduct since the stable scrape—

Tuesday Janry 12 1847 A young man named Goosebecke [Grosbeck—see the November 8th diary entry] to whom I had loaded a spanish saddle which I would not have taken twenty dollars for (on account of the truce) comes down from Monterey and Saltillo and says the saddle was stolen. I blame myself more than I do him—The Ostler in Capt. Crosman's yard (Smith) who was present when I bought the saddle on my horse which I bought of the Texian says that the poney Goosebecke rode away and the saddle passed through here five weeks ago. I have no doubt but that he sold it.

Wednesday Janry 13. 1847 Capt. Walker and Mr. Whiteley his clerk dined with me. This morning the new wagon master of the yard Sherman sent over in the place of a most excellent one Mr. Ainsworth (the latter having been sent to Monterey with a train) was reported absent last night from the yard and this morning. Reported the facts in writing to Capt. Crosman. A new wagon master Mr. Bowen was soon sent over. Learned that Sherman went over early last night to a gambling scrape got in to a frolick and a quarrel and was shot in the back and is now lying ill! Cards and liquor are twin demons!

Thursday January 14—1847 This evening "A. Monroe" was despatched down the river with an express to hurry up the other steam boats to be in readiness to take down Genl. Worth and his troops on their way to join Scott to attack Vera Cruz—Genl. Worth is expected to be here on the 18th inst.—Wrote my brother James M. Smith a long letter on life death and immortality and on domestic relations the ties of brotherhood and with a post script of news—

Friday Janry 15—1847 Last night some rogue stole from behind Capt. Walker's tent his frying pan and skillet and all his best cooking utensils—When it is remembered that these articles are hard to be replaced and very dear—the loss will be regarded as considerable. The boldness of the villain was great—one of his own teamsters most likely while going and returning from Monterey. I had a chance to find out that the teamsters hold the Spartan faith—to steal and not be detected is a sort of merit—a good joke—a boast among them doubtless many of them come from the Penitentiary and it is very certain that many of them will return to the same place...

Saturday Janry 16th 1847 For Monterey a train of 75 wagons start to-day—great trouble and bother about this train—Capt. Walker had put on train some 125 of the refuse wagons of Wool's command—he being a gentleman and his head wagon master Canless—While he was paying off his men to-day a Norther came up and blew his papers about and blew away mine entirely out of my tent. Capt. Crosman and myself were in Capt. Walker's tent when the blow came up—Capt. C. and myself made for my tent and the first thing I saw was my papers streaming out into the chaparral—

Old scribbles, drafts of letters to my wife, orders, scraps of poetry, and this paper just as it is all to the last sentence—How ridiculous would it have been had I not recaptured the Sybilline leases what jests and jibes would not the men and troops have had at the expense of the "quartel maestro". Complaints made again of the Ohio troops—Winfield says 13 barrels of pickles have gone out of 20—Gregory the forage master says forage has gone to a considerable amount and others a barrel of sugar etc. I stated these things to Capt. C. told him of my passing several times through the depot without seeing a sentinel at a late hour at night and suggested that there ought to be employed watch men on our post and then there being two sets of guards of different interests and corps they would watch each other as well as others—He advised that my suggestion be followed—ordered accordingly that two of the new trusty men should be engaged as watch men and that the sentinels be notified and the Ohio officers of the fact—Part of Genl. Worth's command arrived to-day—Some dragoons—Genl. Worth himself and Major Thomas[5]—Artillery expected this evening—infantry to-morrow. This morning I heard that our discharged interpreter Brewer instead of having gone down the river as I supposed had started for Monterey on tuesday last and that on thursday he and his party Grant, Myers, and Reynolds were attacked by some ten or 15 Mexicans and that Brewer was killed. Walking down toward the landing this evening I heard the news confirmed—Poor Brewer is certainly killed and buried—when the guard went in pursuit of him the other day he hid himself—it was reported that he had gone down the river on the "Col. Cross"—I dismissed the subject from my mind. The story as brought here is Brewer was a little ahead—a few feet—the four men were chatting jogging along the road about 20 miles beyond Mier. The chaparral at the place was very dense on both sides. The first warning that he had was the discharge at them of some ten or 12 guns—Brewer was shot in the shoulder and neck lent forward and died on his horse's neck—the horse was very gentle and stood still—Grant and Myers were seized Myers being badly wounded managed to fall close to the chaparral feigning himself dead while they were killing Grant and pursuing Reynolds he slipped into the bushes and got to Genl. Worth's camp and is now at Mier— Reynolds conducted a detachment of troops to the spot and there they found Brewer naked. They buried Brewer but could not find

Grant—Brewer could have continued with Capt. Crosman any length of time he could have made what work he pleased—but "there is a divinity that shapes our ends roughhew them how we will"—gone—cold, cold, cold

"A heap of dust is all remains of thee
Tis all thou art, 'tis all the proud shall be"

It was but the other day that I heard Brewer's voice stimulating the Mexicans to work "*muchachos, muchachos*" etc—Now he is a festering corpse literally "unknelled uncoffined and unknown"—I could never have believed that any Mexican would have killed Brewer—as there *is no life here* or any state of mind or body worth calling life the scripture might have a new reading on its application in reference to the stragglers and small parties—instead of "In the midst of life we are in death" it might read—"In the midst of the Mexicans we are in death"—Seven wagons sent over to haul wood for Genl. Worth's troops who are to encamp on this side when they come

Sunday Janry 17. 1847 The dragoons and artillery of Worth's command arrived this morning and passed over the river—Genl. Worth had Reynolds imprisoned at Mier on suspicion of his being in conspiracy with the Mexicans who attacked him Brewer etc.—He was tried by the Alcalde and released—Much suspicion of him is entertained here, it is said he secreted Brewer at his house and over persuaded to go to Monterey instead of going down the River as Brewer wished to do—It is said also that he fled at the first fire and that he has given contradictory accounts of the affair. Brewer had about $600 with him a fact which it is said was well known to Reynolds. Now if these things be so, taken in connexion with the fact that Brewer was killed at the first fire, it would look like a conspiracy "to a man up a tree"—The officers of the light artillery were much displeased that the dragoons should have crossed the river first, delaying the artillery some half hour. It appears that the artillery has precedence by the regulations or to speak technically "ranks" the dragoons—Several officers tell me that the Mexican officers who fought at Monterey openly declare in Santa Anna's camp that they (the Mexican troops) can not fight the Americans. That we are superior in strength skill bravery gunnery etc. Santa Anna has had several of them arrested for uttering such sentiments and he has issued an order to have arrested and shot as a traitor any one that utters such sentiments again—It appears to me that if such intelligent men as Ortega (I am told that he is one of those arrested) take such sensible views of things that there ought to be peace soon for it is very certain to my mind that our army can and will cut up any force which may dare to face them in the open plain—and to relieve Vera Cruz this is the thing they would have to do and not to defend Vera Cruz would be to surrender every thing in Mexico worth fighting for. Read the bible this evening. I have heard nothing of my application for leave of absence yet—Suppose that I shall not—

Monday January 18th It was quite cold saturday evening and yesterday, so much so that most of the Mexican labourers and seven wagons were at work all day yesterday cutting and hauling wood for Genl. Worth's troops—the infantry—expected here yesterday evening—they did not arrive until to-day and now it is as hot as any day I ever felt in June—Every body in their shirt sleeves. Genl. Worth made his head quarters on board of "The Corvette". The 4th infantry arrived first about 12 o'clock—they marched on board the Corvette without stopping and about an hour afterwards "The Corvette" carrying Genl. Worth and staff and the gallant but unfortunate 4th descended the river all decks crowded and the band of the 4th playing splendidly—got a look at Genl. Worth—I expected to see a young looking man—and he is as to carriage and deportment but his hair is gray. Duncan[6] went on this morning at day light with his battery in company with the rest of the artillerists and the Dragoons—they march by land of course. I am sick to-day. Genl. Jesup and Col. Whiting might at least answer my letters

"Cassius is weary of the sun—

And could wish the affairs of this world (this Mexican world) were undone"

Tuesday January 19th Heard to-day that Genl. Jesup had left Brazos for New Orleans. I presume he did not get my letter—Now the matter is getting serious. If I dont get my leave in a few days I shall have to go to Seralvo—Then I shall be among the lost tribes—then I shall never see any thing or do any thing—then I shall be regular set down as a regular quarter master—and the quarter master's business become a profession—Without the least hope of honor or reward. *There is to be no more fighting along this line. This I now regard as certain.* The time has gone by—The

Mexicans have evidently given up this part of the country. They must concentrate their forces and husband all their resources for a big battle at Vera Cruz—a big battle at San Luis Potosi—a big battle near the city of Mexico. With the preparations which our government is making they will see that the contest in future is not whether they shall hold upper Mexico but for their national existence— This they must see and must either conclude to fight for their fire sides or make peace. The innumerable opportunities furnished the Rancheros along this line to strike a blow and their failure to do so prove that they are but silent spectators of the spoilation of their country without a particle of patriotism or love for their government. Why should they strike for a government which they have only known by its oppressions and against a government which has brought them peace plenty and a prosperity unknown to them before and has protected them against the exactions of their robber chiefs? Now as for my tamely sitting down in a remote Mexican village—filled with canaile white black and brown—a garrison quarter master without the hope of honor or profit—after six months hardships already endured—leaving my wife and children to misery and distress—My affairs to run waste—to end in heavy pecuniary losses and perhaps the loss of life—or permanent decay of health. I shall not stand it unless the leave comes in a few days I must resign. There is a quarter master already at Seralvo—as competent as I could possibly be—He has been placed there by authority superior to that of Capt. Crosman—and I am sure that any neglect or omission were pointed out to him it would be remedied at once. I know the gentleman well and I am sure he has but to have his duty pointed out to him—to do it—This is all that I could do. The rest of Genl. Worth's command are pouring in to-day—They look like heroes—fierce brave brown from the sun rough from service—They are the most cast iron looking men that I have seen yet—

Sant' Anna, Sant' Anna beware the day
When these brave men shall meet you in battle array

"Behold, a people shall come from the North, and *a great Nation* ... They shall hold the bow and the lance: *their voice shall roar like the sea*, and they shall ride upon horses every one put in

array, like a man to the battle, against thee, O daughter of
Babylon!"
(Jerem. Ch 50 ver: 41–42)

Against thee oh city of Mexico!—Last night when I lay down, I was
in a perspiration it was so hot. A Norther came up about midnight
and in spite of all the cover I could heap on me I was cold. It is very
cold to-day putting in requisition big fires great coats etc.—Such is
winter in the city of Camargo! This morning Capt. Walker was in
my tent and talking of Columbia Tenn. the place of his residence led
me to speak of Miss Hill's being there at school and then of her
father Wm. R. Hill Esqr. I was in the act of speaking of Mr. Hill
when the folds of my tent were suddenly lifted and in came Albert
Hill his brother—This was quite a coincidence and considering the
parties the places and the chances might be likely to happen about
once in ten thousand years could the parties live that long—'Tis
night the tattoo is beating the drums rattling; while the bugle
answers from beyond the San Juan. The 5th, 8th and part of the 6th
infantry—regulars, are camped around me. They depart to-morrow.
On to Vera Cruz, on to battle and to blood. What a country is ours!
Under the starry folds of the ensign of the republic gather the
daring and the free of all nations—Hang out that glorious banner,
and all that's brave in Europe and America—the adopted and the
native citizen—springs forward to defend its honor and bear it aloft
untarnished! The time is coming and is now when the name of
American citizen will strike more terror into the hearts of tyrants
and their minions than did that of Roman in the days of old. What
though a hundred heroes fell on the plains of Palo Alto? What
though two hundred heroes have baptized and consecrated with
their blood the soil of Monterey? What though a thousand brave
hearts have ceased to beat on the banks of the Rio Grande and the
San Juan? Higher and higher swells the tide of enthusiasm! The
sons of the republic rally to her call in Myriads—State rivals
State—City answers to City! Thousands and hundreds of thousands
rush forward to supply the places of their dead brothers—Over their
graves they step to death and glory! Woe betide the man who
perverts these elements of grandeur and good to out ruin! Woe
betide the man who evokes the energies of the states and the people
in any other cause than that for which our fathers fought—The

cause of liberty and Right! America was designed to be the defender not the oppressor of man—An asylum for truth, justice, and liberty! And whenever she forgets the old reading and her early teachings and begins a career of conquest and dominion she will begin a career which will end in her overthrow, and in the going down of that sun of popular freedom which has arisen but seldom to gladden the the eyes and the hearts of men—and—now for the last time! Was the *animus* with which our government undertook this war—to uphold right and justice or to play over again the game of *Annexation*? To conquer peace or to conquer territory? That is the question—a question which has been tried and upon which a verdict must be rendered for history. In the mean time—*flagrante bello*—on to the battlefield—on to blood and let the shout still go up "war to the knife and the knife to the hilt—our country—our country always *right or wrong*"—! Our liberties may prove unsafe in our own hands (God grant they may not) but one thing is certain they would be very unsafe in the hands of the Mexicans. We should therefore whip the Mexicans first and then examine the ancient land-marks of our constitution and the principles of the Revolution and see how far we have strayed or are in danger of straying from the line of Right. Having thus whiled away a cold writer's evening and written if not sensible at least enough for one day—I'll now at 10 past 12 to my bunk—Perhaps some of my children are now dead perhaps robbers are now stealing into my house. Oh! Oh! Oh! This is unmitigated misery.

Wednesday Janry 20th 1847 Sold my Mexican horse yesterday for 15 dollars and now comes Albert Hill this morning and wants just such a horse having determined to go by Loredo and San Antonio to see Texas etc.—This is my old luck. An amusing conflict of authority occurred to-day in which Major Wall Ohio Regt. and a Major Brown—regular—were the *figurantes*—Major Wall who has a tender regard for the field work which he has thrown up here watching all trespasses upon and even approaches to it with oriental jealousy discovered in the grand round which he was taking that some regulars not having the fear of Major Wall before their eyes but being moved and seduced by the desire to keep warm—had built a fire (*horresco referens*) in the fortification ditch. It is true that a piercing Norther was blowing, it is true that these brave fellows had fought at Palo Alto Resaca and Monterey and *it may be* that they were appropriating the ditch to the only use that the Americans may ever have for it, yet these considerations constitute no apology to the genius loci for this unhallowed profanation. The demon of discord entered into the heart of the atrabilanous Major—his nostrils dilated—his eyes flashed fire and the poison of asps lubricated his tongue. In a voice of harsh thunder he denounced the trespassers and ordered them under the pains of immediate imprisonment to turn in and go to work on the fortification—the only business for which such lazaroni were fit. Major Brown being hard by and catching the latter part of Major Wall's speech came foreward to the relief of his men and without any preliminary or parley ordered up his guard and bade them to arrest "this fellow" and take him to the guard tent—Major Wall announced his rank—the men remained—some say Major Wall was actually arrested and imprisoned some that the guard did not arrest him but that he escaped the arrest with the greatest difficulty—Major Brown being hard to be convinced (though he was finally) that Major Wall was a Major. I doubt whether history will ever be able to set the matter right—Should I fortunately find out the truth I will record it. One thing is certain Major Wall felt his dignity was invaded as he crossed the river to report to Col. Morgan. In the mean time I believe Major Brown and his men quietly departed on the Aid (steamer) en route for Vera Cruz—

"Oh cruel, cruel Major Brown"—

I would not write this but I marked with indignation this morning while walking down the depot Major Wall's conduct towards some poor little camp boy about 10 years old—The little boy was running over the embankment to get to (Lane's) the sutler's store to buy a paper of pins perhaps for his mama making about as much trace or impression on *the holy ground* as the foot prints of an ordinary sized tom cat: Major Wall sent after him a volley of stern rebuke in a voice of thunder and with the fierceness of lightning—I can now tell an anecdote of a scene in which a regular fared the worst. This evening Mr. Ainsworth our old wagon master arrived from Monterey. He tells me that on his way up about 8 mile from Monterey one of his teamsters (a Dutch man) ran his wagon over a bridge built over one of those irrigating canals which farmers up that way cut to conduct the water from the mountain streams to their fields. The wagon upset happened to be loaded with barrels of sugar which were precipitated into the water. He was using every exertion to recover the barrels as quickly as possible and replace them in the wagon when a Lieutenant (a regular) rode up at the head of some wagons coming down—"Drive your team out of the road sir" said the regular—"I am a wagon master and trying to save these barrels of sugar" said Ainsworth "Damn you" said the regular "I am not here to argue with you but to order you, I am Lieut.————————regt. and am on my way to join Genl. Worth take away your wagon instantly". "But sir" said Ainsworth "in a few minutes I will have the sugar in and I am anxious to get on". "You continue to argue G—d dmn you what is your name?" Ainsworth gave his name pencilling it in his book the officer said he would report him to Capt. Crosman as soon as he got to Camargo—just then the Captain of the escort which went up with the train rode up. On understanding the nature of the controversy he told Ainsworth to hold on and not to move the wagon until he had got in all the sugar—"very well gentlemen" said Ainsworth "you can now settle the matter between yourselves and in the mean time I will load the wagon"—Turning to the Lieut. "Now sir you see the thing has come to a head". This made the Lieut. furious—"Who are you sir that dares to interfere with me" he shouted to the Captain. The Capt. gave his name and Regt.—Capt. of the Ky mounted Regt. —out came the pocket book again and down the lieut. pencilled the name exclaiming while doing so "Sir I will report you to Genl. Worth." "Very well" said the Kentuckian and taking out a memorandum book and pencil; he demanded the name of the Lieut.—The Lieut. gave it and the Capt duly recorded it and as he did so remarked to the Lieut. jeeringly "I shall not think it worth while to report you sir I generally redress my grievances myself"—Here the matter ended—It is reported to-night that "The Corvette" having on board Genl. Worth etc. is fast on a bar about 15 miles below the mouth of the San Juan—That the Genl. is tearing out his hair and in the language of my rough informant "he has cursed the bow off the boat d—ning quarter masters steam boat captains and all creation". If the idea that I have heard thrown out that a feeling of rivalry between himself and Genl. Taylor—(the latter to arrest the former's career, the former to prevent the latter from gaining any credit) caused the capitulation to be true, the boat ought not only to run aground but her boilers ought to burst and blow him sky high. For had the Mexican soldiers been made to lay down their arms at Monterey this war would have been much nearer its close.

Thursday Janry 21st 1847   The "J. E. Roberts" steamer came up to-day and reports Genl. Worth off on "The Corvette" rather and 40 miles on her way. I talked with an officer to-day who was present at the Wall affair and he thus represents it. Two or three Lieutenants and some privates of the artillery Battalion were around their fire in the ditch. Major Wall came forward and stormed at them—The lieutenants for a while paid him no attention thinking it *impossible* that they were addressed in that style. The Major came closer and gave them preemptory orders to come out of the ditch. Lieut. McCowan[7] asked him if he was addressing them—The Major replied in the affirmative "Then sir" said Lieut. McCowan "Who are you sir". "No matter who I am I order you out of the ditch, I have authority here". "What authority sir, who are you what is your rank?" "I have authority, I order you out of this ditch instantly" —The question was asked three times and the same answer given with but little change in phraseology—The Lieutenants say they took the Major (Oh! cruel mistake) to be some drunken teamster. Lieut. McCowan (I did not get the story from him but from another of the same Corps) called out "Corporal bring a file of your men here". The Corporal and the men came, "Take that fellow under arrest". "Fall in sir" said the Corporal to the Major—Major—"I am Major Wall"—Corporal—"It is all one to me sir, you heard the order, fall in".—Major "I am major of the Ohio regt." The Corporal seized him by the arm and marched him off to where the guard tent had stood some thirty or forty yards off in review of the whole battalion. When they got to where the guard tent had stood the Corporal learned that the guard tent had been struck or the guard dissolved preparatory to departure—He therefore marched the Major back to McCowan for further orders. When he did so Major Wall protested his rank and became much excited—one of the *Captains* therefor hearing him protest so bitterly before God and Man that he was the Ohio Major and in command of the post ordered him released—In the evening (after his return from across the river) Major Wall came down to the camp of the battalion in full dress—before, he had on nothing to distinguish him he steps up to Major Brown and asked for McCowan remarking at the same time that he came to arrest him—"Arrest an officer of my command sir, I think you would hardly do that." "Sir" said Major Wall "I am Major Wall and I intend to arrest him". "Sir" said the regular "I am Major Brown and you will do no such thing". Then said Major Wall "I order you to arrest him". Major Brown "I presume that you are at least sufficiently acquainted with the regulations to know that I rank you"—Major Wall "Well what then is my redress?"—Major Brown "I dont know that you have any unless you complain to Genl. Worth"—Major Wall "Very well Genl. Worth was my old tutor" —finis to the Wall and the catter walling of whom and which I would not have written so much but for the sake of veracious history—Repeating what our old wagon master said last night of the Ohio troops I think I will bid them farewell for ever—There was a conversation going on in reference to San Juan D'Ulloa. Ainsworth remarked that "the American Genl. does not know his resources if he did he would send down to Vera Cruz the 2d Regt of Ohio and let them steal the castle. They would soon do it fort guns and every thing else without the loss of a man or the firing of a gun". Col. Morgan, Capt. Caldwell, and several officers I got acquainted with are noble men—The artillery battalion embarked on board the "J. E. Roberts" this evening and will descend the river to-morrow morning at day-break—It was some other troops that went in the Aid or perhaps a part of the same battalion.

Friday Janry 22d 1847 The J. E. Roberts having on board the artillery battalion left this morning at day-break—the "Rough and Ready" and the "Enterprise" came up about 10 o'clock—Albert P. Hill called on me this morning he is going in the Rough and Ready having despaired of making up a party to go through Texas. The vulgar sayings here at this present greeting are "bamos the Ranche" "Nothing else" "Nothing the shorter" the songs "Old Dan Tucker" and "Julianna Johnsing". The most awful oaths salute the ear on every side—The soldiers *et al* are never rebuked for swearing and being afraid to do hardly any thing else they let off steam in volcanic outpourings of their wrath in the way of hard and strange oaths. There is a report to-day that a new dignitary to be styled a Lieutenant General is to be appointed (and that Col. Benton is likely to receive the appointment) to come on and join the army clothed with plenary powers to conclude a treaty whenever the Mexican government shall be ready to do that. In the phraseology of the newspapers "he is to carry the sword in one hand and the olive branch in the other". Speaking of newspapers I met with a good expression to-day "Literary trifles which float on the surface of the newspapers to the shores of oblivion"—Another report is that Benton Crittenden and somebody else are to be appointed commissioners for the purpose and with the powers above referred to—Just now Angel comes galloping up to my tent white with rage i. e., angry to a white heat—A man named Hazlewood (devilish pretty name by the bye I have no doubt that his real name is Smith) had "beat a venetian and traduced the state" not so—but had abused with divers insulting blackguard remarks and oaths free citizens of the republic to-wit the ferry man in the qr. mr.'s employment whereupon Mr. Angel gently rebuked him whereupon said Hazlewood denounced and defied said Angel—whereupon said Angel very properly ordered him to the guard house but changing his purpose *pro majori dignitate* told said Hazlewood to come to my tent as it was his intention to report him—Hazlewood had not arrived when Angel came and I sent a peremptory order to him to come—He came at last—I inquired his business here he was a wagon master in Capt. Arnold's train—I told him he should learn there was authority here to control him—that Mr. Angel was the superintendent of the depot that I was the commissioned officer of the depot that I would sustain Angel. He apologized saying he was sorry he did not know who Angel was or he would not have done as he did and that the like should not happen again. I told him that would do we now understood each other—Thinking the matter so easy he began to have the old man Adam rise in him to argufy—Seeing his disposition I gave him a stern look and told him there could be no more words on the subject that there was nothing further to talk about. He then left—Now here is a lesson on military authority. This man Hazlewood has had much authority as a wagon master over an army of teamsters coming from Saltillo down to this point. He has been for a long time as autocratic as the centurion mentioned in the "bible" and from mere wantonness he must blaze out at the ferrymen to cut a shine as *Captain Hazlewood*—Moral—It is a bad business for a republic to elevate generals to the chief magistracy who have been recently and for a long time acting military commandant. The "Rough and Ready" went down this evening carrying the 5th infantry—Capt. Walker and myself took a short ride Capt. Caldwell came to my tent and conversed—delightful day to-day just cold enough—A friend showed me the following paper as a curiosity which he found in an old newspaper—I begged him to give it to me that it should go to the States if he would—That the document have a fair show for posterity and immortality I place it at the top of a new page

My frend pucket i send you theas purlines hoping you and the rest of the boys is well for i am not my lov to awl. and send me sum knude as sune as you can rite. times is dul. i have no more to say

I stin your frend

god bles the pragines

John B. Roca
i shud lik to be
with you if i wos wel

Saturday January 23d 1847 9 o'clock in the morning—The drum beat brought me to my tent door—Along the Monterey road from their camp were marching towards the river the 6th Infantry— The sun was shining brightly and as the bright and burnished arms flung back the rays of the sun, the officers marching forward with a firm step—officers and men in conscious order of parade while at the sight of the spectators the drummers and fifers seemed to strike and blow as if inspired. I felt what it was to be a warrior. As they drew closer and closer and finally filed off by me for the landing just at that moment I felt that I had rather be one of those gallant men than a monarch on his throne—Philosophers may say what they please but there is innate in man a thirst for battle—a desire to fight—It is the office of Christianity to repress the passion but all its lessons are forgotten at the sight of the unfurled banner the glittering arms the marching column preceded by "the soul stirring drums and the ear piercing fife"—Off goes the "Enterprise" just at this moment (12 o'clock M) carrying the 6th drum and fife playing "Hail Columbia"—Brave gallant men! May you triumph in your hour of trial and realize (it is all the prayer that can be made for the soldier) the soldier's hope—victory—if not *victoria lata, cita morta*. Head ferry man comes and reports this evening that Lieut. Wall[8] of the 2d Regt. Ohio came down to the landing to-day and demanded that he be put over in the large ferry boat reserved for horses wagons and carriages etc. that the small passenger boat was coming over from the other side at the time and within 50 feet of the bank on this side. That Cook the ferry man when ordered by the Lieut. calmly stated to him that the other boat used by foot passengers would arrive in a minute and that it was against the quarter master's orders to use the big boat but for wagons etc. that Lieut. Wall (I hear that he is the son of the Major) said he did not care a d—n for the quarter masters that he was acting under higher authority and struck the ferryman (Cook) with his fist and then struck at him with a tent pole swearing he would kill him—I made a written report with the witnesses names to Capt. Crosman and sent it by the head ferry man. Suggesting that if by the articles of war the Lieut. could order, then the humble ferry man ought to know that when any officer orders he has to obey and thereby save his head and the Lieut. ought to be punished for wanton abuse of his authority, but that I submitted the matter to his better judgement.

Sunday, January 24th 1847   Read the bible—Capt. Walker a. q. m. in a peck of trouble this morning his superintendent having reported 42 mules and one horse as lost—Some of his teamsters have been very mad at not getting their money—They were turned over without a descriptive list and the Capt. can not pay at present, there is no doubt but that they have let the mules get off or perhaps turned them loose as there are too many gone for it to be accidental— The Lieut. acting qr. mr. to the 8th infantry has just applied to me for hand cuffs and balls and chains to secure 3 deserters from their regt. captured and brought back this morning—Mr. Lectura the superintendent of the depot on the other side called at my tent. He is at all times a very grave respectable looking man but on this occasion there was such an air of melancholy about him that I felt uncommon interest in him. He sat some time talking about the wagon road which was left for wagons to conduct wagons to and from the tarpaulins containing the quarter master's and commissary's stores around which runs his immense fort. It appears that the road is too narrow—that two wagons have already been precipitated into the ditch. After talking on this subject sometime, Lectura became silent and thoughtful. I asked him what was the matter, he said "this has been Captain the heaviest day of my life. I got news this morning that they have killed my brother-in-law (Lectura's wife is a Mexican). As mild and kind hearted man as ever lived." "Who killed him," said I? Lectura "Some volunteers, they shot him for his blanket, shot him in the back as he was returning from his field to his house at night, his family was entirely dependent upon his exertions for bread, they are now without a father to provide for them"—"Where did he live?"—Lectura "At a Ranche near Matamoras." "Wife and children did you say how many?" Lectura "A wife and seven children the oldest 8 years old, the youngest 2 months. I tell you Captain I feel very bad, he was one of the best men I ever knew, had they asked him for his blanket he would have given it to them, he was just that kind of man. All the glory which the Americans first gained among these people after the great battles last spring is passing away. The acts of violence the robberies and murders committed by some of the volunteers are fast destroying all the good name which the Americans had gained, the Mexicans are getting afraid to travel afraid to be on the road to come here or go to Matamoras, distrust has taken the place of confidence and love is turning to hatred etc."—Soon afterwards he left me he was greatly distressed and being a man of excellent sense and discretion he seemed to me to feel not less distressed on account of the public than his individual account. In mean time the Mexican *Ladrones* about Seralvo and Mier are keeping the account of outrages between the Mexicans and the Americans well balanced! What a dreadful state is war conducted any way in camp or in battle—in the strife of the field or the partisan foray—still it is a dreadful thing—The worst passions excited, the worst characters turned loose—while the brave and the honourable mind yields to it as a necessity—deploring its horrors—it constitutes a shield to the base and unprincipled and enables them to revel in roguery plunder and blood!

Monday January 25th 1847 Went over to the office as I was returning I met a funeral procession. Some old Mexican well to do in this world had departed to the realities of the next—The corpse was bourne on a litter carried on the shoulders of 5 or six men (the old man's peons I suppose). A Mexican youth clothed in a red flannel or red woolen gown and a white cape was marching some 20 yards in advance holding up with his right hand a wooden cross about two feet long—The priest and his clerk walked immediately before the corpse—The clerk was bawling Latin with a nasal twang to one of those tunes peculiar to the catholic service. The priest wore on the top of his head a black crown which I took to be made of paste board and black cloth—He did not sing he did not cry, he did not laugh look serious or look unhappy—All he did was to go ahead and wipe the sweat from his red fat stoled face with a worky day matter of course earnestness which shocked me. His manner spoke as plainly as manner could speak—this is a damnable bore I wish I was through with it—this is a job for me—a scene in which I have to play a part—the quicker it is over the better. There was a prospect of his not dying with appoplexy before he finished as the church (at the point when I saw them) was only 50 yards off. *Revenous a nos moutons*—Major Wall comes to see me to-day holding in his hand the report I made to Capt. Crosman on saturday complaining of the conduct of Lieutenant Wall at the ferry. He was exceedingly polite and evidently concerned and anxious—After saying that he wished to speak to me upon which we walked one side, he then went to say the young man was his son—not of age—indiscreet— intoxicated—That his conduct placed him in a delicate situation— That Capt. Crosman had said that if he got my consent and the injured man's the thing might drop—He was still going on about his anxiety and unpleasant situation when I stopped him by saying certainly sir with the greatest pleasure so far as it depends on me the charge is withdrawn you need make no further remark on the subject major so far as depends on me there is an end of the matter—His reply was I thank you kindly etc.—I feel very sure that had he been in my place his conduct would have been very different but I have in fact no ill feeling toward him and having made up my mind to resign at the end of the month I would be mean indeed to deny so small a boon to a father already cut to the heart on account of the folly and worthlessness of a drunken son. Were I going to fight Major Wall to-morrow morning my conduct would have been the same. Whatever other sins may be laid at my door no man can charge me with a want of magnanimity—But on the contrary it is well known in Maryland and in Mississippi that I have often borne with a light and sparing hand on the worst enemies I had when I had them in my power. Men who had me in their power I well knew at the time would have pursued me with a slathound vengeance—I can thank God that there is a man a man that I have encouraged and helped up the ladder the young the weak the humble—which I have tried to pluck no man down but in a fair field a just cause and in open warfare and those the haughty and the powerful—that I have ever acted on the motto—*Parcere subjectis et debellare superbos*—Enough of egotism—Major Wright, 8th Infantry, sent down this evening that he wanted 10 wagons at his camp by day-break to morrow morning to take down baggage tents etc. to the landing—"The Brownsville" having come up and unloaded—I ordered them—

Tuesday January 26th 1847 At the first dawn I heard our wagons going to the camp of the 8th—Soon afterwards a part of the 8th marched to the landing and embarked—"The Exchange" (steamer) came up this morning—"The Brownsville" has gone down the River carrying three or four companies of the 8th. "The Exchange" is now taking on a volunteer company from Ky which has been attached or incorporated with the 8th—This learned thru companies to go on the next boat which will be up reported to be the "Col. Cross" —One of our clerks got for me a day or two ago from one of the steamboat captains a New Orleans "Daily Delta" of the 31st of December...I was sitting after supper in Capt. Walker's tent and was in the middle of a long yarn when Mr. Angel came up and stated that Col. Morgan was mounting some Ohio troops and collecting all the men he could find who had horses for the purpose of going to the relief of Capt. Latham who with a mule train was surrounded by Canales and 300 Mexicans and in imminent danger. Mr. Whitely (an Arkansan and now acting as Capt. W.'s clerk) Capt. Walker and myself at once exclaimed that we would like to go. Capt. Walker was to leave on thursday following with his train for Monterey, it was therefore necessary that he should see Col. Morgan and Capt. Crosman to get permission to go. He had his horse saddled immediately. I concluded that propriety required that I should get Capt. Crosman's permission—I placed a note in my messenger's hands for the Captain—The messenger returned informing me that he could not find Captain Crosman. He had gone to his office only. I ordered him back and to seek him at his lodgings. In the mean time I was preparing to start fixing pistols, holsters, etc. Capt. W. returned and said that he could not find Capt. Crosman but as Col. M. had assured him that an escort could not be started until he (M.) returned from the expedition he (W.) thought that would do. My messenger found Capt. C. at his lodgings and returned in a few minutes with his consent for me to go. So Capt. W. Mr. Whitely and myself made ourselves ready with all despatch.

We were armed with swords and pistols. I had two very fine duelling pistols (which I borrowed of Angel) in holsters and two fine Derringer do. in belt. Being ready before the Col. had come over we concluded to go to Lane's sutler's store and get some refreshments. We drank and supplied ourselves with tobacco and returned to our quarters with a couple of boxes of sardines while in the act of devouring the sardines Col. Morgan rode up to my tent and came in. We tendered our services to him to which he made a polite reply and accepted us. In the next moment we were all mounted and off. We left the depot about 10 o'clock at night. Col. Morgan's troop consisted officers and privates of 37 men all told. There were five men volunteers to fight on their own hook—Capt. Walker, Mr. Whitely, Mr. Tree formerly a sergeant major of the 2d Dragoons (who had seen much service) Mr. Rogers (who was the son of one of the Rogers and brother to the other who were killed in Texas last spring) and myself: so the party were in all 42 men. We had a Mexican guide one of the men employed in the qr. Master's Service and an interpreter. Our route lay along the banks of the San Juan. A Norther sprung up about an hour before we started and the weather became intensely cold. The moon would have shone had it not been obscured by heavy clouds. About five miles off at a point where the road wound close to a Ranche situated immediately on the banks of the river we overtook one Mexican man and six Mexican women. There was nothing peculiar about the party only the women were all clad in white and all big with child. They were very polite and the guide said they were going to a fandango. The next thing worthy to note was that we lost our way but we soon regained it and while doing so stumbled on a party of Camanches men women and children. They refused to state what tribe they belonged to the reason of which was the fear of being attacked by some one whom they had injured. They had a considerable camp and a very large fire. The Col. made one of them mount a horse and ride on in front with the guide so as to be certain of the road. The Indian having stated that he knew the road, the Col. caused him to be told (he spoke the Mexican language very well) that he would shoot him if we got lost. We pushed on and soon afterwards about 2 or 3 o'clock in the morning the moon went down and it became extremely dark. The whole party jogged on in silence and many were half asleep. At one time I found I was asleep having dreamt that I had run against a chaparral tree and dodging to avoid it waked up and found that the tree only existed in fancy. There was not a word spoken for a mile or two. Then we came to a tributary of the San Juan a dreadful place the banks of the stream were very high and nearly perpendicular. On the near side close on the water the ground was boggy. The two guides the sergeant major and the interpreter floundered over. The Col. who had a very fine horse next attempted to cross. The horse sank down in a quagmire as if about to be wholly swallowed up. Down went rider and horse—the rider struggled out one way the horse the other. There was then a dead halt but soon Capt. Reynolds passed over on a powerful horse which he had got from Capt. Crosman (most of the horses were very poor and bad being furnished by the qr. mr. on the spur of the occasion the best that he had but they were perfect Roseanantes). There was another halt. I was mounted on a little Mexican poney and finding no one ready to try I being a Captain I went next by picking my way a little higher up I passed over without much difficulty. Then came Col. Morgan (he had been much hurt by the fall though he would not complain) came over next. Then one of the men tried it but just as he got on the edge of the stream his horse almost disappeared and would have immediately drowned had not four or five men rushed in to his assistance. With great labour the horse was got over. Then there was a perfect stand still no one was ready after what they had witnessed to attempt to follow and I thought our expedition was likely to come to an end at least until day break but Col. Morgan ordered all hands to dismount and lead their horses over. The water was not more than knee deep. They seemed unwilling to get themselves wet on so cold a night. But the order was thundered at them with so hearty a G—d d—n you that they were glad to get off. In the mean time Mr. Whitely and Capt. Walker who had been in the rear had got forward and rode over without much difficulty. Most of the others walked over and led their horses. After we had got all over and had progressed a short distance the day broke much to our satisfaction and delight.

Wednesday January 27 1847 We travelled over some beautiful rich lands and reached the village of Aldamas[9] (situated on the west bank of the San Juan) about 10 o'clock being a travel from Camargo of 45 or 50 miles. Col. Morgan held at Camargo some hostages from Aldamas as security for the good behavior of its people. The

Alcalde had sent down a messenger on Monday evening who reached Camargo about daybreak Tuesday giving Col. Morgan in a letter the same information as to Latham's situation as Latham did himself in a letter by another messenger who reached Camargo about 9 o'clock A. M. the same morning. Such was the character of these despatches that no one left Camargo under any other idea but that a fight was certain and against great odds so much so that Mr. Whitely left a letter with Capt. Walker's servant directed to his father informing him of the expedition and containing a statement that if the letter reached him he might rest satisfied we had either fallen or been captured. The servant was directed to put it in the office if we did not return in 4 days. The Alcalde of Aldamas and his cunning spry looking old secretario were very polite and even affectionate in their treatment. Corn was readily furnished for our horses and a fine beef for the men at fair prices. All the people (the village contained I would suppose some three or four hundred inhabitants) were kind, attentive, and complimentary. Nothing was to be heard but *"mucho bueno" "mill gratias" "Si senior"*. The women like women every where else are always kind, but the men were under the potent influence of fear. Almost the only influence which they can be brought to recognize or respect. Col. Morgan immediately upon his arrival despatched a messenger to Latham who had fortified himself at Allacka[10] [La Laja] a Ranche 18 miles off. The plan was to start immediately upon the return of the messenger. In the mean time men and horses ate rested and slept. The messenger returned about 8 o'clock that evening bringing with him a letter from Latham in which he stated that the Mexicans had raised their siege and departed higher up the river having doubtless learned through their *eine Sanis* that succor was at hand. They in fact know always every step the Americans take. This arises from the fact of the government being obliged to employ so many of their treacherous countrymen as muleteers *arreos* interpreters guides etc. the difficulty of distinguishing them. Col. Morgan did not think it necessary to start on that night so we remained at Aldamas until morning.

Thursday January 28th 1847   The next morning we set out early and reached Alacka about 12 o'clock here we got dinner and the mules being all packed and ready the whole party set out together. When we were about to leave Aldamas Walker Whitely Tree Rogers and myself requested Col. Morgan through me as spokesman to allow us to constitute the advance guard. To this he very readily assented ordering us to keep about a hundred yards in advance of the foremost troops and to bring to [him] all Mexican stragglers whom we might see. We ever after rode in advance during the remainder of the expedition and I may say here that there was never met with a dense looking chaparral during the whole of the trip that we did not look for an attack. Col. Morgan divided his force now numbering about 60 men—one third in the front one third on either side of the train about the middle of it and a third in the rear. He rode at the head of the front party but passed frequently to see all right. We reached a ranche on the San Juan 6 miles from Alacka called Mantayka[11] [Manteca]—which I am told signifies lard—a good name as we saw there many fat hogs. We arrived there about an hour by sun and staid there till morning. The land from Aldamas to Alacka with the exception of 3 or 4 miles is as rich as any in the world especially between Alacka and Mantayka. In the Ranche that the officers slept in at Mantayka I noticed the Mexican cradle which is nothing more or less than a shallow circular hammock about three feet in diameter with four cords attached to it quadrangularly and fastened to a beam. The hammock swinging about six inches from the floor which is always earthen never of wood. The little *nino* is placed in this hammock and gently swung to sleep by an older brother or sister. I saw afterwards the same arrangement at several other ranches. At Mantayka Col. Morgan sent out a spy to find the camp of the Mexicans and having done so to join us on the road and lead us to it. This service the poor wretch gladly undertook to perform for a reward of $250 to be paid upon the confirmation of his task. He went off with great confidence and gaiety but he never returned his fate may be judged of by the sequel. Before I go further I will here remark that all the ranches villages and towns which we passed through on our route going and coming we found houses and churches perfect forts port holes in the walls to fire through and battlements on many of them as high as a man's head.

Friday January 29th 1847 We left Mantayka this morning in the same order as the day before and arrived at Rancho Veho [Viejo] or as we dubbed it the big bellied Ranche the head man being a very large Mexican with a large paunch, he bore on his person scars of several wounds and said he had been in early life a soldier and had fought in ten battles this old fellow had a neat little fort being a stone house with port holes for musketry into which he could put his family on emergency and defend himself a long time against Camanches and Robbers. From Mantayka to Rancho Veho is 21 miles. During the whole of to-day's march we supposed every moment that we would be attacked and as the spy did not join us we thought it a plain case that he had proved a traitor or had been cut off. We saw to-day a very large armadillo which we overtook in the road. The old soldier had a great number of beautiful daughters to whom our young men played the amiable. He was better fixed than any Ranchero that I have ever seen. His houses were all comfortable—a plenty of everything corn horses cattle fat hogs in pens chickens turkeys etc. He had also small gardens where grew in great abundance onions and red pepper. Close to his Ranche boils the San Juan in a cataract. I attribute his comfortable situation to superior information derived from travel and observation among a people more civilized and refined than those around him. Such are the triumphs of mind over matter knowledge over ignorance. Had these people sense they would desire to have the laws of the American Union extended over them to shield them from Robbers, their own government and the Camanches to whose inroads in turn they are perpetually exposed and of some of which they live in such constant dread that all the pleasure of their existence must be poisoned. But of this truth I am now convinced that their hatred to the Americans is deep seated. Those who have joined us will become outcasts—with the great mass hatred to Americans will become an inheritance from father to son. I believe if this war is continued beyond May rivers of blood will flow before it ceases while thousands and tens of thousands of our brave men will perish from a twofold enemy—sword and this climate—one thing I am satisfied that the longer the war lasts the more national it will become and the more will disappear the prospect of the two races ever living together in harmony. One or the other must conquer— there may be hollow truces but war to the knife can only give a permanent peace and that kind of war has not yet commenced unless the commencement may be dated from this present period— The officers slept in the old Mexican's fort. About 2 or 3 o'clock in the morning the officer of the guard burst into the house and said guns were firing out among the muleteers who were with the mules in an enclosure about ¾ of a mile off. We all sprung to our feet and seized our arms in two minutes all were armed and out. As we sallied out we found our old soldier up and meeting us loading his gun. He said that the Camanches would be down upon us. The packs had been arranged in a square the evening before and soon officers and men were all ready for the fight. Three or four muleteers came running in and reported that some five or six Mexicans had stolen into the *corral* or enclosure and before they had found them out had got through the gap about a hundred of the mules. That discovering them they had got close on them and fired that the thieves returned the fire—and got off with what they could the firing only prevented their getting the whole of them the firing turned those inside from the gap. Mr. Thompson the contractor's agent and the captain of the muleteers said it was no use to attempt to pursue the thieves until morning that then his Mexicans could see and follow the trail. Every body came to the conclusion that this was but a ruse of Canales or whoever was the head chief of the Mexicans to draw as large a force as possible from the Rancho so that he might fall on the main train at the Ranche that the mules could be no object to such a force and at such a time etc. Col. Morgan taking this view of the subject ordered Lieuts. Brown and Wall to take 23 men and go with Thompson at day light and to endeavour by a forced march to come up with Mexicans and to attack or not attack according to their numbers and according to their direction: that if they found a force which they might deem it unpolitick to attack that they should halt on the ground and despatch a messenger to him.

Saturday January 30th 1847 By day-light in the morning the party set out accompanied by Thompson and some dozen *arrieos* (muleteers) who were to follow the trail in advance and while the fighting was going on to secure the stolen mules. About 11 o'clock a Mexican came as messenger from the party with a note that they had caught up with the Mexicans who were 160 strong that they had declined giving battle and that they wished for aid. The Col. immediately ordered the men he had left of those from Camargo together with Latham and a part of his men to get their horses out and be prepared to start immediately and soon we were on the road.

Our road lay through a thick wilderness, so thick that the thieves had cut the bushes from the path but the evening before—the trees and limbs looked as fresh as if they had been cut only an hour. Down in a glorious lowland shaded by hackberry and muskite through which wound rushing streams of clear water and where under the heavy coating of dead grass was to be seen green grass which resembled wheat, we found a herdsman with an immense heard of goats. As soon as he discovered us he made off with his flock with all the haste he could. Col. M. said he wished him brought back. Rogers and myself started after him crying out "*halto*" this word will always bring a Mexican to a [stop] and as soon as they hear it they hasten to you as fast as possible. He came up saying that he was a poor shepherd (*pastodad*) [*pastor?*]. Rogers told him he must go to the Col. The Mexican said something about his losing his goats (*capaderas*[12])—Rogers brought down his gun and told him *bamos*—He hurried onto the Col. Being questioned he said he had seen no Mexicans did not know any body or any thing, the Col. did not waste time on him but told him to *bamos* which he did with all his might. Soon afterwards in passing between two trees the tops of which the thieves or some body else had cut off the rifle which the Col. was carrying striking against the posts went off but no one was hurt. We reached the "Rancho del Rio Colorado" which we named "the Robbers Ranche" where our friends were about an hour by sun a distance of 18 miles. I had eat no dinner and as I had *to rely on myself* for supper the prospect of going without any thing seemed very great. Turkey and a great number of chickens and a hog or two had been killed and most of them were cooked and eat up but no one had "said Turkey to me". My hope of winging in was growing dimmer and dimmer when I determined to make one desperate effort. I approached a party of some three or four seated around a large fire over which boiled an iron pot. I asked what they were cooking they said chickens. I told them I would like to buy one no they would not sell and could not give which they would gladly do if they had any to spare which they feared they had not. I knew they would as leave eat pork as chicken and that some things could be done as well as others. I hunted up Lieut. Brown the finest fellow of all his party. I proposed to him to buy the chicken together. He readily assented, I put in his hand a half dollar and he put in mine two bits he went off the money was accepted and one of the boys found a large board which he placed on a pile of stones hard by on this we laid our chicken and Brown split it in two lengthwise— It was very fat and large it was well cooked and having a small piece of cracker in my pocket I never enjoyed a meal more in my life. I had more than I wanted and shared my portion with Dr. Donaldson and Morgan. It was very cold in the night and I awoke just before day stiff and shivering I pushed my back up against my next neighbor lying on the floor of the Ranche and doubled up my feet soon got comfortable and again addressed myself to sleep.

Sunday January 31 st   Our misfortune in pursuit of these villains was that from this inferior quality of the horses we were compelled to stop every night and from the smallness of our party and the ascertained number of the foe and the character of the leaders Canales, Carrabajal[13], Remiries the 3 Aldirettes[14] and Felippe Perez (being all fighting men) we expected at every moment to be attacked and that instead of pursuing the foe we should have enough to do to act in defence. At day break next morning all had got something to eat the horses were saddled and we were all ready to depart. But we had 6 prisoners picked up at the Robbers Ranche by the party first sent out who came down on them before they had time to leave. These had to be disposed of. About an hour passed away while the Col. and his adjutant were disposing of them assisted by the counsel of Thompson and others. What to do with them was in fact a knotty question. They swore they were there by accident some by force some as passers by—The Col. finally released three and sent off three to Captain Reynolds (who was left in charge of them at Ranche Veho) tied together by their necks with orders to keep them as prisoners—The Col. then gave orders to burn the Ranche which consisted of one dwelling-house main ranche one out house as a kitchen and one other out house filled with corn shucks fodder and wool—This was a proper order. The Ranche was undoubtedly the head quarters of the Robbers. It was situated in an open space with an almost impenetrable wilderness around on every side—remote from every other haunt or dwelling—Near it (within 100 yards) ran a bold stream of water, 200 yards off was another stream—a quarter of a mile off were high hills gorges and inaccessible retreats. On the side we came a chaparral (thicket) through which only a Mexican could have worked his way. The main building contained lances, escopettes, swords, pistols, and all the appliances of war—In the corners of the room were lance poles, from the beams were suspended innumerable lassos, girths, leather and every thing for saddlery—On the floor were bull hides to be appropriated to the same purpose for which Homer's heroes used them—shields and bedding—There were some signs that women might be there occasionally though there was nothing effeminate—The detachment had been mounted and waiting some time when the Col. and his adjutant and orderly came forward towards us on one side while the three prisoners departed on the other. Immediately thereafter men were seen with brands applied to the three houses—inside and out. The sun just then about ¾ of an hour high began to struggle through some fleecy clouds which had previously obscured it. First arose some patches of smoke Anon it curled rolled away in white volumes then it grew black and threatened like an angry cloud upon which the flittering sun bows danced like lightning then came the volcanic outburst of fire and the robber's ranchero with all the appurtenances thereinto belonging were so far being consumed that nothing short of the cataract of Niagara could arrest the destruction. Being satisfied that our work was accomplished we moved on. It is a dreadful sight to see a dwelling establishment of man consumed by fire. The mind involuntarily dwells on the many happy moments there passed on the feeling of desolation and woe with which men women and children return to the spot so dear to them but to find them selves houseless homeless and destitute of every comfort of life—All the numberless and nameless articles of convenience and enjoyment which they had prized destroyed forever. Theirs is the lot "To under go/Each outrage of the cruel foe/Their fields laid waste their cot laid low"—Perhaps these villains forced themselves on an innocent family who would have wished nothing more but to pass their lives in peace and happiness and succumbed willingly to superior power. But enough of this. We rode foreward in the order before spoken of—Two of the *arreros* just ahead of the advanced guard with Thompson. One of them had lost 6 mules his own property. He was so skilled in mule feet tracks that he could tell the tracks of his own mules among ten thousand—After we had left the Ranche about 200 yards Mr. Thompson called our attention to a horse track with a notch in the hoof tending toward the Ranche. We were now satisfied that they had sent back a spy to watch our movements and were entirely convinced that as the stolen mules must have been weary from the march the day before and the flight in the night that they would place themselves in an ambush in some one of the many favourable positions and attack us—There was "A stillness like to death/And the brave man held his breath"—As we passed the deep and narrow passes through chaparral walled up in many places to the very path, for nearly 8 miles we had to ride single file expecting at every moment to see the fire and hear the shout of the foe—But on we rode secure and passed the river Colorado[15] (pronounced Colorao) 8 miles from the Ranche. Just before we did so the fresh tracks of a woman in the dust tending towards the Ranche were plainly to be seen. I could but think that she was one of the tenants of the Ranche who seeing the smoke and the flames had started to go back with the vain hope of rescuing something from the ruins. On we went as fast as our horses could travel and came to the Ranche Las Tabbeles on the Cappadera River[16] 10 miles from the Robber's Ranche—We found it altogether deserted except for one man and woman—The Col. made the man (who to all our enquiries had nothing to reply but *quin sabe*) to mount his horse and ride with us. We crossed the Cappadera River about fifty yards wide but a dashing terrible torrent. I was fearful that my horse would be swept away but with a free use of the spurs I got him across and all got over safe—Lovlier lands deep loamy rich soil (coated with a matting of dead grass under which flourished in perpetual verdure the green pasturage) from the Robber's Ranche to two miles beyond the Cappadera river the eye of man never beheld—A mile after we crossed the Cappadera in a beautiful shady sequestered spot we came on a flock of goats and sheep numbering I would suppose 300. It was a beautiful sight. Near them was a boy and a dog. The Col. ordered the boy in, the everlasting Rogers was on him in the twinkling of an eye with the rifle brought down and the terrible world "*halto*". The old Mexican fearful that the boy in his innocence would tell the truth as to where the robbers passed spurred his horse to join the *Muchaco*—crying out *muchaco muchaco*. His object was at once understood and "*halto*" was shouted to him by a dozen voices—He looked around but persevered several spurred toward him and looked askance he still seemed disposed to "dare his damnation" but fortunately he espied the imperturbable Tree drawing a bead on him (as it is technically called) and quicker than thought his horse was turned and bamosing back. A mile further and the robbers to bother us moved their mules about in every direction but the faithful *arrieros* in front true as blood hounds circled around and soon struck off a trail to the right through the chaparral and then for 28 miles we passed through some of the most desolate barren waterless murderous looking region that was ever known. Not a drop of water flint rock, the dry beds of spring rivers gullies caverns and parched sand banks. In the morning it was very hot—a july day—but fortunately for man and horse—about 12 o'clock a cloud overcast the sun and a delightful breeze sprung up. After we had travelled thus about 25 miles away in the distance Thompson pointed us to a stone Ranche on a high hill—said that it was the other great rendezvous of the Robbers and that he had seen men and mules descending the hill. Off we put for the Ranche at full speed over rocks and gullies up hill and down dale and when reached the foot of the hill one Mexican was seen speeding away he was brought. Five others were seen with some mules and horses having just crossed the San Juan. Our *arreros* examined the trail and pronounced with confidence that they were not of our party, so skillful had they shown themselves in their line that their pronouncements were taken as conclusive on the principle of—"*Curque in sua arte credendium est*." We ascended to the Ranche—Here we found every thing abundant—corn jerked beef, oranges, lemons, dried tamarinds etc.—and there were abundant evidences that fair senioras and seniorettas had been but recent inmates of the Ranche— And as a sign of their industry there was to be found a pair of wool cards. No one was at the Ranche. We then pushed on to China[17] —about 3 miles off—Crossing the San Juan at a most romantic beautiful spot—The current was very rapid and deep and those who rode poneys were glad to get off with wet feet. Into China we rode having travelled that morning more than 30 miles—We reached there at 3 or 4 o'clock. We rode into the Plaza in good order making an imposing appearance as we could being in all 58 men. The Col. ordered Mr. Thompson (who can speak Mexican as well or better than he can English) to find out the Alcalde and demand quarters of him—Soon Thompson returned with the Alcalde who said the best place the Town would afford was the Priest's house for the officers and the priest's yard and lot for the men and horses. The

Priest's establishment was on the N. E. corner of the Plaza. We drew up in front of it. The Priest's house or palace (a very uncommon luxury) was two stories high. With a balcony and iron rails running around the front of it. Soon the priest came out on the balcony displaying in his manner and carriage the utmost hateur and contempt—Cocking his hat on the top of his head and drawing a chair to the iron railing he proceeded very deliberately to count our force pointing with his finger as he did so—Tree and Rogers regarded this proceeding as *contra jus getium* and as denoting as spy and they only wanted the Col.'s permission to arrest his progress with a ball through his head. Doubtless he deserved to be shot but as frequently happens he did not get his deserts—The Alcalde approached close under the balcony and taking off his hat gave him to understand that his quarters were to be required *por el Colonel e Los soldados Americanos*—The Priest replied most contemptuously that he did not wish their company that the last Colonel that had staid with him had stolen his watch and thinking he had gone too far he qualified his words by saying he did not mean to say this Col. would steal that the Alcalde must get some other place. The Alcalde and Thompson rode off but soon returned with the report that there was no other place in the Town half so good as the Priest's. Thereupon the Col. ordered the bars to the Priest's yard to be pulled down and without further ado we rode and secured our horses and the officers took possession of one of the largest and most agreeable halls I ever saw. It was about 30 feet long and 15 wide—It contained every thing that heart could wish. Windows with iron railings in front and protected by wooden shutters so constructed as to admit as much or as little air and light as might be agreeable or convenient, settees otomans, chairs, in abundance—In one corner was a sort of wardrobe of the richest robes blankets etc. in another a very fine bed with embroidered coverlids baskets containing female dresses and fixings—behind which was a splendid bath tub on the upper part of which was thrown a rich scarlet cloak of diminutive proportions showing that in that corner slept the *seniora* (Bye the Bye Col. Morgan slept on the seniora's bed and I slept on a settee hard by using every night for a covering to my head and shoulders her scarlet cloak. The Senior slept in the next room the priest's sanctum—into which the room we slept in opened by regally constructed folding doors which opened more glibly and noiselessly than any folding doors I ever saw) In another corner was on a sort of a rack a splendidly embroidered silver mounted saddle and hard by a stool upon which [MS torn] in reverend neglect— about a dozen books in Latin principally on theological subjects— and about ½ dozen more in Spanish one of which was poetry and the other nothing more nor less than—Voltaire's Maid of Orleans— From the walls looked down frown the living canvas in pious rebuke at us hereticks the holy virgin Saint Anthony and the boy saint (to be found everywhere) and some other of the holy ones of the church triumphant. There was no mistaking the *seniora* she was well dressed had a staid matronal lady like appearance most general- ly to be found in the next room working at the needle and not visiting the kitchen over once or twice a day—There was an other woman much younger well made tight tidy pert buxom always stirring through a little lame in one foot there was no mistaking her—she was the servant maid—The first evening the priest was very mad at every thing he would come in look around retreat through his folding doors and return again before you could say Jack Robertson—He had a thousand complaints to make, the horses were tied too near his kitchen, the soldiers were burning his wood etc.—I should have stated that we ascertained from an American (one cast away Dr. Bullock who resided at Cadarreto [Cadereyta] and here now on a professional visit to China) that the robbers numbering about 150 men left China about 10 o'clock in the morning. To have pursued them in the then condition of our horses with the start they had would have been madness—night would have overtaken us before we could have overtaken them. We could not travel in the night because we could not track them after dark—they could travel night and day *ad libitum*. We gave the Alcalde six or seven dollars to have a supper and breakfast for us—We had little or nothing at either meal wretched coffee and huge wretched tortillas, not enough of either—The inhabitants were no where to be found every house was shut up as if it were a city of the dead—if we accidentally stumbled on a Townsman or Towns- woman and asked them for eggs chickens etc. it was "*quin sabe*" "*no di*" "*no entiende*" all the time. Never did I see Mexicans look so hostile and contemptuous—But Lord how the tune was changed next day.

Monday February 1st 1847   Col. Morgan had the Alcalde brought before him this morning and caused him to be told that unless he furnished 82 good pack mules to supply the place of those stolen by their friends who had been harbored by the Town the day before that he would lay the Town [MS torn] He gave him till 5 o'clock to get the mules. He also ordered him to have the officers taken care of and furnished with abundance of the best fare the Town and season would admit. This threat acted like a charm. The agents of the Alcalde were hurrying in every direction. The streets swarmed with anxious faces the tenants of the poor hackals in the suburbs were moving off (war always falls heaviest on the poor the ignorant like every other calamity) whenever we met the citizens off went the hat and the most gracious salutations were made. The old priest came in and sat with us and became jocular and even merry. He commenced with me a conversation in Latin (finding I had one of his books in my hands) but we did not get on very well. His conversation was a confusion of tongues half spanish half Latin—I used the term *homo bellicosus*—he corrected me by saying—*non bien—activo—bellicoso— passivo—bellicosus*—he again asked me upon coming into the room *apprend lectio?* I thought then it was time to stop which I was glad to do having given our company sufficient fun already. After the threat we fared most sumptiously. The officers were divided into 2 parties (5 in one 7 in the other including of course us of the advanced guard) and were assigned to two aristocratic families where we had cushioned chairs to sit on, china to drink out of silver spoons—coffee chocolate kid mutton, *frijoles*—wheat bread etc. all in great profusion—We got a fiddle and one of our party played all day monday the rest singing dancing sleeping etc. Monday night— the Alcalde came with a thousand excuses—he had failed to get more than 45 mules he begged another day—Thompson begged that it would be granted—Col. Morgan very reluctantly consented— This morning Thompson found a fellow who he said belonged to the robber gang he was brought before Col. Morgan and having a most dogged look and replying to every thing *quin sabe* and the Alcalde testifying against him. Col. Morgan ordered him to be hanged—a rope was fixed to the limb of the tree in the priest's yard a noose made and put round his neck he looked perfectly resigned and never winced just as the soldiers were drawing the rope tight and about to swing him off the priest said he would get him to state all he knew. The priest Thompson and the fellow went into a room and the fellow stated to the priest where the robbers and mules were—They were he said at a Ranche or village called Passa siccata[18] [Paso del Zacate]—30 miles below on the road to Camargo.

Tuesday February 2d 1847 We passed the day pretty much as we did the day before—with the exception that in the morning the priest sent word that the fiddle was wanted to use in the Church— we were glad of this wishing to attend mass by way of variety but after the bells rang twice the church doors still remained closed. Upon enquiring the reason we were told the Priest had too bad a headache to say mass this morning—The whole matter was a ruse to get away the fiddle. This we thought a cute joke in the old priest. The old priest is a spry large respectable looking old fellow of 60. I never saw a more sensual countenance in my life—He was the impersonation of epicurism—

Wednesday February 3d The priest Dr. Bullock and the Alcalde particularly the former were constantly trying to find out what road we were going to take the whole time—We gave out that we were all going in a body to Monterey. After we had mounted our horses this morning about sun rise (the Alcalde had furnished more than the number of mules) Col. Morgan held a sort of counsel at the head of the command whether we should divide the force—a part to go to Rancho Veho with Thompson and the mules and the rest to proceed on the East bank of the San Juan (the side we were on) to Camargo. I was among the first to speak and said what I wanted to know was which was our direct route to Camargo? I was told we would save at least a day by going the China road (the East Bank). Then said I I vote for going down the nearest route (leading by Papa Siccata) and as in all other cases of honor and duty leave consequences to take care of themselves. It should be never said we went out of our way. This was the general voice. No said Col. Morgan that's not it but may not the mules be captured and the detachment destroyed. Thompson said with Capt. Latham and 22 men he could carry the mules safe—Then it was determined that we would go in a body to the river and there divide this we did. Latham and his men and Thompson with the mules crossed the river—We 36 men all told wheeled to the right for Camargo—We passed several ranches hugging the San Juan. The young men were all absent no body to be seen but old men women and children all

fit to bear arms gone—We reached Papa Ciccata about 11 o'clock—
The Alcalde seemed to be expecting us. He said the robbers had
gone the back track we were perfectly satisfied that this was a
lie—There we found a regular built stone fort on a hill overlooking
and commanding the village and the surrounding country. The Col.
demanded a fresh horse for the guide getting which we proceeded—
we then passed for 10 miles through an out of the way cut throat
looking country (following the guide implicitly) though Rogers and
Whitely as brave men as ever lived rode by his side or as close to
him as the nature of the road would admit with orders to shoot him
should we get lost. These orders were communicated to and well
understood by him—It was indeed a most serious time all conversation stopped every body communed with his thoughts. The silence
was broken by observing a vulture attacking a crow. In vain the
crow soared—the vulture soared still higher—they ascended almost
out of sight at last the crow fagged out began to give in—blow after
blow was struck and finally the crow fell to the ground the vulture
on top of him. Again the party became silent, more desolate became
the scenery when to the right of the path suspended from a limb of
a muskite tree all beheld an object that made the brave man
furious—while it horrified all. About 50 yards from the path in a
little open spot hung a dead man by the heels. Col. Morgan cried
out "G—d d—n them I know what it means keep your places my
lads be ready they are about here in ambush". "Men" addressing
himself to the advance he said "two or three of you ride up and see
if you can make out what it is". Rogers the guide myself and one or
two others I forget who being intent on the object rode close to the
horrid spectacle. The feet of the man across each other were lashed
tight to the tree—the head was within a half inch of the ground, his
hands lassoed one over the other in front rested on his forehead—
his shoes were on a pair of blue cotton pants reaching to his
waist—his shirt stripped down half way his arms were spread out
like a cloth on the ground leaving his back and head exposed to
view—His back was shockingly burnt—the blood had gushed out
of his nostrils and mouth. Oh God what a horrid death did that
poor man die!—they had first horribly burnt him and while yet alive
they had tied him up by the heels to perish by the gravitation of his
own blood! None but devils incarnate could have been even hired to
do such a thing, what then were they who did it willingly! The most

of our company thought he had been hanging there for from 10 to 20 days—I believe he had been hanging there not more than 3 days and I believe *he was our spy*. We were told at China that the robbers carried through the Town a Mexican tied. This sight told us what to expect if we were ever taken prisoners—We had not gone 200 yards before we came to a small prairie—The Mexican guide stopped short as if a bullet had passed through his brain—looking to the right of the prairie he cried out *Cavallos muchos cavallos ombres— uno—dos—tres—cuatro—cincquo, six, ocho—muchos*—all exclaimed there they are now—Close up said Col. Morgan and stand in your places, let no man stir. I will ride forward and see what it means—he rode two or 300 yards he and Capt. Walker both of whom had fine horses—Soon Col. Morgan returned "I see a great number of men—they are pouring out and saddling their horses, we will form a square and fight them here". Those who could see good said that there appeared to be at least 300 horses perhaps 400—Every body saw that all we had to do was to fight to the last and die like men. The advance would have suffered first and perhaps most but I believe there was no man of us but what was ready to fight and stand and die with his comrades—There was an awful expectancy— arms were examined and made ready—Tree suggested to the Col. that since our force was small and theirs large, perhaps it was best to go on to the chaparral where we might [fight] under cover to more advantage—Yes said Morgan we will pursue our course and fight them whereever they appear—"forward in front". On we went at the same pace we had been travelling all the morning if any thing slower for all eyes were up the prairie soon the chaparral obscured our view. When we emerged on top of a hill about a ¼ of a mile off, the cry was they come—here they come—we halted and looked— there was the dust but it was rolling the other way like the riders were spurred by the devil—Then we concluded that their object was to deceive us by their pretended flight make a detour and attack us in ambush at the many favourable points along the road—collect all the forces and have (as the saying is) the game dead—Then the excitement and expectancy again ran high—intense—From every thick chaparral we expected a wide spread blaze of fire the iron hail and the avenging shout; but no! safely still we rode on to Ranche La lahaya [La Laja?] on the San Juan 18 miles from Papa ciccata— We reached there about an hour by sun—Demanded the Alcalde—

Alcalde not at home—there was a substitute a dark cut throat looking ruffian. There was no other young man at the place except one who was very officious helping us to hunt up the Alcalde corn etc. Soon he mounted his horse and without any connection or any thing to draw out the remark he rode up to the Col. and said he supposed he would stay there all night. Yes said the Col. without being at all disconcerted—Said he I live at another ranch I wanted to know if you would stay all night because if so in the morning I will go with you to Camargo. I asked the Col. why he did not stop him he said he understood him perfectly well that he was there as a spy on his actions to find out if we stay all night, if I stopped him they would send another and then our purpose would be suspected— The Col. gave secret orders to start at moon rising 9 or 10 o'clock and he and myself lay down in a bed in a hackal made of fodder. Just as we went to sleep, a soldier threw open the door and said horses were coming. We all seized our arms but soon found the alarm was occasioned by two or 3 Mexican boys who had been to water their horses—At moon rising we started and rode on to Camargo a distance of 30 miles. We reached Camargo a little before day break—the day broke before I got to my tent having performed in continuous travel in one day and night of 75 miles—We passed all sorts of elegant places for attack but we were unharmed—unchallenged. When I got home I found a letter from Col. Whiting refusing me leave of absence and stating that he had not received the letter I enclosed to Col. Davis—That my statement of reasons for leave was too brief and general. I had relied on my letter to Col. Davis—I will now resign I have seen no fight it is true but I have done all I could to get into one—There are a plenty of men possessed of qualities physical and mental and of youth and vigor who disencumbered from other ties would better suit the place I hold than I do and would gladly take it—I have served out my six months for which time I originally volunteered. I have been here three months longer than I expected when I left home—But these reasons have no weight—I resign solely on account of my wife—I have all men of gallantry on my side and the ladies. I forgot to say that the stone Ranche on the high hill on the opposite side of the river from China was burnt by order of Col. Morgan on Monday evening—This was suiting the action to the word and taught the burghers of China what they might expect—*Vale! Vale! Vale!*

Saturday February 6th 1847   The Brownsville is up—Capt. Crosman a most extraordinary thing has gone on a visit to Clay Davis at the mouth of the San Juan—When he returns I resign and go in the Brownsville—*Vale—Vale—Vale*

Notes

CHAPTER I: *August 11–October 14, 1846*

    1. Executive Document No. 65, 31st Congress. "Message from the President of the United States communicating the report of Lieutenant Webster of a survey of the gulf coast at the mouth of the Rio Grande," July 27, 1850, 3–4. Brazos Island was a barrier island off the coast of Texas bounded on the east and west respectively by Laguna Madre and the Gulf of Mexico and on the north and south respectively by Brazos Santiago Pass and Boca Chica. The island extended for about three miles north of the mouth of the Rio Grande. In 1846, Boca Chica was a shallow inlet that could be waded across from the island to the mainland, but it has since silted over.

    2. Haskell M. Monroe, Jr., and James T. McIntosh, eds. *The Papers of Jefferson Davis* (Baton Rouge: Louisiana State University Press, 1971) vol. 1, liii–lxv, vol. 3, 22-52, 123-162. Robert McElroy, *Jefferson Davis: The Unreal and The Real* (New York: Harper and Brothers, 1937), 22-38. Brainerd Dyer, *Zachary Taylor* (Baton Rouge: Louisiana State University Press, 1946), 96-98, 239. Jefferson Davis, at the time a Congressman from Mississippi, joined the First Mississippi Regiment in July 1846 at New Orleans and immediately began to exert strong leadership tempered with wisdom. One of the great weaknesses of American volunteer militia had always been the election of officers by the rank and file. Quite often the man elected to lead was the most popular, or else he promised the least amount of drilling and unpleasant

duty. The practical result of such a system of elected leaders was the creation of unruly and undisciplined soldiers. Davis had made no such promises to obtain the leadership of the Mississippi Regiment, and he pushed the men to their limits and shaped the regiment into a fine fighting unit. Several of the young soldiers wrote home during the first months of enlistment to complain about Davis and his excessive demands regarding drill and discipline, but the letters of complaint became letters of praise when the regiment was placed in peril. The First Mississippi quickly became known as the finest volunteer regiment in Taylor's army, and the resulting praise for Davis that filled newspapers in the United States served to focus national attention on him and move his career from a position of regional to national prominence. Davis and his regiment were put to their sternest test on February 23, 1847, at the battle of Buena Vista. The American defensive positions, taken across Angostura Pass, were thinly manned and outnumbered by the Mexican attackers. When Davis and his Mississippians reached the battlefield that morning they were met with a grim scene: the divisions of Lombardini and Pacheco had turned the American left flank, and defeat was imminent. An American volunteer regiment on the left had bolted in terror from the advancing divisions of Mexican infantry and fled the battlefield. Davis was ordered to place his regiment in the path of the two divisions and stall the Mexican breakthrough until reinforcements could be shifted. All eyes on the battlefield turned toward Davis and his 347 men as they resolutely advanced in good order upon a force of Mexican soldiers estimated by observers to be as large as 5,000 men. The Mississippians withheld fire until they were close to the Mexicans, then delivered a volley into the head of the column that drove it back upon its reserves. The unequal contest continued until enough time could be bought to bring up American reserves. Later in the day, Davis arrayed the Mississippi regiment and the Third Indiana Regiment into a *V* formation which enabled American forces to bring a powerful converging fire to bear on a Mexican cavalry charge. The Mississippi regiment suffered very high casualty rates as a result of its gallantry. Davis was shot through the foot early in the day but refused to leave the field with his painful wound and commanded the regiment throughout the battle.

3. Cadmus Wilcox, *History of the Mexican War* (Washington: Church News Publishing Company, 1892), 610. Col. Henry Whiting was assistant quartermaster-general and was brevetted brigadier general for gallantry at Buena Vista. He died on September 16, 1851.

4. Monroe and McIntosh, *The Papers of Jefferson Davis*, vol. 2, 59. Dr. Seymour Halsey was born in New Jersey in 1802. He had settled in

Vicksburg by the late 1830s, and he joined the First Mississippi Regiment as a private in June 1846. Appointed as a volunteer surgeon by President James K. Polk in October, Halsey was placed in charge of the volunteer division hospital in Monterrey. He was later assigned to the First Mississippi Regiment at Saltillo and served as commander of the smallpox hospital at Monterry in April 1847. Halsey remained in Mexico to treat the sick and wounded after the First Mississippi Regiment returned home and was honorably discharged on July 20, 1848. He returned to Vicksburg where he died on July 16, 1852.

5. National Archives (DNA) Microfilm Series M-863, Records of the Adjutant General's Office, Compiled Service Records, Mexican War, hereafter referred to as Compiled Service Records. Pvt. Thomas J. Ellis, Co. A (The Yazoo Guards), First Mississippi Regiment.

6. Monroe and McIntosh, *The Papers of Jefferson Davis*, vol. 3, 11, 16-19, 250. Col. Jefferson Davis had indeed become vexed at not receiving the shipment of percussion rifles. The shipment had been expected since July when the First Mississippi Regiment had been stationed at New Orleans awaiting transportation to Brazos Island. As a stopgap measure the men had been issued the standard weapon of the Mexican War, the Model 1825 musket, a smoothbore weapon of .69 caliber with a flintlock ignition system. This weapon was suited for the military tactics of the day which required volley firing at close range followed by a charge with the bayonet. Davis, however, believed that his men, who were for the most part hunters and sportsmen, would never rely on the questionable accuracy of a musket and preferred instead the increased range of a rifle and the reliability of a percussion ignition system. The model 1841 percussion cap rifle, mass-produced by Eli Whitney, Jr. at the Whitney Arms Company in Hartford, Connecticut, was the weapon Davis selected for his regiment. The rifles were not fitted for the bayonet, and the Mississippians had to arm themselves with short sabers and Bowie knives for action at close quarters.

7. Executive Document No. 65. Point Isabel was a small village on the Laguna Madre, about five miles northwest of the Brazos Santiago Pass. An extensive supply depot was established there during the war and an earthen fort, Fort Polk, was thrown up around the depot. The only wall of the fort remaining today forms the embankment upon which the lighthouse is situated.

8. Joe Penix, "McClung—Death's Ramrod," *Clarion Ledger*, Jackson, Mississippi, April 3, 10, 17, 1955. A Mississippian, "Sketches of Our Volunteer Officers—Alexander Keith McClung," *Southern Literary Messenger*, vol. 21, 1855. Dunbar Rowland, *Mississippi* (Spartanburg: The Reprint Company Publishers, 1976), vol. 3, 184-85. Alexander Keith

McClung was a man of mystery and excitement who was often found in dangerous situations and seemed to have a penchant for duelling, according to the accounts of his contemporaries. He was born either in Fauquier County, Virginia, in 1811, or Mason County, Kentucky, in 1812, depending upon which source is quoted. His mother was a sister of John Marshall, chief justice of the United States Supreme Court, and his father was related to the Breckenridges of Kentucky. McClung moved to Mississippi from Kentucky in 1832. An ardent Whig, he edited newspapers, served as a federal marshall, and dabbled in state politics. When war with Mexico threatened, McClung organized the Tombigbee Guards and was elected its captain. The Guards became Company K of the First Mississippi Regiment, and McClung was elected lieutenant colonel by the regiment.

On September 21, 1846, the First Mississippi Regiment, as a part of the volunteer division, advanced on the eastern side of Monterrey. The volunteers were placed under a severe cross fire from two forts, Teneria and the Citadel. A sudden lull in cannon fire from Fort Teneria presented an opportunity for attack, but Davis, even with his military training, could not act without an order from a superior officer. McClung, with the daring and instinct of a duelist, was not about to let the laurels of victory slip away through inaction. Leaping in front of his old company, he called to the men, "Charge! Charge! Tombigbee volunteers follow me!" At a saner and more rational time, his men would have probably recognized this as an illegal order, but the volunteers he had raised for this company knew him personally, and the fire in his eyes bespoke action. McClung led the charge on Fort Teneria and was the first American to enter its walls. Minutes later while in the fort, he was felled by a Mexican ball which severely wounded him (see Franklin Smith, December 2, 1846). After recuperation from this wound, McClung returned to Mississippi in 1847 to run for the United States Senate. However his eloquence and the war wounds which caused him to use crutches were not enough, and his Democrat opponent Winfield Scott Featherston was elected. In 1849, President Zachary Taylor appointed McClung chargé d'affaires to Bolivia, but he was soon recalled after he killed an Englishman in a duel. McClung returned to Mississippi, where in 1851 he was again defeated in a bid for a seat in Congress. Over the next few years McClung succumbed to increasingly longer periods of dark melancholia which were accompanied by extended bouts of heavy drinking. He became quarrelsome with friends and incurred heavy debts. Finally, on March 25, 1855, after his application for appointment as colonel of a newly formed regiment of "voltigeurs" was rejected in Washington, he committed suicide in his hotel room in Jackson, Mississippi.

9. Compiled Service Records. Pvt. Spotswood H. Davis, Co. I (Marshall Guards), First Mississippi Regiment.

A poem, "Burial of the Volunteer," written by R. J. of the Marshall Guards, Mi. Vol's, to memorialize the deaths of Pvt. Davis and the other volunteers who died on Brazos Island, appeared in the *Holly Springs Gazette*, Holly Springs, Mississippi, October 3, 1846. The first verse reads as follows:

> *With slow and measured tread we bore*
> *Our comrade to his resting place,*
> *On Santiago's barren shore,*
> *And sorrow sat on every face—*
> *For he, the young and stout of frame*
> *And fearless heart had fallen low,*
> *Without a chance for battle fame,*
> *Before his arm could reach the foe.*

R. J. Of the Marshall Guards, Mi. Vol's.

10. John Frost, *Pictorial History of Mexico and the Mexican War* (Philadelphia: Thomas, Copperwait and Co., 1848), 266-68. Camargo is a small Mexican town situated on the east bank of the Rio San Juan about four miles above the junction of that river and the Rio Grande. Camargo is about 140 miles from Brownsville as the crow flies but is at least twice that far for someone travelling along the Rio Grande. The town consisted of about 2,000 inhabitants in early 1846, but many fled after a disastrous overflow of the Rio San Juan in June 1846 that destroyed a large portion of the town. A volunteer soldier wrote, "The town was once very beautiful; and, from the ruined walls, we saw the houses must have been quite pretty. It contains three plazas, in the middle one of which are situated the finest buildings, and where still stands a neat little church." Camargo became a vast supply depot during the war, and the tents of thousands of American soldiers lined the Rio San Juan on both sides near Camargo.

11. Nathan Brooks, *A Complete History of the Mexican War 1846-1848* (Chicago: The Rio Grande Press Inc., 1965), 92, 96-97. Allen Nevins, *Polk: The Diary of a President 1845-1849* (New York: Longmans, Green and Co., 1952), 162. Tom Lea, *The King Ranch* (Boston: Little, Brown and Company, 1957), vol. 1, 36.

The *Col. Cross* was a river steamer named for Col. Trueman Cross, the deputy quartermaster of General Taylor's forces at Brownsville. Colonel Cross, who left the American camp on April 10, 1846, for a horseback ride, was reported missing by nightfall. His body was found April 19, 1846, and it was rumored among the Mexicans of the area that he had been murdered by a band of men led by Roman Falcon. Colonel Cross was buried near Fort Brown, but his body was later exhumed and transported to Washington, D. C., to be buried there with honors on November 9, 1846. The *Col. Cross* made the fastest passage from the mouth of the Rio Grande to Camargo in 1846-47 of all the steamers, plying the river with a time of sixty-one hours and fifty-five minutes, of which ten hours and fifty-eight minutes were devoted to stops.

12. Wilcox, *Mexican War*, 614; Lea, *King Ranch*, vol. 1, 247. Capt. John Sanders, West Point graduate, Engineer Corps., Bvt. Maj., Monterey. He died on July 29, 1858, at Fort Delaware, Delaware. Capt. Sanders had been sent up the Mississippi Valley to purchase steamboats for the U. S. government to move men and supplies up the Rio Grande. The steamers purchased were: *Hatchee Eagle, Whiteville, Troy, J. E. Roberts, Brownsville, Mentoria, Rough and Ready, Major Brown, Undine, Colonel Cross, Corvette,* and *Telegraph*. In addition, the following steamers were chartered for Rio Grande service: *Big Hatchee, Exchange,* and *W. N. Mercer*. Several additional steamers were chartered at a later date.

13. John Y. Simon, *The Papers of Ulysses S. Grant, 1837-1861* (Carbondale: Southern Illinois University Press, 1967), vol., 1, 99, "To Julia Dent," July 2, 1846. Heavy rains had fallen on the lower Rio Grande watershed during the spring and summer of 1846. Ulysses S. Grant, on duty with the Fourth Infantry, wrote to his future wife from Matamoros on July 2, 1846, "If it is a Paradise where it rains about four hours each day then Matamoras is the place. . . . Matamoras will be very sickly this Summer. The whole of this country is low and flat and for the last six weeks it has rained almost incessantly so that now the whole country is under water."

14. "From the Marshall Guards," *The Holly Springs Gazette*, September 18, 1846. Pvt. William A. Martin, Co. I (the Marshall Guards), First Mississippi Volunteer Regiment.

15. Paul Horgan, *Great River: The Rio Grande in North American History* (New York: Holt, Rinehart, and Winston, 1968), vol. 1, 83-89. The beautiful native palm, *Sabal texana* inspired the Spanish explorer Alonzo de Pineda in 1519 to name this river "Rio de las Palmas" because of abundant stands that fringed the banks of the Rio Grande and reached far inland. By 1846, Franklin Smith noted that the palm forest extended "for twenty miles on the east side of the river." The current range of this beautiful natural resource is less than twenty acres.

16. Executive Document No. 65. Burrita is a small Mexican village situated on the south side of the Rio Grande about ten miles from the mouth of the river. An 1847 map indicates only about eight huts in the village and a small American army camp.

17. Monroe and McIntosh, *The Papers of Jefferson Davis*, vol. 2, 678. Capt. Kemp S. Holland was born in Virginia ca. 1803 and settled in Marshall County, Mississippi, where he served a term as a representative to the state legislature. In June 1846 he was appointed captain and assistant commissary of subsistence for the First Mississippi Regiment. He became ill in Mexico and was granted a leave of absence on November 25, 1846, but he died December 4 on board the steamer *J. E. Roberts*, while descending the Rio Grande. He wa buried at the mouth of the Rio Grande, but later his body was exhumed and buried in Mississippi.

18. Wilcox, *Mexican War*, 639. Capt. William R. Montgomery, West Point graduate, Eighth Infantry, Bvt. Palo Alto and Resaca de la Palma, promoted to Bvt. Lt. Col. after Molino del Rey, wounded at Resaca and Molino; Brig. Gen., Union Army, Civil War. He died May 31, 1871, at Bristol, Pennsylvania.

19. Benjamin Franklin Scribner, *Camp Life of a Volunteer a Campaign in Mexico or a Glimpse of Life in Camp by "One Who Has Seen the Elephant"* (Philadelphia: Grigg, Elliot, and Co., 1847), 43. The rancho was situated about a mile south of the present town of Santa Maria, Texas. This settlement was described as "several thatched huts, a neat little white brick house, and a large cotton press. . . . we found that the buildings were owned by a gentleman from New Orleans. . . . . he sends his cotton into the interior to market." The ruins of the white brick building sit in an open field about a mile from the present banks of the Rio Grande. Written on one outside wall in the stucco is the inscription "Gen. Zachary Taylor's Headquarters, 1845" [*sic*]. It is quite possible that Santa Maria was an evening stopover point for all the steamboats moving up the river from Brownsville, and that General Taylor might have spent a night in this building.

20. "From the Marshall Guards," *The Holly Springs Gazette*, September 18, 1846. Pvt. Joseph Bridges, Co. I (The Marshall Guards), First Mississippi Volunteer Regiment.

21. Compiled Service Record. Pvt. John M. Kincaid, Co. I (The Marshall Guards), First Mississippi Volunteer Regiment.

22. Dumas Malone, *Dictionary of American Biography* (New York: Charles Scribner's Sons, 1933), vol. 14, 306. Maj. Gen. Robert Patterson was born on January 12, 1792, in County Tyrone, Ireland, the son of a revolutionary. His father was banished from Ireland and moved to America, settling in Delaware County, Pennsylvania. Patterson fought in the War of 1812, rising to the rank of colonel in the Pennsylvania militia and later to the rank of captain of the Thirty-second Infantry of

the U. S. Army. He returned to Pennsylvania in 1815 and established himself as a grocer, becoming in time a commission merchant. With the beginning of the Mexican War, he became a major general of volunteers and was left behind to command American troops on the Rio Grande when General Taylor marched on Monterrey from Camargo. In November 1846, Patterson and his forces marched overland from Camargo to Tampico to join forces with General Scott for the invasion of central Mexico. He commanded a division at Cerro Gordo and led the advance into Jalapa. After the war, Patterson acquired extensive holdings in sugar and cotton plantations and owned some thirty cotton mills in Pennsylvania. He served briefly as major general of Union volunteers in 1861 and participated in the battle of Bull Run. He resigned his commission and returned to Pennsylvania, where he died on August 7, 1881.

23. Wilcox, *The Mexican War*, 613. Maj. Abraham Van Buren, West Point graduate, Paymaster, Bvt. Lt. Col. for the battles of Contreras and Churubusco. He died on March 15, 1873 in New York City.

24. Francis B. Heitman, *Historical Register and Dictionary of the United States Army, From Its Organization September 29, 1789, to March 2, 1903* (Urbana: University of Illinois Press, 1965), vol. 1. 265. Archibald W. Burns was born in New Jersey where he enlisted as a volunteer on July 2, 1846, and served as a paymaster. He was honorably discharged on April 1, 1849.

25. Heitman, *Army Register*, vol. 1, 825. Robert B. Reynolds was a native of Tennessee, where he enlisted as a volunteer on June 26, 1846. He served as Capt., A. Q. M., and became a paymaster on March 3, 1847, being promoted to Maj. on March 2, 1849. He resigned his commission on June 23, 1861.

26. Heitman, *Army Register*, vol. 1, 524. John C. Henshaw, who was born in New York, was commissioned a 2d Lt. of the Seventh Infantry in July 1839. He received promotions to 1st Lt. on July 21, 1844, to Capt. on March 3, 1847, and to Bvt. Maj. on August 20, 1847, for gallantry and meritorious conduct at the battles of Contreras and Churubusco. He was discharged on January 9, 1856.

27. Monroe and McIntosh, *The Papers of Jefferson Davis*, vol. 2, 223-24. Maj. Alexander B. Bradford was born in Tennessee in 1790 and served his native state with distinction before moving to Mississippi. In Tennessee he was a lawyer, a senator in the state legislature in 1837, and a major general in the state militia. Bradford entered a volunteer regiment as a private during the Seminole War and was soon elected colonel of the Tennessee regiments. He led a daring charge at the Withlacooche River that brought him fame. Bradford moved to

Holly Springs, Mississippi, in 1839, where he was active in Whig politics and was elected to the state legislature from Marshall County. In 1846 he was elected captain of the Marshall Guards (Co. I, First Mississippi Regiment). When the regiment was organized in Vicksburg, Bradford received a plurality of the votes for colonel, but refused to accept the position unless he was elected by a majority. On subsequent ballots, Jefferson Davis received the majority, and Bradford was elected major. Bradford was noted for his bravery in Mexico, and after the battle of Monterrey wrote a friend, "I was in the fight, saw everything and was exposed fifteen hours to cannon balls, grape canister, and musketry, grazed seven times but escaped unhurt." An admirer of Bradford wrote about him, "The pomp and circumstance of war gave him the purest enjoyment and he had the high personal courage that caused him to love danger for its own sake." Bradford returned to Mississippi after the war and was active in Whig politics, being elected to the state legislature in 1851. In 1861, although he was seventy-one years old, he was suggested as an officer in the Confederate Army. Bradford served the Confederacy, although not in the military, and resumed his law practice after the war in Bolivar County, Mississippi, where he died in 1873.

28. Brooks, *Mexican War*, 163. Reynosa is a Mexican city about seventy miles northwest of Matamoros on the Rio Grande. On June 1, 1846, the Alcalde of Reynosa applied to General Taylor in Matamoros for relief from the ill treatment of the Mexican irregular forces known as "rancheros." Taylor sent the First Infantry, a section of Bragg's battery of artillery, and Price's Texas Rangers to occupy the city. The occupation occurred without opposition on June 4, 1846.

29. Wilcox, *Mexican War*, 611. Capt. Edmund A. Ogden, West Point graduate and Asst. Quartermaster. He died on August 3, 1855, at Fort Riley, Kansas.

30. Monroe and McIntosh, *The Papers of Jefferson Davis*, vol. 3, 43. *The Southron*, Jackson, Mississippi, April 16, 1847. Capt. John L. McManus was born in 1816 and resided in Jackson, Mississippi, before the Mexican War, where he served as clerk of the circuit court. Elected captain of the Jackson Fencibles, which became Co. E of the First Mississippi Regiment, he served with distinction at the battle of Monterrey. Although stricken with illness and unable to lead his company at the battle of Buena Vista, he insisted upon being placed on horseback and aided in defending the camp and wagon park. McManus resigned because of ill health and returned to Jackson greatly enfeebled. "He left the city weighing about one hundred and eighty pounds; he is now

reduced to ninety." He was a resident of Grangeville, Louisiana, at his death in 1895.

31. Wilcox, *Mexican War*, 610. Capt. George H. Crosman, West Point graduate and Quartermaster, was Capt. and Asst. Q. M. July 7, 1838, Maj. and Q. M. March 3, 1847, brevetted for Palo Alto. For his services in the Civil War as Q. M. to the Union Army, he rose to the rank of Bvt. Brig. Gen. and Bvt. Maj. Gen.

32. Malone, *American Biography*, vol. 14, 603. Gideon Johnson Pillow was born in Tennessee on June 8, 1806. He practiced law with James Knox Polk, later president of the United States, and was appointed by him in 1846 as a brigadier general of volunteers. He served under General Taylor, who left Pillow's Brigade behind in Camargo to guard supply lines when the army advanced on Monterrey in August 1946. From Camargo, Pillow was transferred to Scott's army and moved to central Mexico for the invasion of Vera Cruz. Pillow was promoted to major general and was twice wounded in the Mexico City campaign. In 1861, he was appointed senior major general of the Provisional Army of Tennessee and suffered rather disastrous results at the battles of Belmont and Fort Donelson. He was relieved from duty and held no other important command thereafter. The Civil War bankrupted him, and he continued to practice law in Memphis after the war. Pillow died near Helena, Arkansas, on October 8, 1878, and is buried in Memphis.

33. Scribner, *Camp Life of a Volunteer*, 49. Justin Smith, *The War With Mexico* (New York: The Macmillan Company, 1919), vol. 1, 229-30. Cerralvo is a Mexican town about fifty miles southwest of Camargo along the main line of advance of the American army to Monterrey. During the war the town claimed about 1800 citizens. The buildings are mainly of stone with many of the private residences containing formal gardens watered by the many springs of crystal clear cold water that emerge from the ground south of the town and are circulated throughout the city by a system of canals. B. F. Scribner of the Indiana volunteers made the following entry in his diary about Cerralvo; [Dec] 23d. [1846] "We pitched our tents near the old Spanish town of Ceralvo, which bears the impress of an antiquated fortress, and reminds one of the dilapidated castles we read of in romances. The houses are built of gray stone, with loopholes for windows. Through the centre of the town runs a beautiful clear stream, spanned by bridges and arches. There is also a cathedral with chimes and a towering steeple. It is said to be 166 years old."

34. Compiled Service Records. Pvt. Alfred Patton, Co. G (The Raymond Fencibles), First Mississippi Volunteer Regiment.

35. *Diccionario Porrua Historia, Biografia, y Geographia de Mexico*

(Mexico City: Editorial Porrua, 1965), vol. 1, 101. Pedro Ampudia was born in 1805 in Havana, Cuba. He came to Mexico in 1821 and fought against the Spanish, participating in the assault on the St. Juan de Ulloa Castle at Vera Cruz. After Santa Anna deposed Bustamente as president in 1840, Ampudia became a general in the Army of Mexico. He participated with General Woll in an invasion of Texas in 1842 and led the troops that captured Col. William S. Fisher and his Texans at Mier, Mexico, on December 26, 1842. Shifted to southern Mexico, he fought against separatist forces in the Yucatan, commanding the siege of Campeche. During the war with the United States, Ampudia commanded the defenses of the city of Monterrey. After the fall of that city to the Americans he proceeded to San Luis Potosi, where he was appointed quartermaster general of the forces raised by Santa Anna for the defense of Mexico. Ampudia fought at the battle of Buena Vista. After the war, Ampudia was active in politics, becoming governor of the state of Nuevo Leon in 1854. He died in 1868.

36. *Diccionario*, vol. 2, 1577-78. Mariano Paredes y Arrillaga (1797-1849) was the interim president of the Republic of Mexico from January 4, 1846, to July 28, 1846. Balbontin states that General Paredes was overthrown by a party whose members had as their slogan, "Federation and Santa Anna."

37. *Diccionario*, vol. 2, 1922-25. Antonio Lopez de Santa Anna Perez de Lebron was born in Jalapa, Vera Cruz, on February 24, 1794. After a limited education he was apprenticed to a merchant but elected for the life of a soldier and was accepted as a cadet in the Fijo de Vera Cruz Regiment. Santa Anna joined forces with Augustin de Iturbide late in the struggle for independence from Spain, helping to drive the Spanish from Mexico. But shortly thereafter, Santa Anna led a revolt that toppled the government of Iturbide. In 1829 the Spanish attempted to retake Mexico, and Santa Anna led the Mexican army that expelled the invaders. For his services to Mexico, he was elected president in 1832, but he seized control of the government, violating the consitution by assuming dictatorial powers. Several Mexican states revolted, and Santa Anna headed an army to crush the revolts in the states of Zacatecas and Coahuila Y Tejas. Santa Anna's army marched into Texas but was defeated by an army of Texas settlers led by Sam Houston at the battle of San Jacinto on April 21, 1836. Santa Anna was captured by the Texas army and while a prisoner signed a treaty acknowledging the independence of Texas, but the treaty was later rejected by the Mexican Congress. Returning to Mexico, Santa Anna took up arms for his country in 1838 to repulse the French from the city of Vera Cruz, where he lost a leg to a French cannonball. He was elected president of

Mexico again and served from 1841 to 1844, but a revolt against his government forced him to flee the county. In 1846 after war was declared by the United States against Mexico, Santa Anna returned to Mexico from exile. With great energy he quickly organized an army in San Luis Potosi and marched north to oppose the American forces under Gen. Zachary Taylor. The two armies engaged in the battle of Buena Vista on February 23, 1847. Victory was in the grasp of Santa Anna and his men, but the outnumbered and gallant American forces repeatedly blunted the Mexican attacks and at the close of day Taylor's soldiers still held the field. The Mexican forces abandoned the field of battle on February 24, and Santa Anna retreated to San Luis Potosi. Santa Anna continued to command the Mexican army until the fall of Mexico City, when he again fled the country. He returned to Mexico in 1853 and became president of Mexico for the third time but was again overthrown and exiled. After the death of Benito Juarez, Santa Anna was allowed to return to Mexico, where he died in Mexico City in 1874.

38. Wilcox, *Mexican War*, 653. Thomas Marshall was appointed brigadier general of volunteers by President Polk in 1846. Marshall had earlier recruited and organized Kentucky volunteers for the war with Mexico. He died on March 28, 1853, in Kentucky.

39. *Ibid.*, 113-14. Cadmus Wilcox reported seeing these unusual defenses and wrote, "I saw what was reported at the time in the newspapers as General Pillow's fortifications, with the ditch on the inside. Being recently from West Point, with our minds full of what the text books prescribed in such cases, I and my classmates were greatly amused, and one, Lieut. James Stuart of South Carolina, mounted on a Texas mustang, and riding as a fast gallop, leaped both parapet and ditch."

40. J. H. Smith Transcripts, Latin American Collection, University of Texas at Austin, "General Orders," 75. General Patterson's order for noncombatants to leave Camargo by the 17th did not reflect a fear of Mexican attack, but the worry that gamblers, whiskey sellers, prostitutes, and general camp followers would turn Camargo into the type of open town that Matamoros had become. Orders issued from Camargo on October 14, 1846, by General Patterson forbade the movement of goods or persons by steamboat to any points on the Rio Grande without the express approval of an officer. Patterson, for the most part, managed to keep the rowdy American volunteer soldiers and teamsters in check, and Camargo was described by observers in official reports as "peaceful."

41. Thomas Jefferson Green, *Journal of the Texian Expedition Against*

Mier (Austin: The Steck Company, 1935), 82. Mier, a small town about thirty miles west of Camargo, gained fame in the United States as the place where a group of Texan invaders were captured by Mexican forces under Gen. Pedro Ampudia on December 25, 1842. This group of men became known as the Mier prisoners.

42. Dyer, *Zachary Taylor*, 250. Col. Joseph P. Taylor was the chief officer in Mexico for the Department of Commissary and Subsistence of the United States Army. He returned to the United States because of health problems in the middle of 1847. He was the brother of Gen. Zachary Taylor.

43. Monroe and McIntosh, *The Papers of Jefferson Davis*, vol. 2, 602. Col. Bennet Riley was born on November 27, 1787. In the War of 1812, he fought at Sackets Harbor, New York, as an ensign rifleman. A career military officer, he became a second lieutenant in 1814 and a captain in 1818. In 1829 he escorted a large merchant train from St. Louis to Santa Fe and back. He was brevetted colonel for his services in the Black Hawk and Seminole Wars in 1840 and brigadier general and major general for his bravery at Cerro Gordo and Contreras. After the war he commanded the Tenth Military District and was ex officio provisional governor of the state of California. Riley died of cancer in Buffalo, New York, on June 9, 1853. Fort Riley, Kansas, was named in his honor. He is often quoted by Mexican War historians and biographers for his famous quip to his old friend Jefferson Davis, whom he met in the streets of Camargo on August, 1846: "Well my son, here we are again. Good luck to you, my boy! As for me-six feet of Mexican soil, or a yellow sash!" His bravery in Mexico won him the yellow sash of a general officer.

44. Wilcox, *Mexican War*, 630. Capt. James W. Anderson, West Point graduate, Second Regt. Infantry. He died of wounds received at the battle of Churubusco, Mexico.

45. James K. Greer, *Colonel Jack Hays* (New York: E. P. Dutton and Co., 1952), 16-19. John Coffee Hays had four brothers: William Hays, James Hays, Gen. Harry Thompson Hays, and Robert B. Hays. Robert B. Hays, a Texas surveyor and an associate of Col. Jack Hays while he was in Texas, is probably the man Franklin Smith met.

46. *Diccionario*, vol. 1, 345; Green, *Mier Expedition*, 281-88. Antonio Canales (1800?-52?) was a lawyer born in Monterrey, Nuevo Leon. In 1842 he participated in the capture of Texan soldiers who had invaded Mier, and for his brutal treatment of the prisoners became infamous throughout Texas. When war was declared by the United States against Mexico, he formed the rancheros of northern Mexico into a guerilla

band that harassed American supply lines. He became governor of the state of Tamaulipas in 1851.

47. Wilcox, *Mexican War*, 656. Col. Henry R. Jackson, Regiment of Georgia Volunteers.

48. George W. Smith and Charles Judah, *Chronicles of the Gringos* (Albuquerque: The University of New Mexico Press, 1968), 287-89. The Jaspar Greens, a company of the Georgia Volunteer Regiment under the command of Capt. John McMahon, had a well-deserved reputation for violence. On the night of August 31, 1846, while boarding the steamer *Corvette* for passage to Camargo from near the mouth of the Rio Grande, the Greens became involved in a donnybrook. After an exchange of unpleasant remarks, the Greens attacked the Kenesaw Rangers, one of the other companies of the Georgia regiment, with clubs, pistols, and knives. Capt. McMahon drew his sword and rushed into the affray in an attempt to quell the riot, as did Col. Edward Baker and about twenty-five of his men from the Fourth Illinois Regiment. McMahon, who had been drinking, attacked Col. Baker and the two exchanged thrusts. When order had been restored, the casualty list included Capt. McMahon, who had been stabbed through the cheek with a bayonet, Col. Baker, who had been shot in the back of the head, a dead lieutenant, a dead corporal, and a dead private. McMahon was convicted of drunkenness on duty and mutinous conduct but was allowed to keep his sword because of "the palliating character of the testimony."

49. Monroe and McIntosh, *The Papers of Jefferson Davis*, vol. 3, 39. Capt. James H. R. Taylor (c. 1820-67), born in North Carolina, was a lawyer from Holly Springs, Mississippi. Elected captain of Co. I (The Marshall Guards) of the First Mississippi Regiment, he served in that capacity throughout his term of enlistment. Taylor served a term in the state legislature in 1852, then briefly as lieutenant colonel of the Fifteenth Tennessee Infantry in 1861 and returned to Mississippi to be elected to the state senate.

50. Compiled Service Records. Ferdinand Bostick, Co. A (The Yazoo Guards), First Mississippi Volunteer Regiment.

51. Wilcox, *Mexican War*, 637. Capt. Forbes Britton, West Point graduate, Seventh Regt. Infantry. He died on February 14, 1861 in Austin, Texas.

52. Brooks, *Mexican War*, 106. This man was quite possibly Pvt. R. R. Morehead of the First Tennessee Volunteer Regiment, listed as missing in action in the battle of Monterrey. He was probably left behind in Camargo when the regiment moved to Monterrey.

53. Compiled Service Records. Pvt. James Boyd, Co. G (Raymond Fencibles), First Mississippi Volunteer Regiment.

54. Monroe and McIntosh, *The Papers of Jefferson Davis*, vol. 3, 46; Joseph E. Chance, *The Second Texas Infantry—From Shiloh to Vicksburg* (Austin: Eakin Publications, 1984), 13-14, 76. Capt. William P. Rogers, born in Georgia, was raised on a plantation outside of Aberdeen, Mississippi. In Aberdeen, he practiced law and edited a Whig newspaper. He became captain of Co. K, First Mississippi Regiment (The Tombigbee Guards), until the regiment was mustered out in June, 1847. Rogers kept a diary of his experiences while in Mexico which closely agrees with many of the observations reported by Franklin Smith. After the war he was appointed consul to Vera Cruz, resigning the post in 1851 to move to Texas. He practiced law at Washington-on-the-Brazos and later in Houston. As colonel of the Second Texas Infantry, Rogers was killed on October 4, 1862, while leading his regiment on a charge on Union lines at Corinth, Mississippi.

55. Compiled Service Records. Pvt. William R. Rhea, Co. B (The Wilkinson Guards), First Mississippi Regiment.

56. Monroe and McIntosh, *The Papers of Jefferson Davis*, vol. 3, 31. Douglas Hancock Cooper (1815-79) was a Wilkinson County, Mississippi, planter and attorney who was elected captain of Co. B (The Wilkinson Guards) of the First Mississippi Regiment. After the Mexican War, he became federal agent to the Choctaw Indians in 1853. He was Confederate superintendent of Indian affairs and in 1863 became a brigadier general in the Confederate Army. After the Civil War, he resided at Fort Washita.

57. Wilcox, *Mexican War*, 688. Capt. George W. McCowan, Second Regiment of Tennessee Volunteers.

58. *Ibid.*, 626. Capt. Thomas W. Sherman, West Point graduate, Third Regiment of Artillery, Bvt. Maj. Buena Vista; Brig. Gen., Union Army, Civil War. He died on March 16, 1879, at Newport, Rhode Island.

59. *Ibid.*, 682. Maj. William Wall, Second Regiment of Ohio Volunteers.

60. *Ibid.*, 612. Capt. Amos B. Eaton, West Point graduate, Dept. of Commissaries and Subsistence, Bvt. Maj. Buena Vista; Brig. Gen. Sub., Union Army, Civil War. He died on February 21, 1877 in New Haven, Connecticut.

61. *Ibid.*, 671. Lt. Col. William H. Watson led the Battalion of Maryland and District of Columbia volunteers in the attack on the eastern side of Monterrey on September 21, 1846, where he was killed.

62. Walter P. Webb, *The Handbook of Texas* (Austin: The Texas State Historical Association, 1952), vol. 1, 690. John R. Kenly, *Memoirs of a*

Maryland Volunteer (Philadelphia: J. B. Lippincott and Co., 1873), 171-72. Richard Addison Gillespie was born in Kentucky and moved to Texas in 1837. In Texas, Gillespie was noted as an Indian fighter. He was a member of Jack Hays's ranger company and was wounded in the battle of Walker's Creek in June 1844. In the Mexican War, he led the Hays Regiment of Rangers overland from San Antonio to capture Laredo and took the men on from there to capture Mier in July 1846. Gillespie was killed leading the charge on the Bishop's Palace at Monterrey on September 21, 1846. He was buried near where he fell, but his body was later moved to San Antonio, Texas, and reburied in the Odd Fellows Cemetary. The other bodies moved to Maryland for reburial included Herman Thomas of Hartford County, Maryland, and George Pearson of Baltimore, Maryland, soldiers in the Baltimore Battalion. The commanding officer of the Baltimore Battalion, William H. Watson, of Baltimore, and the daring artillery officer Randolph Ridgely completed the complement of bodies being sent home.

63. Malone, *American Biography*, vol. 3, 371-72. William Orlando Butler was born in Jessamin County, Kentucky, on April 19, 1791. He graduated from Transylvania College in 1812, and when war was declared he joined the army as a private. He took part in the battle at the River Raisin on January 18 and 22, 1813, where he was captured by the British. Butler was exchanged and returned to Kentucky, where he raised a company which he led under Andrew Jackson against Pensacola. His bravery at the battle of New Orleans won the unstinted praise of Jackson and a brevet majorship. Butler resigned from the army in 1817 to study law. In 1846 he was appointed major general of volunteers by President Polk and was second in command to General Taylor at the battle of Monterrey. He received a leg wound during the action in the streets of Monterrey on September 21, 1846, and returned home to Kentucky to recuperate. Later he joined General Scott's army and was present for the capture of Mexico City. In 1848 he was the Democratic candidate for vice-president of the United States, but his ticket, led by Lewis Cass, was defeated. He died in Carrollton, Kentucky, on August 6, 1880.

64. Malone, *American Biography*, vol. 20, 513-14. Gen. John Ellis Wool was born in Newburgh, New York, on February 29, 1784. An orphan with little formal education, he raised a company of volunteers in Troy, New York, when the War of 1812 was declared. On April 14, 1812, he was commissioned a captain in the Thirteenth Infantry. He was severely wounded at the battle of Queenstown and was promoted to major in the Twenty-ninth Infantry on April 13, 1813. For bravery at Plattsburg, Wool was promoted to brevet lieutenant colonel, and on

April 29, 1816, was again promoted to the rank of colonel and inspector general of the army. For ten years of service in one grade, he was promoted to brevet brigadier general on April 29, 1826. At the outset of war with Mexico in 1846, he was ordered to Cincinnati where he prepared and mustered in 12,000 volunteers in six weeks. On August 14, 1846, Wool arrived in San Antonio to lead his command on an invasion of the Mexican state of Chihuahua. He led a force of 1,400 men on a 900-mile march through enemy country, arriving at Saltillo on December 22, 1846. Wool served gallantly at the battle of Buena Vista and was voted a sword by Congress "for his distinguished services in the War with Mexico and especially for the skill, enterprise and courage" at Buena Vista. He was promoted to brevet major general for his heroism. He retired on August 1, 1863, and died on November 10, 1869, in Troy, New York.

65. *Ibid.*, vol. 17, 106-7. James Shields was born on May 12, 1806, in Altmore, County Tyrone, Ireland. He received a good education in Ireland but yearned for adventure and came to America in 1826. He settled in Kaskaskia, Illinois, where he participated in Democratic politics and practiced law. In 1836, he served in the state legislature, and he was later state auditor. He served efficiently, but Whig criticism of his office caused him to challenge Abraham Lincoln to a duel. The duel was never fought and the two men became good friends. Shields was named to the supreme court of Illinois and was later appointed by President Polk to a commisionship of the general land office in Washington, which he resigned upon the declaration of war with Mexico. He was commissioned brigadier general of Illinois volunteers. For gallantry at the battle of Cerro Gordo, where he was seriously wounded, Shields was promoted to brevet major general. At Churubusco, he led the charge of New York Irish and South Carolina volunteers. After the war, he was elected to the United States Senate from Illinois. Lyman Trumbull defeated his bid for re-election in a closely fought race, and he moved to Minnesota to settle on his land grant. He was appointed brigadier general of volunteers on August 19, 1861, and led Federal troops in the Shenandoah Valley, gaining recognition at Winchester and Port Republic. He resigned his commission on March 28, 1863. Shields died on June 1, 1879, while on a lecture tour at Ottumwa, Iowa.

66. Horgan, *Rio Grande*, vol. 2, 713, 782. The *Major Brown*, named for Maj. Jacob Brown, who was killed in the siege of Fort Texas, not only ascended the rapids but continued on to Laredo with a complement of supplies for the garrison there. Shortly after the steamer's

arrival, the depth of the water in the Rio Grande lowered and the *Major Brown* remained trapped at Laredo for two years.

67. Wilcox, *Mexican War*, 610. Capt. George Lincoln, Asst. Adj. Gen., Bvt. Capt., Palo Alto and Resaca de la Palma. He was killed at the battle of Buena Vista on February 23, 1847, while heroically attempting to rally volunteer troops to make a stand against advancing Mexican forces.

68. *Ibid.*, 630. Lt. Schuyler Hamilton, West Point graduate, First Regt. Infantry, Bvt. 1st Lt. and Capt., Monterrey and Mill Flores; Maj. Gen., Union Army, Civil War.

69. The "New Camargo" referred to by Franklin Smith is known locally as "Villa Nueva." The deserted village of stone and adobe buildings is located about two miles southwest of Camargo on a hill above the floodplain of the Rio San Juan and on the west side of that river.

70. Smith and Judah, *Gringos*, 287. Lt. Col. Thomas Y. Redd, Regiment of Georgia Volunteers.

71. Webb, *Handbook of Texas*, vol. 1, 962. Col. Henry L. Kinney was born near Shusshequin, Pennsylvania, on June 3, 1814. He moved to Texas in 1838, settling at Brownsville. By 1841 he was engaged in ranching and trading at Corpus Christi, a town he helped to found. Gen. James Pinckney Henderson appointed Kinney to the staff of Texas volunteer officers, and he served in northern Mexico during the first part of the Mexican War. At the close of the war, Kinney returned to Corpus Christi, where he conducted a lucrative trading operation involving many ships and a fleet of wagons. Kinney served as a senator in the state legislature for the first four sessions. In 1854 he went to Nicaragua on a filibustering expedition. With the backing of New York financiers, Kinney contracted for 30 million acres of land for which he had pledged to pay $500,000. He hoped to establish an empire with a new form of government, but all his plans failed and his main financial backer withdrew his support. Kinney returned to Texas where he was elected to the state legislature, but he resigned in March 1861 because he was opposed to secession.

72. Roger T. Peterson, *A Field Guide to the Birds of Texas and Adjacent States* (Boston: Houghton Mifflin Company, 1963), 69. The sighting of bald eagles (*Haliaeetus leucocephalus*) south of Camargo is a rare event for contemporary bird watchers.

73. *Ibid.*, 75. The birds sighted were either Gambel's quail (*Lophortyx gambelli*) or the scaled quail (*Callipepla squamata*).

74. Robert Lonard, *The Woody Plants of the Lower Rio Grande Valley, Texas* (Austin: The Texas Memorial Museum Press, 1990), 140-41. The

Capsicum annuum var. *minus* or chile piquin, grows in abundant supply throughout the Rio Grande Valley of Texas and is used to add zest to insipid foods.

75. Wilcox, *Mexican War*, 637. Lt. Lewis A. Armistead, West Point graduate, Sixth Regt. Infantry, Bvt. Capt. and Maj., Contreras, Churubusco, and Molina del Rey, wounded at Chapultepec; Brig. Gen., C. S. A. He was killed July 3, 1863, at the battle of Gettysburg, Pennsylvania.

76. *Ibid.*, 671. Lt. Benjamin F. Owen, Battalion of Maryland and District of Columbia Volunteers.

77. Charles D. Spurlin, *Texas Veterans in the Mexican War* (Nacogdoches: Erickson Books, 1984), 208. Stephen Smith, age twenty-two, is listed on the muster roll of Captain Shivors's company, Texas Foot Volunteers, as a private.

78. Peterson, *A Field Guide*, 124, 233. This bird is thought to be either the groove-billed ani (*Crotophaga sulcirostris*) or the boat-tailed grackle (*Cassidix mexicanus*).

79. Edward Nichols, *Zach Taylor's Little Army* (Garden City: Doubleday and Company Inc., 1963), 150. Stephen Smith was probably describing the death of nine volunteers from the First Tennessee Regiment who were killed by a single cannonball fired from the Citadel, a Mexican fort north of Monterrey.

80. Malone, *American Biography*, vol. 10, 135-36. Albert Sidney Johnston was born on February 2, 1803, in Washington, Mason County, Kentucky. He attended schools in western Virginia and Transylvania University. Appointed to West Point in 1822, he graduated with honors in mathematics in 1825 and was commissioned a second lieutenant. He resigned his commission on April 24, 1834, because of his wife's health. After her death in 1835, he joined the Republic of Texas Army as a private. He was appointed adjutant general, and by his seniority he assumed command of the Texas army on January 31, 1837. Felix Huston, jealous of Johnston's position of command, challenged him to a duel. Both parties fired five shots from dueling pistols without injury, but a sixth exchange struck Johnston in the right hip, inflicting a serious wound. On December 22, 1838, he was appointed secretary of war for the Republic of Texas. When war was declared against Mexico, Johnston was commissioned colonel of the First Texas Rifle Volunteers, and he served at Monterrey under General Butler as inspector general. After the Mexican War, he was recommissioned in the United States Army and in 1858 served as brevet brigadier general to quell the Mormon uprising in Utah, which he was able to do without resorting to force. Johnston resigned his commission in the United States Army, was appointed general in the

Confederate Army, and took command of the Western Department. He was killed in the battle of Shiloh on April 6, 1862, and is buried in Austin, Texas.

81. Henry Barton, *Texas Volunteers in the Mexican War* (Waco: Texian Press, 1970), 49-50; Alexander Lander, *A Trip to the Wars Comprising the History of the Galveston Riflemen, Formed April 28, 1846, at Galveston, Texas; Together With The History of the Battle of Monterey; Also, Descriptions of Mexico and its People* (Monmouth: Illinois, printed at the "Atlas" Office, 1847), 79-81. William R. Shivors, a Mississippian, was looking eagerly for a fight. In Mississippi he was a member of the Claiborne Rifles, one of the many volunteer militia companies that converged on Vicksburg in June 1846, hoping to be selected to serve in the First Mississippi Regiment. From the 18,000 eager volunteers, only about 1,000 were selected, and the Rifles was one of the companies that failed the final muster. The Rifles travelled to Galveston at their own expense and on June 20 were mustered in as Company K of the First Regiment of Texas Foot Rifles. After many adventures (including the "killing of a rattlesnake while at Point Isabel that was thirteen feet four inches long and weighed 35 pounds"), the regiment arrived at Camargo on August 28. As three-month volunteers, the regiment's term of enlistment had expired, and to their colonel's amazement, most of the men refused to re-enlist. William Shivors quickly assembled eighty-two men from the defunct regiment who still wanted to fight and formed an independent company. When Shivors approached General Taylor to inquire if the company could be mustered in, the answer was, "'Yes—yes—I will take all such men as these.—Egads! they're all captains.' He then called his son-in-law, a surgeon of the regular army, and told him to inspect the company; and he didn't care if he reported that they all had consumption— he would 'take 'em any how.'"

82. Malone, *American Biography*, vol. 20, 536-37. William Jenkins Worth was born in Hudson, Columbia County, New York, on March 1, 1794. He received a common school education and was in the mercantile business when the War of 1812 began. He was appointed first lieutenant in the Twenty-third Infantry and was selected by Gen. Winfield Scott as his aide-de-camp. Worth fought with great valor at Chippewa and Lundy's Lane, receiving a serious wound in the latter battle. The wound, at first thought to be fatal, kept him confined to his bed for a year and left him lame for the remainder of his life. At the rank of brevet major, Worth became commandant of the United States Military Academy, a post that he held from 1820 to 1828. He was promoted to colonel in 1838 and assumed command of the Eighth Infantry, which fought with valor in the Seminole War. He led the

American division that captured the heights on the western side of Monterrey and was promoted to brevet major general on September 23, 1846, for this action. Worth was awarded a sword by Congress on March 2, 1847, for his gallantry at Monterrey. He was transferred to Scott's army and fought in all the battles in central Mexico from Vera Cruz to Mexico City, always exhibiting great skill and personal initiative. After the war he was placed in command of the Department of Texas. He died from cholera on May 7, 1849.

83. Monroe and McIntosh, *The Papers of Jefferson Davis*, vol. 3, 77; Wilcox, *Mexican War*, 669. Balie Peyton was born in Tennessee in 1803 and educated to be an attorney. He served as a Whig congressman from 1833 to 1837. Peyton was living in New Orleans and practicing law when the Mexican War began. He joined the Fifth Regiment of Smith's Brigade of Louisiana Volunteers as a colonel and waited out his three-month term of enlistment in the camps along the Rio Grande without seeing any action. Still eager to fight, he became a volunteer aide-de-camp to General Worth and participated in the battle of Monterrey. Peyton died in Nashville, Tennessee, on August 19, 1878.

84. Wilcox, *Mexican War*, 666. Col. William R. McKee, West Point graduate, Second Regiment of Kentucky Volunteers. He was killed February 23, 1847, at the battle of Buena Vista.

85. Joseph M. Nance, *After San Jacinto* (Austin: University of Texas Press, 1963), 251. The Federalist forces of Antonio Zapata arrived in the border town of Guerrero (now under Falcon Lake) on January 7, 1840, and Zapata "found two of men, a *gauchupin* by the name of Jefferys . . . and a Mexican by the name of Mandeole [*sic*], who had deserted a day or two before. Both men were exacting a money contribution from the inhabitants of the town; and when questioned about their conduct; declared that they had been sent there by Canales to collect funds for the army. Zapata, however, placed them under arrest until he left the place."

86. Wilcox, *Mexican War*, 687. Capt. William R. Caswell, Regt. of Tennessee Mounted Volunteers.

87. *Ibid.*, 616. Lt. Thomas J. Brereton, West Point graduate, Ordnance Dept., Bvt. 1st Lt., Palo Alto and Resaca de la Palma. He died on September 18, 1870, in Yonkers, New York.

88. Heitman, *Register*, vol. 1, 452. Richard D. Gholson was a native of Kentucky and volunteered for the military on June 26, 1846. He was a Capt., A. C. S., and was honorably discharged on June 30, 1847.

89. Wilcox, *Mexican War*, 613. Maj. George A. McCall, West Point graduate, Third Regt. Infantry, Bvt. Lt. Col., Palo Alto and Resaca de la

Palma; Maj. Gen., Union Army, Civil War. He died on February 25, 1868, in West Chester, Pennsylvania.

90. *Ibid.*, 682. Col. George A. Morgan, West Point graduate, Second Regt. Ohio Volunteers and Fifteenth Regt. Infantry, Bvt. Brig. Gen., Contreras and Churubusco; Brig. Gen., Union Army, Civil War.

CHAPTER 2: *October 15–November 7, 1846*

1. Peterson, *Field Guide*, 169. The white-necked or Chihuahuan raven (*Corvus cryptoleucus*) is widely seen in southern Texas and northern Mexico.

2. Wilcox, *Mexican War*, 618. Ripley A. Arnold, West Point graduate, Second Regt. Dragoons, Bvt. Palo Alto and Resaca de la Palma. He was murdered September 6, 1853, in Fort Graham, Texas.

3. *Ibid.*, 659. Col. Edward Dickinson Baker, Fourth Illinois Volunteer Regt.; Maj. Gen., Union Army, Civil War. He was killed October 21, 1861, at the battle of Balls Bluff, Virginia.

4. *Ibid.*, 613. Maj. Robert H. Hammond, Paymaster. He died June 2, 1847.

5. *Ibid.*, Maj. Andrew J. Coffee, West Point graduate, Paymaster, Bvt. Lt. Col., Buena Vista.

6. Monroe and McIntosh, *The Papers of Jefferson Davis*, vol. 2, 672. Capt. Reuben Downing, a clerk of the Hinds County, Mississippi, circuit court from 1843 to 1847. He was elected captain of the Raymond Fencibles, Co. G of the First Mississippi Regiment on June 2, 1846. He had previously served in the state militia as captain (1841) and colonel (1845). During the battle of Monterrey he was wounded in the right arm and hospitalized. He received a medical leave of absence, and returned to his company in February 1847 in time to participate in the battle of Buena Vista. He returned to Hinds County, Mississippi, after the war.

7. Wilcox, *Mexican War*, 630. Maj. George W. Allen, Second Regt. Infantry, Bvt. Lt. Col., Palo Alto and Resaca de la Palma. He died on March 15, 1848.

8. *Ibid.*, 633. Maj. Gouverner Morris, West Point graduate, Fourth Regt. Infantry, Bvt. Maj., Palo Alto and Resaca de la Palma. He died on October 18, 1846.

9. *Ibid.*, 618. Capt. Charles A. May, Bvt. Maj., Lt. Col. and Col., Palo Alto, Resaca de la Palma and Buena Vista. He died on December 24, 1864.

10. J. Lee and Lillian J. Stambaugh, *The Lower Rio Grande Valley of Texas* (Austin: The Jenkins Publishing Co., 1974), 89. Henry Clay

Davis was born in Kentucky and came to Texas in 1833. After the Texas Revolution, he lived in Camargo, Mexico. While there he married Maria Hilaria de la Garza, granddaughter of Francisco de la Garza Martinez, and came into possession of Porcion 80, a grant of land which came to be known as Rancho Davis. Davis built a two-story brick home on the site, which overlooked the Rio Grande River. The settlement that he established would later come to be known as Rio Grande City.

11. Wilcox, *Mexican War*, 682. Charles O. Joline, Adjutant, Second Regt. Ohio Volunteers; Maj., Union Army, Civil War. He died on February 15, 1885.

12. Webb, *Handbook of Texas*, vol. 1, 795–96. James Pinckney Henderson was born in Lincolnton, North Carolina, on March 31, 1808. He attended Lincoln Academy and the University of North Carolina and was admitted to the North Carolina Bar to practice law in 1829. Henderson came to Texas in June 1836, was commissioned as a brigadier general, and was sent back to the United States to recruit soldiers for the Republic of Texas Army. He returned to Texas leading a company of North Carolina volunteers in November 1836. Under the Republic of Texas, Henderson served as attorney general, secretary of state, and minister to England and France. In 1844, Henderson was sent to Washington with Isaac Van Zandt to negotiate a treaty of annexation with the United States which was later rejected by the United States Senate. He was elected governor of Texas in November 1845. When the Mexican War was declared, Henderson took personal command of the Texas volunteers in the field while he was still governor and delegated the duties of the office to his lieutenant governor. He led the Second Texas Mounted Regiment at the battle of Monterrey and was appointed by General Taylor as one of the commissioners to negotiate for the surrender of the city. Henderson was later appointed a major general in the United States Army. He returned to Texas after the war to practice law and was appointed by the legislature in 1857 to serve the unexpired term of Thomas J. Rusk in the United States Senate. He died in Washington, D. C., on June 4, 1858, and is buried in the state cemetery in Austin, Texas.

13. Compiled Service Records. Pvt. William I. Wilkinson, Co. B (The Wilkinson Guards), First Mississippi Volunteer Regiment. He was killed at the battle of Buena Vista, February 23, 1847.

14. *Ibid.*, Pvt. W. T. S. Durham, Co. D. (The Carroll County Guards), First Mississippi Volunteer Regiment. He was discharged for disabilities on October 12, 1846, in Monterrey, Mexico.

15. Webb, *Handbook of Texas*, vol. 2, 119; Barton, *Texas Volunteers*,

25, 26; Lander, *A Trip to the Wars*, 12, 19. Ephraim W. McLane was born in Christian County, Kentucky, in 1816, and came to Texas in 1836. He bought the schooner *Columbia*, which he ran between Velasco and New Orleans until she was wrecked in 1837. In 1838 he joined an expedition to search for a reported silver mine in the Washita Mountains. McLane served in the Texas Rangers and at the beginning of the Mexican War organized the Galveston Riflemen, who elected him captain. The Riflemen formed a company of Col. A. S. Johnston's First Regiment of Foot Rifles. Johnston's regiment was enlisted to serve for ninety days, and by the time they reached Camargo in August 1846, their period of enlistment had expired. McLean joined Captain Shivor's independent company and served at the battle of Monterrey with distinction. After the war he joined the gold rush to California and is said to have built the first lighthouse in the San Francisco harbor. McLean returned to Galveston, where he died on January 31, 1896.

16. Compiled Service Records. Pvt. Marcellus A. Foute, Co. E (The Jackson Fencibles), First Mississippi Volunteer Regiment. He was discharged for disability on October 12, 1846, in Monterrey, Mexico.

17. Wilcox, *Mexican War*, 630. Maj. Carlos A. Waite, Second Regt. Infantry, Bvt. Lt. Col. and Col., Contreras, Churubusco and Molino del Rey; Col., Union Army, Civil War. He died May 7, 1866.

18. Hudson Strode, *Jefferson Davis: American Patriot 1808–1861* (New York: Harcourt, Brace and Company, 1955), 172–74. Col. Jefferson Davis was returning to Mississippi to attend to domestic problems. While at Monterrey his wife, Varina Howell Davis, had written him a letter describing the "alarming condition" of her health. Fearing the worst, Davis received a sixty-day furlough and rushed to her side. She had mysteriously recovered by the time Davis had completed the arduous three-week journey to Mississippi. Some biographers feel that her illness was brought on by the discovery that Davis had included his two sisters and his brother Joseph in his will to share his estate with Varina. Her indignation over this discovery and her growing dislike for Joseph Davis (in whose home she lived as a guest while Colonel Davis was away in Mexico) probably brought on the illness.

19. Monroe and McIntosh, *The Papers of Jefferson Davis*, vol. 2, 24. Capt. John Willis was born June 30, 1819, in Vicksburg, Mississippi. The son of a prominent state politician, Willis was educated at Transylvania College in Kentucky and the College of New Jersey (now Princeton). In May 1846, he was elected captain of the Vicksburg Southrons, the militia company which became Co. G of the First Mississippi Regiment. He participated in the battle of Monterrey and shortly thereafter

received a furlough to return home. Captain Willis returned to Mexico in January 1847 but contracted pneumonia and arrived too late to participate in the battle of Buena Vista. Willis returned to Vicksburg after the Mexican War and lived there until 1874, when he moved to Panther Burn, a plantation in northwest Sharkey County, Mississippi. He died there on January 16, 1906.

20. *Ibid.*, vol. 3, 24–76; Wilcox, *Mexican War*, 93–100; Grady and Sue McWhiney, *To Mexico With Taylor and Scott 1845–1847* (Waltham: Charles Scribner's Sons, 1969), 50–71. The attack of September 21, 1846, on the eastern side of Monterrey had been a mismanaged affair. A brigade of the First, Third, and a portion of the Fourth regiment and the Washington and Baltimore Battalion were led into a street surrounded by stone buildings from which a heavy fire was poured on them. A large casualty list, especially among the officers, resulted. The Mississippi, Tennessee, and Ohio volunteer regiments were a bit luckier and faced off against Fort Teneria, a four-gun earthen lunette. A spontaneous charge led by Lt. Col. A. K. McClung and the men of the First Mississippi captured Fort Teneria. Colonel Davis then tried in vain to organize an attack against Rincon del Diablo, a two-gun earthen fort to the east of the captured Teneria. Davis and a small party of Mississippians moved so close to Diablo that the defenders could not depress the cannons to fire upon them. Davis was awaiting the arrival of the remainder of his regiment, which he had ordered forward, when he received a confused order from General Hamer, the volunteer division commander, to retreat from his advantageous position.

21. David C. Roller and Robert W. Twyman, editors, *The Encyclopedia of Southern History* (Baton Rouge: Louisiana State University Press, 1979), 1026–27. John Randolph, or John Randolph of Roanoake, was a brilliant orator and politician from Virginia who served eleven terms in the House of Representatives and one term in the Senate. He became the principal spokesman for southern sectionalism and agrarian interests. Randolph was appointed minister to Russia in 1830–31. "He had a mordant wit and erratic personality that was the consequence of a disease which plunged him into periods of insanity."

22. Malone, *American Biography*, vol. 12, 34–36. George McDuffie was born August 10, 1790, in Columbus County, Georgia. He graduated from South Carolina College in 1813 with a reputation as a debater and orator. He served two terms in the South Carolina legislature and in 1821 began a career as a representative in the United States Congress. In 1834 he resigned his seat to become governor of South Carolina and capped his political career with a term in the United States Senate from 1842 to 1846. "In Congress he quickly acquired

reputation as a ready, eloquent, and sensational debater, and the news that he intended speaking rarely failed to fill the galleries. His speeches, usually extemporaneous, were always delivered as if he were in a frenzy of passion. They were characterized by their noise and fury, extravagance of phrase, and denunciatory quality, though on occasions he could also be persuasive. His voice was fine and powerful, his memory unfailing, his face expressive, his fluency never failed, and always he 'pounded the air with his fists.'" McDuffie died on March 11, 1851, on his plantation Cherry Hill in the Sumter District of South Carolina.

23. Horgan, *Rio Grande*, vol. 2, 703–4. The *American Flag* was a newspaper published in Matamoros whose first issue appeared two weeks after the American occupation of that city. The publisher, Gen. Hugh McCleod, originally titled the newspaper *The Republic of the Rio Grande And The People's Friend*. His avowed intention was trying to persuade "the people of the states of Tamaulipas, Nuevo Leon, Coahuila, and Chihuahua to an appreciation of the merits of a separate Northern Mexican federation." This bilingual journal failed and was sold to new owners who renamed it the *American Flag*. The biweekly publication of this newspaper continued for two more years in Matamoros.

24. Heitman, *Register*, vol. 1, 868. Henry Scott, a native of New York, was commissioned a volunteer Capt., A. C. S., from Illinois. He was honorably discharged on June 30, 1847.

25. Wilcox, *Mexican War*, 612. Presley H. Craig, surgeon, died August 8, 1848.

26. *Who's Who In America: Historical Volume 1607–1896* (Chicago: A. N. Marquis Co., 1963), 198. Rice Garland was a prominent congressman, judge, and attorney from Louisiana. He was born in Lynchburg, Virginia, about 1795, and served in the 23–26 Congresses of the United States as representative from Louisiana and as a judge of the Louisiana Supreme Court from 1840–46. He practiced law in Brownsville, Texas, from 1846–61 and died there in 1861.

27. Wilcox, *Mexican War*, 621. Capt. Stephens T. Mason, Regiment of Mounted Rifles. He died of wounds received at the battle of Cerro Gordo, Mexico, May 15, 1847.

28. Webb, *Handbook of Texas*, vol. 2, 854. Capt. Samuel H. Walker was born in Maryland about 1810. He fought in the Indian Wars in Georgia and Florida, and went to Texas in 1836. In 1839 he was sent to New York to negotiate the purchase of arms for the Republic of Texas. He met with Samuel Colt and suggested several modifications of the existing model of revolver. The modified revolver developed by Colt became known as the Walker Colt. Walker fought against Woll's invasion of Texas in 1842 and in December 1842 was captured by the

Mexicans at Mier. Walker joined Gen. Zachary Taylor on the Rio Grande as a scout in April 1846 and performed valuable services before the battle of Palo Alto. He fought at the battle of Monterrey in operations against the west side of the city with General Worth's division. Walker transferred to Scott's army and was active in central Mexico against Mexican guerrillas. Walker was killed while leading a charge into Huamantla, Tlaxcala, on October 9, 1847. He is buried in San Antonio, Texas.

29. Wilcox, *Mexican War*, 621. Lt. Thomas G. Rhett, West Point graduate, Regiment of Mounted Rifles, Bvt. Capt., Puebla; Maj., C. S. A.. He died on July 28, 1878, in Baltimore. Maryland.

30. *Ibid.*, Capt. Andrew Porter, West Point graduate, Regiment of Mounted Rifles, Bvt. Maj. and Lt. Col., Contreras, Churubusco, and Chapultepec; Brig. Gen., Union Army, Civil War. He died on January 4, 1872.

31. Bruce Catton, *Michigan: a Bicentennial History* (New York: W. W. Norton and Co., 1976), 90. George B. Porter was appointed territorial governor of Michigan by President Andrew Jackson. Porter died in 1834.

32. Compiled Service Records. Cpl. John B. Markham, Co. C (The Vicksburg Southrons), First Mississippi Volunteer Regiment. He was severely wounded at the battle of Monterrey and was discharged Oct. 20, 1846. Lt. Hugh M. Markham, Co. H (The Vicksburg Volunteers), First Mississippi Volunteer Regiment. He resigned October 19, 1846.

33. *Ibid.*, Either Pvt. Walter A. Thompson, Co. I, or Pvt. William Thompson, Co. F, First Mississippi Volunteer Regiment.

34. Monroe and McIntosh, *The Papers of Jefferson Davis*, vol. 2, 160. Fulton Anderson was a Jackson, Mississippi attorney.

35. Catton, *Michigan*, 62–63. Gen. Isaac Hull, in the early stages of the War of 1812, led American volunteers from Detroit across the St. Claire River to destroy a British post in Malden. The attack faltered, and the American party recrossed the river to Detroit only to be followed by the British forces under the command of Maj. Gen. Sir Isaac Brock. Hull complied with the British demand for the surrender of Detroit, and the city was handed over to the British on August 16, 1812.

36. Webb, *Handbook of Texas*, vol. 2, 13–14; Monroe and McIntosh, *The Papers of Jefferson Davis*, vol. 3, 66. Gen. Mirabeau B. Lamar was born near Louisville, Georgia, on August 16, 1789. He served as secretary to Gov. George M. Troup, edited the *Enquirer*, a Columbus, Georgia, newspaper, and was elected to one term as a state senator in Georgia. After a brief trip to Texas in 1835, he returned to Georgia to

settle his affairs and moved to Texas. He joined the Texas army as a private and as a result of his gallantry and heroism rose to the rank of colonel and commanded the cavalry. Lamar was elected the first vice-president of the Republic of Texas and the second president. Lamar's term of office as president is probably best remembered for his proposal to establish a system of public education endowed by public lands, which was enacted on January 26, 1839. In the Mexican War he served as inspector and adjutant for J. Pinckney Henderson's Texas division. Lamar served gallantly at Monterrey, and his service was remembered fondly by Jefferson Davis in a speech delivered three decades later: "At Monterey, with a bright red vest, heedless of danger, [Lamar] rushed into the thickest of the fray, and, with the cry of 'Brave boys, Americans are never afraid!', at the head of the gallant Second regiment, charged home to victory. He was an ideal Texan—a man of rare genius and tender affection."

37. Wilcox, *Mexican War*, 610. Col. George Croghan, Inspector General. He died on January 8, 1849.

38. *Ibid.*, Capt. Randolph Ridgely, West Point graduate, Asst. Adjutant General, Bvt. Capt., Palo Alto and Resaca de la Palma. He died on October 27, 1846, at Monterrey, Mexico.

39. *Ibid.*, 634; Horgan, *Rio Grande*, vol. 2, 67. Lt. Theodoric Porter, West Point graduate, Fourth Regiment Infantry. He was killed April 19, 1846, by Mexican guerrillas near the present city of Brownsville, Texas.

40. Wilcox, *Mexican War*, 630. Maj. William A. Graham, West Point graduate, Second Regt. Infantry. He was killed September 8, 1847, at the battle of Molino del Rey, Mexico.

41. *Ibid.*, 614; Justin Smith, *Mexican War*, vol. 1, 451. Capt. Alexander J. Swift, West Point graduate, Engineer Corps. He died April 24, 1847, in New Orleans, Louisiana. Justin Smith reported that Swift, with a complement of ten sergeants, ten corporals, thirty-nine artificers, thirty-nine second-class privates, and two musicians had been sent to Metz, France, at the outbreak of war with Mexico to study the French army's Corp of Engineers.

42. Webb, *Handbook of Texas*, vol. 2, 929. Capt. George T. Wood was born in Randolph County, Georgia, on March 12, 1795. At the age of nineteen he organized a militia company that fought in the Creek Indian War at Horseshoe Bend. Wood came to Texas in 1839, locating in the present San Jacinto County, where he operated a large plantation. He was a state senator in 1845. When the Mexican War began, Wood resigned from the senate and organized the Second Texas Mounted Volunteers, who fought with great bravery at Monterrey. The regiment

was active from July 4 to October 1, 1846, when it was released from further duty. Wood had so distinguished himself by his actions at Monterrey that he was elected the second governor of Texas in 1847. He died at his plantation on September 3 (5?), 1858, and is buried there.

43. Brooks, *Mexican War*, 156. The four peculiarly constructed wagons reported by Franklin Smith carried the pontoon bridge that General Taylor had repeatedly requested from the War Department. From Matamoros, on May 18, 1846, Taylor had written the War Department on the occupation of Matamoros, "My very limited means of crossing rivers prevented a complete prosecution of the victory of the 9th instant. A ponton [*sic*] train, the necessity of which I exhibited to the department last year, would have enabled the army to cross on the evening of the battle...to destroy entirely the Mexican army."

44. Wilcox, *Mexican War*, 609. Brig. Gen. Nathan Towson, Bvt. Maj. Gen., Mexico. He died on July 20, 1854.

45. Webb, *Handbook of Texas*, vol. 1, 354. Edward Clark was born on April 1, 1815, in Georgia. He moved to Alabama where he studied and later practiced law. Clark came to Texas in 1842 and settled at Marshall. He was elected to the Texas legislature and during the Mexican War served on the staff of Gen. James Pinckney Henderson. Clark fought in the battle of Monterrey. After the war he served as secretary of state from 1853 to 1857 during the term of Gov. Elisha M. Pease. He was elected lieutenant governor in 1859, running on the same ticket as Sam Houston, and became the eighth governor of Texas in 1861 when Houston refused to take the oath of allegiance to the Confederacy. Clark raised the Fourteenth Texas Infantry during the Civil War and was wounded at the battle of Pleasant Hill. He rose to the rank of brigadier-general before the close of the war. He died at Marshall, Texas, on May 4, 1880, and is buried there.

46. *Ibid.*, 789. Col. John Coffee Hays was born at Little Cedar Lick, Wilson County, Tennessee, on January 28, 1817. He came to Texas in 1837 and settled in San Antonio. He was employed as a surveyor and in 1840 became the captain of a ranger company. Hays and his company served with great distinction in many battles with the Indians and fought the Mexicans in 1842 at the battle of the Salado. During the Mexican War, Hays led the First Regiment of Mounted Volunteers, at the rank of colonel, and fought with great bravery at Monterrey and later at Mexico City. After the war, Hays followed the gold rush to California and served as sheriff of San Francisco County. He died near Piedmont, California, on April 25, 1883.

47. Wilcox, *Mexican War*, 615. Capt. Thomas B. Linnard, West

Point graduate, Topographical Engineers, Bvt. Maj., Buena Vista. He died on April 24, 1851, at Philadelphia, Pennsylvania.

48. *Ibid.*, 625. Lt. John F. Roland, West Point graduate, Second Regiment Artillery, Bvt. Capt. and Maj., Palo Alto, Resaca de la Palma, and Monterrey. He died on September 28, 1852, at Castle Pinckney, South Carolina.

49. *Ibid.*, 666. Capt. Speed S. Fry, Second Regiment of Kentucky Volunteers; Brig. Gen., Union Army, Civil War.

50. *Diccionario*, vol. 1, 290–91. Nicolas Bravo (1786–1854) was a leader in the Mexican struggle for independence from Spain. He was president of the Republic of Mexico from October 26, 1842, until May 4, 1843, and again from July 28, 1846, to August 4, 1846.

51. *Ibid.*, 303–4. Anastacio Bustamente (1780–1853) was born in Jiquilpan, Michoacan, and educated to be a physician. He served as president of Mexico twice, 1830–32 and 1837–39.

CHAPTER 3: *November 8, 1846–January 7, 1847*

1. Wilcox, *Mexican War*, 666. Capt. William T. Willis, Second Regiment of Kentucky Volunteers. He was killed at the battle of Buena Vista, Mexico, February 23, 1847.

2. *Ibid.* 665. Capt. John Shawhan, Regiment of Kentucky Cavalry. He was wounded at the battle of Buena Vista, Mexico, February 23, 1847.

3. Dyer, *Zachary Taylor*, 215; Nevins, *Diary*, 159. Maj. Robert W. McLane was the bearer of dispatches from President Polk and Secretary of War William Marcy. Polk confided with McLane as to the nature of the orders and would later write in his diary, "We had a full conversation in relation to the despatch and its objects." McLane left Washington on October 22 and reached General Taylor in Monterrey by November 12.

4. Compiled Service Records. Pvt. Marshall M. Smith, Co. E (The Jackson Fencibles), First Mississippi Volunteer Regiment. He was discharged for disability, November 2, 1846, Monterrey, Mexico.

5. Wilcox, *Mexican War*, 635. Col. William G. Belknap, West Point graduate, Fifth Regt. Infantry, Bvt. Col. and Brig. Gen., Palo Alto, Resaca de la Palma, Buena Vista. He died November 10, 1851.

6. Eleanor D. Pace, ed., "The Diary and Letters of William P. Rogers, 1846–1862," *Southwestern Historical Quarterly*, vol. 32, 262. Guardado Abajo is a small Mexican village about nine miles up the Rio Grande from Camargo, on the route to Monterrey taken by General Taylor and the American army. The village is referred to locally by a shortening of

the name Guardado which sounded like "Wardaw" to Franklin Smith and "wardo" to Capt. William P. Rogers. Pace had mistakenly thought the village name to be "Nordo."

7. Wilcox, *Mexican War*, 666. Capt. Wilkinson Turpin, Second Regiment of Kentucky Volunteers.

8. *Ibid.*, 665. Col. Humphrey Marshall, Kentucky Cavalry; Brig. Gen., C. S. A.. He died on March 28, 1872, at Louisville, Kentucky.

9. Green, *Mier*, 443. Wilson M. Vandyke, who was born in Georgia, was a resident of Jackson County, Texas. He is listed by Gen. Thomas Jefferson Green as having been captured with the Texan forces at Mier.

10. Edward Nichols, *Zach Taylor's Little Army* (Garden City: Doubleday and Company, 1963), 39, 54. Col. William Whistler, the sixty-six-year-old veteran of the War of 1812 who once led the Third Infantry Regiment, was relieved of command by General Taylor at Brownsville because of a drinking problem.

11. Wilcox, *Mexican War*, 682. Capt. Edwin D. Bradley, First Ohio Volunteer Regiment; Col., Union Army, Civil War.

12. *Ibid.*, 688. Capt. William B. Walton, First Tennessee Volunteer Regiment.

13. Compton Smith, *Chile Con Carne* (New York: Miller and Curtis, 1857), 315–16. Puntiagudo was a small Mexican village located about fifty miles west of Camargo along the main road to Monterrey. The village was thought to be sympathetic to the Mexican guerrillas who waylaid American travelers and wagon trains on the way to Monterrey. In the words of Compton Smith, by late 1847 "on the passage of Colonel Curtiss, of the 3rd Ohioans, this pretty village [Puntiagudo] was laid in ashes, in retaliation for some depredations which had been committed upon some of our trains, while on the road; and of which, there is no doubt, these people were entirely innocent." The town, however, survives to this day, and is now known as General Trevino. American retaliation for guerrilla warfare was widespread in northern Mexico. Compton Smith described the road to Monterrey as "marked with devastated fields, and the smoking ruins of villages and ranchos, where the advancing columns of our army had met with shelter and friendly receptions. Such are the horrors of war: the innocent and friendly peasantry are oftenest made to suffer the penalties."

14. Wilcox, *Mexican War*, 617. Capt. Philip Kearny, First Regiment of Dragoons, Bvt. Maj., Contreras and Churubusco; Maj. Gen., Union Army, Civil War, killed September 1, 1862, at the battle of Chantilly, Virginia.

15. Heitman, *Register*, vol. 1, 1021. Nathan Weston, Jr., was a native

of Maine and was commissioned as a volunteer paymaster on June 24, 1846. He resigned on June 30, 1847.

16. Wilcox, *Mexican War*, 624. Lt. Henry J. Hunt, West Point graduate, Second Regiment of Artillery, Bvt. Capt. and Major, Contreras, Churubusco, and Chapultepec, wounded at Molino del Rey; Brig. Gen., Union Army, Civil War. He died February 11, 1889, at Soldiers' Home, Washington, D. C.

17. *Ibid.*, 617. Lt. Richard S. Ewell, West Point graduate, First Regiment of Dragoons, Bvt. Capt., Contreras and Churubusco; Lt. Gen., C. S. A.. He died on January 25, 1872, at Spring Hill, Tennessee.

18. Wilcox, *Mexican War*, 681. Col. Alexander M. Mitchell, First Ohio Volunteer Regiment, wounded at Monterrey. He died on February 28, 1861, at St. Joseph, Missouri.

19. *Ibid.*, 682. Capt. John B. Armstrong, First Ohio Volunteer Regiment.

20. *Ibid.*, Capt. Edwin D. Bradley, First Ohio Volunteer Regiment; Col., Union Army, Civil War.

21. Malone, *American Biography*, vols. 15–16, 315–16. John Anthony Quitman was born on September 1, 1798, in Rhinebeck, New York. He was educated by his father for the ministry and finished his formal education at Hartwick Academy in Oswego, New York. He moved to Delaware, Ohio, studied the law, and was admitted to practice in 1821. He then went to Natchez, Mississippi, where in 1827 he was elected to the state legislature. From 1827 to 1835 he served as chancellor of the state of Mississippi. He was elected to the state senate in 1835 and was defeated in 1836 in his bid for a seat in Congress. In 1836 he organized a company of volunteer militia to aid the Texas settlers in their revolution against Mexico, but the company arrived in Texas too late to participate in the action. When the Mexican War was declared, Quitman was commissioned as a brigadier general of volunteers and served under General Taylor at the battle of Monterrey. He was later transferred to General Scott's army and led the attack on Mexico City. Quitman was appointed military governor of Mexico City, and on April 14, 1847, was promoted to the rank of major general. In 1849, he was elected governor of Mississippi but resigned the office in 1850 when he was indicted by a federal grand jury in New Orleans for violation of the neutrality laws. He had been associated with Lopez, a revolutionary who was attempting to overthrow the Spanish rule of Cuba. The case against Quitman was dismissed after one of his indicted associates was tried and a jury found him not guilty. He was elected to Congress in 1855 and 1857. He died at his home near Natchez on July 17, 1858.

22. Jose R. Alvarez, ed., *Enciclopedia de Mexico* (Cuidad de Mexico,

1978), Tomo 9, 295. The explanation given for the origin of the name for the city of Monterrey is incorrect. The city was named for the Spanish Viceroy of Mexico, the Conde de Monterey, appointed to the office in 1600. He established the first colony in the province of Nuevo Leon, which was named in his honor. At the time of the Mexican War, the name of the city was spelled "Monterey." The modern spelling is "Monterrey."

23. Wilcox, *Mexican War*, 611. Capt. Ebenezer S. Sibley, West Point graduate, asst. Quartermaster, Bvt. Maj., Buena Vista; Lt. Col., Union Army, Civil War. He died on August 4, 1884, at Detroit, Michigan.

24. *Diccionario*, vol. 1, 139. Mariano Arista (1820–55) was a noted cavalry officer born in San Luis Potosi. He commanded the Mexican forces defeated by Gen. Zachary Taylor's army at the battles of Palo Alto and Resaca de la Palma. Arista was the president of Mexico from 1851 to 1853.

25. Wilcox, *Mexican War*, 622. Capt. Lucien B. Webster, West Point graduate, First Regt. Artillery, Bvt. Maj. and Lt. Col., Monterrey and Buena Vista. He died on November 4, 1853, at Fort Brown, Texas.

26. Monroe and McIntosh, *The Papers of Jefferson Davis*, vol. 3, 31. Lt. William Purnell Townsend (1822–82) was a resident of Lowndes County, Mississippi, before the Mexican War. He lived there after the war until 1852, when he moved to Texas and settled in Robertson County. He served as captain in Hood's Brigade during the Civil War and was later major of the Fourth Texas Infantry until he was wounded. He returned to Texas after the Civil War and died in Calvert.

27. James K. Greer, *A Texas Ranger and Frontiersman: The Days of Buck Barry in Texas 1845–1906* (Dallas: The Southwest Press, 1932), 40; private correspondence. James Buckner Barry reports seeing the same repulsive sight: "The dogs came back after the surrender so hungry and starved that they ate the dead men who were overlooked or buried in shallow graves. I saw these dogs eating on the carcasses of the men." Not all Americans were buried in shallow graves where they fell; the soldiers of the Third Infantry, for example, were buried in a cemetery enclosed by a stone fence. The cemetery was located in the vicinity of Ojo Nogal, near the American camp at Santo Domingo. As late as 1965 the cemetery could still be found, but the headstones were all those of Mexicans. The old Mexican practice of disinterring the dead (see Franklin Smith, December 29) makes it seem likely that the American soldiers' bodies were gradually displaced over the intervening years.

Americans killed at the battle of Buena Vista were buried in two locations: on the eastern edge of the present Agricultural Campus of the Coahuila Agriculture Station, at the site of the Hacienda Buena Vista, and a second location in downtown Saltillo at the intersection of Avenida Benito Juarez and Matamoros. A visitor to the downtown Saltillo site on June 11, 1965, reported, "The original wall surrounding the graveyard enclosure has been torn down, however, the old foundation is still visible. Other walls made of adobe from materials on the spot have numerous human bones visible and easily removed with a knife or screw driver." In 1900, a Colonel Scully of the Q. M. Corps of the United States Army was sent to Saltillo to investigate reports on the desecration of American soldiers' graves. A letter written by Colonel Scully on July 31, 1900, to the Office of the Adjutant General of the United States Army in Washington, D. C., recommended that "These remains [bodies interred at the Saltillo site] be removed to the San Antonio, Texas National Cemetery where they can be decently and revently [sic] interred and cared for." Apparently Colonel Scully's recommendation was never adopted.

28. Malone, *American Biography*, vol. 19, 83. David Emanuel Twiggs was born in Richmond County, Georgia, in 1790. A career officer, he rose through the ranks from lieutenant to colonel, and with the latter rank he joined General Taylor in south Texas when the war with Mexico was declared in 1846. Twiggs fought well at Palo Alto and Resaca de la Palma and was promoted for his gallantry to the rank of brigadier general. Twiggs was brevetted a major general for his part in the capture of Monterrey, and on March 2, 1847, Congress voted him a sword with a jeweled hilt and a golden scabbard for gallantry at Monterrey. He transferred to Scott's army in central Mexico and led the attack on Cerro Gordo. After the war he commanded several departments in the South, and on February, 1861, surrendered all troops and supplies in the Department of Texas to the Confederates without firing a shot. A known southern sympathizer, he was dismissed from the United States Army and promptly received a commission as major general in the Confederate Army. He was assigned command of the district of Louisiana, but being too old to take the field, he resigned. He died on July 15, 1862.

29. McWhiney and McWhiney, *To Mexico with Taylor and Scott*, 50–71; Wilcox, *Mexican War*, 93–101. The statue of the Virgin Mary surmounting a pillar marked the west end of the Purisma Bridge, a heavily armed *tete-de-pont* which was key to the defenses of eastern Monterrey. From this stronghold on September 21, 1846, deadly fire was brought to bear on the American attackers, and the Mexican defenders held their position throughout the day.

30. Wilcox, *Mexican War*, 609. Brig. Gen. Persifor F. Smith, Bvt.

Maj. Gen., Monterrey, Contreras, and Churubusco. He died on May 17, 1858, at Fort Leavenworth, Kansas.

31. *Ibid.*, 657. John J. B. Hoxey, surgeon, Battalion of Georgia Volunteers.

32. *Ibid.*, 666. Lt. Col. Henry Clay, Jr., Second Regiment Kentucky Volunteers. He was killed on February 23, 1847, at the battle of Buena Vista, Mexico.

33. Compton Smith, *Chile Con Carne*, 76–77. Other American observers in Cerralvo also reported this story. Dr. S. Compton Smith, a surgeon stationed in Cerralvo at this time, reported, "An epidemic prevailed amongst the children, and visited every family. The disease was of a malarious origin, and was strictly confined to the younger children. It rarely attacked those of twelve years and upwards; whilst adults were entirely exempt from the disease. It was of a dysentaric nature, and readily yielded to quinine, so long as the very limited quantity of that medicine, with which I had been supplied, held out; but that failing; and having no substitute, I was pained to see them dying around me hourly.

"The priests asserted that the disease was caused by the presence of the heretical Americans; and many of the common people believed this ridiculous assertion."

34. Monroe and McIntosh, *The Papers of Jefferson Davis*, vol. 2, 111. Capt. John McNitt Sharp was born in Tennessee on November 22, 1795, but soon moved to Yazoo County, Mississippi, and settled on a 3,000-acre plantation near Benton. He served one term in the state legislature in 1840, and in 1846, he organized the Yazoo Guards, which became Co. A of the First Mississippi Regiment. The company served on detached duty at Cerralvo, Mexico and did not participate in the battle of Monterrey. Captain Sharp led his company at the battle of Buena Vista and was severely wounded. He returned after the war to his plantation, Cedar Grove, where he died on May 20, 1862.

35. *Ibid.*, vol. 3, 131. Capt. William Delay was born in Kentucky in 1814. He settled in Oxford, Mississippi, where he edited several Democratic newspapers, including the *Oxford Organizer*. He organized the Lafayette Guards, a militia unit that later became Co. F of the First Mississippi Regiment, and he served as captain of that company while it was in Mexico. After the Mexican War, Delay returned to Oxford, where he served as postmaster in the years before the Civil War. He organized and was captain of Co. C, Ninth Mississippi Infantry, from 1861 to 1862 and was county probate clerk from 1862 to 1867. He died in 1871.

36. Malone, *American Biography*, vol. 14, 122. William Owsley was the Whig governor of Kentucky from 1844 to 1848.

37. Wilcox, *Mexican War*, 639. Capt. George S. Wright, West Point graduate, Eighth Regiment Infantry, Bvt. Maj., Lt. Col., and Col., Contreras, Churubusco, and Molina del Rey; Brig. Gen., Union Army, Civil War. He died on July 30, 1864.

38. *Ibid.*, 629. Maj. Edgar S. Hawkins, West Point graduate, First Regt. Infantry, Bvt. Maj., Fort Brown. He died on November 5, 1865, Flatbush, New York.

39. Compiled Service Records. Pvts. Elijah A. Peyton and John C. Peyton, Co. H (The Vicksburg Volunteers), First Mississippi Regiment. They were discharged for disability, December 2, 1846, Monterrey.

40. Wilcox, *Mexican War*, 613. Maj. Andrew J. Coffee, West Point graduate, Paymaster, Bvt. Lt. Col., Buena Vista.

41. *Ibid.*, 665. Capt. Cassius M. Clay, Kentucky Cavalry; Maj. Gen., Union Army, Civil War.

42. *Ibid.*, Capt. Thomas F. Marshall, Kentucky Cavalry.

43. *Ibid.*, Capt. Johnson Price, Kentucky Cavalry.

44. Monroe and McIntosh, *The Papers of Jefferson Davis*, vol. 2, 198, 299. Jefferson Davis resigned his seat in Congress to accept the command of the First Mississippi Regiment, and a special election was held in Mississippi in the latter part of 1846 to fill the unexpired term. The Democratic candidate Henry T. Eller was victorious over his Whig opponent Peter B. Starke.

45. *Ibid.*, 678, vol. 3, 92–93. In a letter to Elizabeth Maury Holland, Col. Jefferson Davis offered condolences to her for the loss of her husband, Capt. Kemp S. Holland. The body of Captain Holland was interred at Holly Springs, Mississippi, on February 24, 1847. Elizabeth Maury Holland was a sister of the famous oceanographer, Matthew Fontaine Maury.

46. Harry Oberholser, *The Bird Life of Texas* (Austin: University of Texas Press, 1974), vol. 1, 432. The birds sighted were quite possibly green parakeets (*Aratinga holochlora*), now rarely found in Hidalgo and Cameron Counties in Texas.

47. Wilcox, *Mexican War*, 632. Capt. James M. Smith, Third Infantry Regiment. He died on December 4, 1847.

48. Monroe and McIntosh, *The Papers of Jefferson Davis*, vol. 3, 414. Col. Jefferson Davis received Franklin Smith's letter requesting a furlough.

49. *Ibid.*, Vol. 2, 330. Joseph Howell was Col. Jefferson Davis's brother-in-law. Howell attended school at Princeton, New Jersey, and later at Edge Hill, Pennsylvania. He was a lawyer and accountant by profession, and when war was declared with Mexico he joined the

Vicksburg Southrons (Co. C, First Mississippi Regiment) despite his sister Varina Howell Davis's fears that "his six feet and seven inches would make him a target for the enemy." Howell fought in the battle of Monterrey and was discharged on December 5, 1846, for illness. He did not return home but took a job in the quartermaster's depot at Camargo as a clerk in the clothing department. He later became superintendent and continued his employment in that position until July 1848.

50. Lester R. Dillon, *American Artillery in the Mexican War* (Austin: Presidial Press, 1975), 19, 20, 23, 25; Lander, *Trip to the Wars*, 17; Scribner, *Camp Life*, 20. Samuel Ringgold developed tactics for the use and deployment of the six-pounder Paixhan horse artillery that played such a decisive role in the American victories at Palo Alto and Buena Vista. The leader of a dashing corp of artillerists that included Randolph Ridgeley, James Duncan, and Braxton Bragg, Ringgold was widely respected and admired both by his fellow officers and by the American public. While deploying one of his batteries during the battle of Palo Alto, Ringgold was struck by a Mexican four-pounder solid shot that tore away the flesh from both legs above the knees and killed his fine thoroughbred mount David Branch, reported to be the fastest horse in the American army. He refused to be taken from the field until the battle was over, when he was gently transported to Point Isabel. A naval surgeon worked to ease his pain, but little could be done to save his life. He died on May 11, 1846, and was buried at Point Isabel, Texas. Lander reports seeing an improvised monument on the battlefield of Palo Alto, picketed with Mexican gun barrels, that marked the location where Ringgold had been wounded. Scribner described Major Ringgold's grave in Point Isabel as "enclosed with a wooden fence, the rails of which are filled with holes, so as to admit musket barrels. These form the palings, the bayonets serving as pickets. Two boards painted black serve for tombstones." The body of Ringgold was later exhumed from this site and moved to Baltimore, Maryland, where it was buried with civic and military honors on December 22, 1846.

51. Wilcox, *Mexican War*, 624. William C. deHart, West Point graduate, Capt., Second Regiment of Artillery. He died in Elizabethtown, New Jersey on April 21, 1848.

52. Jerry D. Thompson, *Sabers on the Rio Grande* (Austin: Presidial Press, 1975), 146–49, 153. Lt. Bryant P. Tilden, West Point graduate, Second Regt. Infantry, wounded at Contreras. He died on December 27, 1859, in Olean, New York. Tilden had just returned from an expedition on the steamboat *Major Brown* up the Rio Grande from the mouth to Laredo (see diary entry for October 1). His experience on

this trip formed the basis for a monograph that he wrote and gave the impressive title *Notes on the Upper Rio Grande: Explored the Months of October and November, 1846, on board the U.S. Steamer Major Brown Commanded by Captain Mark Sterling of Pittsburgh. By Order of Major General Robert Patterson, U. S. A. Commanding the Second Division, Army of Occupation, Mexico* (Philadelphia: 1847).

53. Scribner, *Camp Life*, 46. B. F. Scribner, a private in the Second Indiana Regiment stationed at Camargo, reported the same incredible scene at the Camargo cemetery (see diary entry for December 18, 1846): "What a sight to behold. The ground was strewed with skull bones and partly decayed remains of humanity. Every new grave they dig they disinter a body ... to make room for another coffin."

54. Wilcox, *Mexican War*, 618. Capt. Seth B. Thornton, Second Regt. Dragoons, severely wounded on the Rio Grande. He was killed in action August 18, 1847, at San Antonio, Valley of Mexico.

55. *Ibid.*, 613; Samuel E. Chamberlain, *Recollections of a Rogue* (London: Museum Press Limited, 1957), 121. Maj. Roger S. Dix, West Point graduate, Paymaster, Bvt. Lt. Col., Buena Vista. He died on January 7, 1849, Hillsboro, Pennsylvania. Chamberlain reported that Maj. Dix made heroic efforts to steady the green volunteer troops at Buena Vista who were exposed to heavy enemy fire for the first time. "Major Dix, a paymaster, mounted on a gigantic Bay horse, seized the National Colors from the standard bearer of the regiment and waving them over his head led the men back again where they done [*sic*] good service."

56. Wilcox, *Mexican War*, 634; private communication. Lt. Archibald B. Botts, West Point graduate, Fourth Regt. Infantry. He died on January 1, 1847, in Camargo, Mexico. Lieutenant Botts represents only one of an estimated 1,500 American soldiers who were buried around Camargo, a village referred to by American soldiers as a "graveyard." In August 1980, hurricane Allen caused extensive flooding on the Rio San Juan in the Camargo area. The resulting erosion of the river banks unearthed many graves of American soldiers, readily identifiable to the natives of that area because "they were buried in coffins." Local souvenir hunters collected nails from the remains of the coffins, uniform buttons, and even the bones of the "gringos."

57. Compiled Service Records. Pvt. Edward H. Gregory, Co. K (Tombigbee Guards) First Mississippi Regiment. He was discharged December; 12, 1846, in Monterrey, Mexico, having "procured a substitute," H. P. Lyon.

58. *Who's Who 1607–1896*, 85. Tristam Burges was a noted orator,

congressman, and politician from Rhode Island. Born on February 26, 1770, he served in the 19–23rd Congresses as a representative from Rhode Island. He was a professor of oratory at Brown University and a prominent member of the Federal Party.

59. Compiled Service Records. Lt. Fredrich J. Malone, Co. F (The Lafayette Guards), First Mississippi Volunteer Regiment. He resigned October 31, 1846, and re-enlisted as Pvt. January 15, 1847.

CHAPTER 4: *January 8–February 3, 1847*

1. January 8, 1814, was the date of General Jackson's victory over the British at New Orleans.

2. Justin Smith, *Mexican War*, vol. 1, 541. In the latter part of December 1846, Col. Charles May and his dragoons had escorted a topographical engineering party into Santa Rosa Canyon, south of Linares, Mexico. The rear guard of the party was attacked, and ten dragoons and the baggage wagons were captured by the Mexicans.

3. Wilcox, *Mexican War*, 688. Lt. James L. Scudder, First Regiment of Tennessee Volunteers. He was severely wounded at Monterrey, September 21, 1846.

4. *Ibid.*, 636. Capt. William H. T. Walker, West Point graduate, Sixth Regt. Infantry, Bvt. Maj. and Lt. Col., Contreras, Churubusco, and Molino del Rey; Maj. Gen., C. S. A.. He was killed July 22, 1864, at the battle of Atlanta, Georgia.

5. *Ibid.*, 610. Maj. Lorenzo Thomas, West Point graduate, Asst. Adjutant General, Bvt. Lt. Col., Monterrey; Brig. Gen., Union Army, Civil War. He died on March 2, 1875, in Washington, D. C.

6. *Ibid.*, 612. Capt. James Duncan, West Point graduate, Bvt. Maj., Lt. Col., and Col., Palo Alto, Resaca de la Palma, and Monterrey. He died on July 3, 1849, in Mobile, Alabama.

7. *Ibid.*, 628. Lt. John P. McCown, West Point graduate, Fourth Regiment Artillery, Bvt. Capt., Cerro Gordo; Maj. Gen., C. S. A. He died on January 22, 1879, in Little Rock, Arkansas.

8. *Ibid.*, 682. Lt. Elliot D. Wall, Second Regiment Ohio Volunteers.

9. Las Aldamas is a small village located about thirty miles southwest of Camargo on the left bank of the Rio San Juan.

10. The name "Allacka," probably a phonetic spelling, is thought to refer to the rancho by the name of La Laja, which refers to the geologic outcroppings of ledgestones that appear in this region along the banks of the Rio San Juan.

11. Marilyn McAdams Sibley, ed., *Samuel H. Walker's Account of the*

Mier Expedition (Austin: The Texas State Historical Association, 1978), 39–42; Florence S. Johnson, *Old Rough and Ready on the Rio Grande* (Waco: Texian Press, 1969), unnumbered page. Walker, one of the Mier prisoners, kept a diary of his captivity in Mexico. The Texian prisoners were herded from Matamoros to Monterrey along a route that coincided with the trail taken by Franklin Smith's party. From Walker's diary, the entry for 23rd reads in part, "at 12 o'clock came to a village called Mantaca [*sic*]. Encamped in a corral." The village of Manteca appears on a map reproduced in Johnson. It is located about fifty-five miles southwest of Camargo on a tributary of the Rio San Juan. This picturesque little village is now known as Las Herreras.

12. The word *"capadero"* is literally translated as the act of castration. It is applied to the act of castrating cattle.

13. Webb, *Handbook of Texas*, vol. 1, 294; Teresa Griffin Viele, *Following the Drum* (Lincoln: University of Nebraska Press, 1984), 191–93. Jose Maria Jesus Carbajal was born in San Francisco de Bexar (now San Antonio, Texas). He worked as a saddlemaker in Lexington, Kentucky, in 1823 and was educated at Bethany, Virginia. Carbajal returned to Texas where he was employed as a surveyor. In 1835, to evade arrest for fomenting rebellion in Texas, he fled to New Orleans. While there, he banded together with other revolutionaries to charter a ship that would bring supplies for the Texan forces. The ship was captured by the Mexicans, and Carbajal was placed in prison, first at Brazos Santiago, then at Matamoras. He escaped prison and returned to Texas, where he was elected as a delegate to the Convention of 1836 at Washington-on-the-Brazos. Carbajal commanded a force of American volunteers in 1839 that defeated a Mexican centralist army near Mier, and he was one of the leaders in an effort to form an independent republic in northern Mexico. In 1846, he led a force of irregular guerilla troops known as rancheros, under the command of Gen. Antonio Canales, which harassed the American army in northern Mexico. Between 1850 and 1853 he was associated with several military forays from Texas into Mexico that came to be known as the Merchant's War. An eyewitness account of his attack on Camargo in 1853 is found in Viele, as is a description of his personal appearance. He spent his latter years involved in the revolutionary turmoil that was occurring in Mexico. He served as governor of the state of Tamaulipas and San Luis Potosi in 1865. He died in Soto la Marina, in Tamaulipas, in 1874.

14. Andrew J. Sowell, *Early Settlers and Indian Fighters of Southwest Texas* (New York: Argosy-Antiquarian Ltd., 1964), 48–49; Joseph D. McCutchan, ed., Joseph M. Nance, *Mier Expedition Diary* (Austin:

University of Texas Press, 1978), 49, 51, 53. Trinidad Aldrette was a lieutenant in the guerilla army of Antonio Canales. Before the war he had lived on the Guadalupe River near Victoria, Texas. At Mier, on December 31, 1842, he assisted in the capture of a party of Texans, led by Thomas Jefferson Green, that had invaded Mexico. This incident became known as the "Mier Expedition." Aldrette murdered one of the Texans, a young man named Joseph Berry, in cold blood. Joseph McCutchan, one of the Mier prisoners, wrote in his diary, "A guard found the body of Berry's which was naked and pierced with fourteen lance holes. This act, as subsequently ascertained, was perpretrated by Capt. Elduret [*sic*] with the cold blooded ferocity of a coward and barbarian. Berry's thy [*sic*] was broken by his fall on the previous evening, and when the enemy found him in the house, he was unable to raise himself up; and in this situation Elduret was dastardly enough to murder him. This act was boasted of by Elduret's friends as a feat of bravery!" Aldrette returned to Texas after the Mexican War and was killed there by the brothers of Joseph Berry in an act of revenge.

15. The tributaries of the Rio San Juan are not designated by names on modern maps of this region. However, this tributary could be the one locally referred to at present as Rio Salinas.

16. Sibley, *Samuel H. Walker*, 41. The Capadero River is a local designation of one of the many branches of the Rio San Juan that drains this rugged country. Walker attempted to spell phonetically the name of this place also: "25th. At 5 miles came to Capisaro [*sic*] on the river of the same name, a branch of the St. John." The village of Capadero was probably a yearly meeting place for local ranchers where cattle and other livestock from a common grazing area were branded and the young males were castrated. The name is also associated with rodeos, which probably provided entertainment whenever the ranchers of this area met to perform their annual chores. The small tributary probably derived its name, Rio Capadero, from the village of the same name.

17. John J. Delaney, *Dictionary of Saints* (Garden City, Doubleday and Company, 1980), 136. China is a little village located about seventy-five miles southwest of Camargo on the Rio San Juan. The city derives its name in a curious way from one of the saints, Philip De Las Casas, born in Mexico City on May 1, 1571. De Las Casas belonged to the Franciscan Order. On a return trip from the Phillipines to Mexico in 1596, the ship on which he travelled was driven off course by a storm onto the coast of Japan. He was arrested there and crucified the following year with twenty-five other Christians at Nagasaki on February 5. Around 1776, this tiny settlement in northern Mexico built a

church to honor Saint Felipe de Jesus. They named it Saint Felipe de Jesus de China, since the generic name "China" was applied to all oriental locations. The village that grew up around this church took the same name. Over the years the village became known simply as China, and to this day it celebrates February 5th with a fiesta in honor of St. Felipe de Jesus.

18. Sibley, *Samuel H. Walker*, 40. Walker was an involuntary visitor to the village of Paso del Zacate. His entry for the 21st reads in part, "Marched 20 miles to a small village on the St. John called the Pass Suarte [*sic*] and encamped in a corral for the night." Johnson's map shows Paso del Zacate to be about forty-five miles southwest of Camargo on the Rio San Juan. This village, now known as Estation Zacate, is on the rail line from Matamoras to Monterrey.

Bibliography

To indicate firsthand accounts, memoirs, and diaries written by Americans who participated in the campaign, I have closed the citation with "acct." The majority of these accounts of the Mexican War parallel, and in many cases are identical to, the observations recorded in Franklin Smith's manuscript. Especially interesting eyewitness reports of the battles of Monterrey and Buena Vista can be found in *The Papers of Jefferson Davis*, vol. 3.

Books

Biographical and Historical Memoirs of Mississippi. Chicago: The Goodspeed Publishing Company, 1891. acct.

Diccionario Porrua Historia, Biografia, Y Geografia de Mexico. 2d ed. Mexico City: Editorial Porrua, 1965.

National Cyclopedia of American Biography. New York: James T. White and Co., 1906.

Who's Who In America Historical Volume 1607–1896. Chicago: The A. N. Marquis Co., 1963.

Alcarez, Ramon. *The Other Side or Notes for the History of the War Between Mexico and the United States*. New York: Burt Franklin, 1970 (originally published 1850).

Allsopp, Fred W. *Albert Pike: a Biography*. Little Rock, Arkansas: Parke-Harper Company, 1928.

Balbontin, Manuel. *La Invasion Americana, 1846 a 1848*. Mexico: Gonzalo A. Esteva, 1883.

Barton, Henry. *Texas Volunteers In The Mexican War*. Waco: The Texian Press, 1970. acct.

Brooks, Nathan. *A Complete History of the Mexican War 1846–1848*. Chicago: The Rio Grande Press Inc., 1965.

Carleton, James Henry. *The Battle of Buena Vista, with the Operations of the "Army of Occupation" for One Month*. New York: Harper & Brothers, 1848. acct.

Catton, Bruce. *Michigan: a Bicentennial History*. New York: W. W. Norton and Co., 1976.

Chamberlain, Samuel E. *Recollections of a Rogue*. London: Museum Press Limited, 1957.

Chance, Joseph E. *The Second Texas Infantry*. Austin: Eakin Publications, 1984. acct.

Claiborne, J. F. H. *Life and Correspondence of John A. Quitman*. New York: Harper & Brothers, 1860.

Crawford, Ann Fears. *The Eagle The Autobiography of Santa Anna*. Austin: The Pemberton Press, 1967.

Davis, Reuben. *Recollections of Mississippi and Mississippians*. Oxford: University and College Press of Mississippi, 1972.

Duncan, Robert Lipscomb. *Reluctant General: The Life and Times of Albert Pike*. New York: E. P. Dutton & Co., 1961.

Dillon, Lester R. *American Artillery in the Mexican War 1846–1847*. Austin: Presidial Press, 1975.

Dyer, Brainerd. *Zachary Taylor*. Baton Rouge: Louisiana State University Press, 1946.

Eisenhower, John S. D. *So Far From God: The U. S. War With Mexico 1846–1848*. New York: Random House, 1989.

French, Samuel G. *Two Wars: An Autobiography of Gen. Samuel G. French*. Nashville: Confederate Veteran, 1901.

Frost, John. *Pictorial History of Mexico and the Mexican War*. Philadelphia: Thomas, Copperwait and Co., for James A. Bill, 1848.

[Giddings, Luther.] *Sketches of the Campaign in Northern Mexico in Eighteen Hundred Forty-Six and Seven*. New York: George P. Putnam, 1853. acct.

Gregg, Josiah. *Diary and Letters of Josiah Gregg*. Edited by Maurice G. Fulton. 2 vols. Norman: University of Oklahoma Press, 1944.

Green, Thomas J. *Journal of the Texian Expedition Against Mier*. Austin: The Steck Co., 1935.

Greer, James K. *Colonel Jack Hays*. New York: E. P. Dutton and Co., 1952.

Greer, James K. *A Texas Ranger and Frontiersman: The Days of Buck Barry in Texas 1845–1906*. Dallas: The Southwest Press, 1932. acct.

Heitman, Francis B. *Historical Register and Dictionary of the United States Army, From Its Organization September 29, 1789, to March 2, 1903*. 2 vols. Reprint. Urbana: University of Illinois Press, 1965.

Henry, William S. *Campaign Sketches of the War in Mexico*. New York: Harper & Brothers, 1847.

Horgan, Paul. *Great River: The Rio Grande in North American History*. 2 vols. New York: Holt, Rinehart, and Winston, 1968.

Johnson, Florence Scott. *Old Rough and Ready on the Rio Grande*. Waco, Texas: Texian Press, 1969.

Kenley, John R. *Memoirs of a Maryland Volunteer*. Philadelphia: J. B. Lippincott and Co., 1873.

Lander, Alexander. *A Trip to Texas Comprising The History of the Galveston Riflemen, Formed April 28, 1846 at Galveston, Texas; Together With The History of The Battle of Monterey; Also Descriptions of Mexico and Its People*. Monmouth (Ill.): Printed at the "Atlas Office," For the Publisher, 1847. acct.

Lea, Tom. *The King Ranch, vol. 1*. Boston: Little, Brown and Company, 1957.

Lonard, Robert. *The Woody Plants of the Lower Rio Grande Valley, Texas*. Austin: The Texas Memorial Museum Press, 1990.

Lynch, James D. *The Bench and Bar of Mississippi*. New York: E. J. Hale, 1881. acct.

Lytle, William M. *Merchant Steam Vessels of the United States, 1807–1868*. Edited by Forrest R. Holdcamper. Mystic, Conn.: Steamship Historical Society of America, 1952.

McCutchan, Joseph D. *Mier Expedition Diary*. Edited by Joseph Milton Nance. Austin: University of Texas Press, 1978.

McElroy, Robert. *Jefferson Davis: The Unreal and the Real*. New York and London: Harper and Brothers Publishers, 1937.

McIntosh, James T. *The Papers of Jefferson Davis*. Vol. 2, *June 1841–July 1846*. Baton Rouge: Louisiana State University Press, 1974. acct.

————. *The Papers of Jefferson Davis*. Vol. 3, *July 1846–December 1848*. Baton Rouge: Louisiana State University Press, 1981. acct.

McWhiney, Grady and Sue McWhiney. *To Mexico With Taylor and Scott 1845–1847*. Waltham: Blaisdell Publishing Co., 1969. acct.

Malone, Dumas. *Dictionary of American Biography*. New York: Charles Scribner's Sons, 1933.

May, Robert E. *John A. Quitman: Old South Crusader*. Baton Rouge: Louisiana State University Press, 1985.

Meade, George. *The Life and Letters of George Gordon Meade, Major General, United States Army, vol. 1*. New York: Charles Scribner's Sons, 1913.

Myers, William Starr. *The Mexican War Diary of George B. McClellan.* Princeton: Princeton University Press, 1917. acct.

Nevins, Allan. *Polk: The Diary of a President 1845–1849.* New York: Longmans, Green, and Co., 1952.

Nance, Joseph Milton. *After San Jacinto.* Austin: University of Texas Press, 1963.

Nichols, Edward. *Zach Taylor's Little Army.* Garden City: Doubleday and Company Inc., 1963.

Owen, Tom (The Bee-Hunter). *Anecdotes of Zachary Taylor and The Mexican War.* New York: D. Appleton & Company, 1848.

Peterson, Roger T. *A Field Guide to the Birds of Texas and Adjacent States.* Boston: Houghton Mifflin Company, 1963.

Risch, Erna. *QuarterMaster Support of the Army: A History of the Corps 1775–1939.* Washington: QM Historian's Office, Office of the QM General, 1962.

Robinson, Fayette. *Mexico and Her Military Chieftans.* Glorieta: The Rio Grande Press, Inc., 1970.

Roland, Charles. *Albert Sidney Johnston: Soldier of Three Republics.* Austin: University of Texas Press, 1964.

Roller, David C., and Robert W. Twyman. *The Encyclopedia of Southern History.* Baton Rouge: Louisiana State University Press, 1979.

Rowland, Dunbar. *Mississippi.* Spartanburg: The Reprint Co. Publishers, 1976. acct.

Samson, William H. *Letters of Zachary Taylor from the Battlefields of the Mexican War.* Privately printed, Rochester, NY, 1908.

Scribner, Benjamin Franklin. *Camp Life of a Volunteer: a Campaign in Mexico or a Glimpse at Life in Camp by "One Who Has Seen the Elephant."* Philadelphia: Grigg, Elliot and Co., 1847. acct.

Simon, John Y. *The Papers of Ulysses S. Grant.* Vol. 1, *1837–1861.* Carbondale: Southern Illinois University Press, 1967.

Singletary, Otis A. *The Mexican War.* Chicago: The University of Chicago Press, 1960.

Smith, Compton. *Chile con Carne.* New York: 1857. acct.

Smith, George W., and Charles Judah. *Chronicles of the Gringos.* Albuquerque: The University of New Mexico Press, 1968. acct.

Smith, Justin. *The War With Mexico.* 2 vols. New York: The Macmillan Company, 1919.

Sowell, Andrew Jackson. *Early Settlers and Indian Fighters of Southwest Texas.* New York: Argosy-Antiquarian Ltd., 1964. acct.

Spurlin, Charles D. *Texas Veterans in the Mexican War.* Nacogdoches: Erickson Books, 1984.

Stambaugh, J. Lee, and Lillian J. Stambaugh. *The Lower Rio Grande Valley of Texas*. Austin: The Jenkins Publishing Co., 1974.

Strode, Hudson. *Jefferson Davis: American Patriot 1808–1861*. New York: Harcourt, Brace and Company, 1955.

Tennery, Thomas D. *The Mexican War Diary of Thomas D. Tennery*. Norman: University of Oklahoma Press, 1970.

Thompson, Jerry. *Sabers on the Rio Grande*. Austin: Presidial Press, 1975.

Vigil y Robles, Guillermo. *La Invasion De Mexico Por Los Estados Unidos En Los Anos De 1846, 1847, y 1848*. Mexico, 1932.

Wallace, Edward. *Destiny and Glory*. New York: Coward-McCann, Inc., 1957.

Webb, Walter P. *The Handbook of Texas*. Austin: The Texas State Historical Association, 1952.

Wilcox, Cadmus. *History of the Mexican War*. Washington: Church News Publishing Company, 1892.

Government Documents

Executive Document No. 65, 31st Congress. "Message from The President of the United States communicating the report of Lieutenant Webster of a survey of the gulf coast at the mouth of the Rio Grande," July 27, 1850.

Executive Document No. 13, 31st Congress. "Letter from The Secretary of War, transmitting a report on the route of General Patterson's division from Matamoras to Victoria," December 19, 1850.

Manuscripts and Collections

National Archives (DNA) Microfilm Series M-863, Records of the Adjutant General's Office. Compiled Service Records, Mexican War.

Spurlin, Charles D. Manuscript on the Mexican War, unpublished.

McDonald, Laurier B. Private correspondence.

The Mexican War Diary of James C. Browning, handwritten manuscript. Mexican War Collection, Mississippi Archives, Jackson, Mississippi.

The Justin Smith Manuscripts. Pan American Collection, Barker Library, University of Texas at Austin, Austin, Texas.

Bloom, John Porter. "With the American Army into Mexico, 1846–1848." Dissertation, Emory University, Atlanta, 1956.

Newspapers

The Vicksburg Whig, Vicksburg, Mississippi. 1846 and 1847. acct.

Holly Springs Gazette, Holly Springs, Mississippi. acct.

The Southron, Jackson, Mississippi. acct.
Clarion-Ledger, Jackson, Mississippi. acct.
The Picket Guard, Saltillo, Mexico, April 19, May 10, 1847. acct.

Articles

A Mississippian. "Sketches of Our Volunteer Officers. Alexander Keith McClung." *Southern Literary Messenger*, vol. 21, 1855.

Backus, Electus. "Details of the Controversy Between the Regulars and Volunteers, in Relation to the Part Taken By Each in the Capture of Battery No. 1 and Other Works At the East End of the City of Monterey, on the 21st of September, 1846." *Historical Magazine*, vol. 10, 1866. acct.

Backus, Electus. "A Brief Sketch of the Battle of Monterey; With Details of That Portion of it, Which Took Place At the Eastern Extremity of the City." *Historical Magazine*, vol. 10, 1866. acct.

Balboutin, Manuel. "The Siege of Monterey." *Journal of the Military Service Institution of the United States*, vol. 8, 1887. acct.

Balbotin, Manuel. "The Battle of Angostura Pass (Buena Vista)." *Journal of the Military Service Institution of the United States*, vol. 8, 1887. acct.

Benham, H. W. "A Little More Grape." *The Vedette*, vol. 2, Æ4, January 1881. acct.

Buchanan, A. Russell. "George Washington Trahern: Texan Cowboy Soldier from Mier to Buena Vista." *The Southwestern Historical Quarterly*, vol. 58, 1954. acct.

Estes, William E. "Something About the First Mississippi Rifles." Undated newspaper article, Mexican War Documents, Mississippi Archives, Jackson, Mississippi.

Jacobs, Wm. H. "Interesting Letters from an Officer on the Rio Grande." *The Vedette*, volume number unknown, December 1888.

O'Neal, H. F "Aleck McClung and Jefferson Davis at Monterey." *The Vedette*, vol. 5, #1, January 1884.

Pace, Eleanor D. "The Diary and Letters of William P. Rogers, 1846–1862." *The Southwestern Historical Quarterly*, Volume 32, 1929. acct.

Penix, Joe. "McClung-Death's Ramrod," *Clarion-Ledger*, Jackson, Mississippi, April 3, April 10, April 17, 1955.

Phillips, George. "A Little More Grape, Captain Bragg." *The Vedette*, vol. 3, #9, June 1882.

Pike, Albert. "A Sketch of the Battle of Buena Vista," *Arkansas State Gazette*, Little Rock, Arkansas, April 24, 1847.

Rowland, Dunbar. "Political and Parliamentary Orators and Orations of

Mississippi." *Publications of the Mississippi Historical Society*, vol 4, 1901.

———. "Badge Members of the National Association of Veterans of the Mexican War." *The Vedette*, vol. 3, #8, May 1882.

———. "Death of a Mississippi Rifleman." *The Vedette*, vol. 3, #12, December 1882.

Index